COMPUTER ARCHITECTURE

COMPUTER ARCHITECTURE

(For the Students of B.Tech Computer Engineering and Information Technology)

By

NIRMALA SHARMA
Assistant Professor
Department of Computer Engineering
University College of Engineering
Rajasthan Technical University, Kota
Rajasthan

UNIVERSITY SCIENCE PRESS

(An Imprint of Laxmi Publications Pvt. Ltd.)

BANGALORE • CHENNAI • COCHIN • GUWAHATI • HYDERABAD
JALANDHAR • KOLKATA • LUCKNOW • MUMBAI • RANCHI
NEW DELHI

Published by :

UNIVERSITY SCIENCE PRESS

(An Imprint of Laxmi Publications Pvt. Ltd.)
113, Golden House, Daryaganj,
New Delhi-110002

Phone : 011-43 53 25 00
Fax : 011-43 53 25 28

www.laxmipublications.com
info@laxmipublications.com

First Edition : 2009

OFFICES

© **Bangalore**	080-26 61 15 61	© **Chennai**	044-24 34 47 26
© **Cochin**	0484-239 70 04	© **Guwahati**	0361-254 36 69, 251 38 81
© **Hyderabad**	040-24 65 23 33	© **Jalandhar**	0181-222 12 72
© **Kolkata**	033-22 27 43 84	© **Lucknow**	0522-220 95 78
© **Mumbai**	022-24 91 54 15, 24 92 78 69	© **Ranchi**	0651-221 47 64

UCA-9361-150-COMPUTER ARCHITECTURE **C—17317/09/04**

Typeset at : Kalyani Computer Services, New Delhi. Printed at : Repro Knowledgecast Limited, Thane

This book is dedicated to
my father Mr. L.C. Sharma
and all my family members

Contents

PREFACE

It gives me a great pleasure in presenting the first edition of the book "Computer Architecture."

This book is based on the latest syllabus prescribed by Rajasthan Technical University, Kota for B.Tech. V semester computer engineering, V semester Information Technology.

The syllabus of RTU is covered in eight chapters as following:

Chapter 1, *Digital Fundamentals,* focuses on the basic knowledge of digital electronics and number systems. This chapter fulfils the requirements up to the mark.

Chapter 2, *Register Transfer Language,* contains concept of bus and timing in register transfer along with the various types of microoperations like arithmetic and logic microoperations.

Chapter 3, *CPU Organisation,* deals with the heart of the computer system—Central processing unit. It includes various types of addressing modes and instruction formats.

Chapter 4, *Pipelining and Parallel Processing,* describes how instructions are executed in parallel manner using the technique pipelining. Various types of techniques to achieve parallelism has been discussed.

Chapter 5, *Computer Arithmetic,* describes the design and implementation of various arithmetic algorithms using various digital components.

Chapter 6, *Microprogrammed Control Unit,* contains the basic organisation of microprogrammed control unit.

Chapter 7, *Memory Organisation,* describes the concept of various types of memories like RAM, ROM, Cache and associative memory. It includes a very interesting concept–Virtual memory organisation.

Chapter 8, *Input-Output Organisation,* deals with the introduction to peripherals and their interfacing. DMA based data transfer is also discussed.

An honest attempt has been made to present each concept in easy and lucid language. Important solved examples have been added for better examination preparations.

All friendly suggestions and criticism for the improvement of the book will be greatly acknowledged and appreciated.

—Author

Acknowledgement

This book has been made possible through the direct and indirect co-operation of various persons, for whom I wish to express my appreciation and gratitude.

I am highly indebited to the authors of various reference books, which I have consulted in giving final shape to this book.

I would like to place on record my gratitude to all of family members whose timely and never failing encouragement has been a great source of inspiration in sustaining our interest in completing this book.

I am also extremely thankful to my publisher for his co-operation and his editorial team to provide excellent layout to the book.

—Author

SYLLABUS

COMPUTER ARCHITECTURE (5 IT 4)/ (5 CS 2)

UNIT-1 : REGISTER TRANSFER LANGUAGE

- Data movement around registers.
- Data movement from/to memory, arithmetic and logic microoperations.
- Concept of bus and timing in register transfer.

UNIT-2 : CPU ORGANISATION

- Addressing Modes.
- Instruction Format.
- CPU organisation with large registers, stacks and handling of interrupts and subroutines instruction pipelining.

UNIT-3 : ARITHMETIC ALGORITHM

- Array multiplier, Booth's algorithm.
- Addition subtraction for signed unsigned numbers and 2's complement numbers.

UNIT-4 : MICROPROGRAMMED CONTROL UNIT

- Basic organisation of microprogrammed controller, Horizontal and Vertical formats, Address sequencer.

UNIT-5 : MEMORY ORGANISATION

- Concept of RAM/ROM, basic cell of RAM, Associative memory, Cache memory organisation, Vertical memory organisation.
- I/O ORGANISATION: Introduction to Peripherals and their interfacing.
- Strobe based and handshake-based communication, DMA based data transfer, I/O processor.

Chapter 1

DIGITAL FUNDAMENTALS

1.1 INTRODUCTION

The digital circuits can be classified into two broad categories: Analog system and digital system. Analog systems deal with variables having continuous nature while the digital system defines variables having discrete values. Digital system defines the term digit. The term digital in digital circuits is derived from the way the digital circuit perform operations by counting the digits. A digital circuit operates with binary numbers.

To understand the operation of a digital computer the knowledge of number system, is very essential so in this chapter first we study about number system and methods of conversion from one to another then in next section we discuss about complements that is necessary in arithmetic digital operations.

For constructing the digital circuit knowledge of logic gates, combinational circuits, sequential circuits and digital components are required. These all are covered in this chapter. Computer codes are the format in which input and output are specified so we take brief idea about computer codes. All these are the basic digital fundamentals.

So we are going to cover the following topics:

1. Number system
2. Complements
3. Logic gates
4. Computer codes
5. Combinational circuits
6. Sequential circuits
7. Digital components.

1.1.1 Decimal Number System

The most familiar number system is decimal number system. To represent any number this system uses 10 digits (0 to 9). Thus, decimal number system is said to have a Base or Radix of 10. The weight of each digit depends upon the relative position of that digit in the number.

Let the number is $(678)_{10}$. This can be represent as: $600 + 70 + 8$

$$= 6 \times 10^2 + 7 \times 10^1 + 8 \times 10^0$$

The weight of I^{st} digit 8 $= 8 \times 10^0$

The weight of IInd digit 7 $= 7 \times 10^1$

The weight of IIIrd digit 6 $= 6 \times 10^2$.

The above expression can be generalised as the weight of nth digit of the number

$$= n^{th} \text{ digit} \times (10)^{n-1}$$

$$= n^{th} \text{ digit} \times (\text{Base})^{n-1}$$

digit is considered from right hand side.

1.1.2 Binary Number System

To understand the operation of a digital computer the knowledge of binary system is essential.

Binary number system deals with two digits 0 and 1, so the base or radix of the binary number system is 2. In short a binary digit is known as a bit. All computer systems use binary number system for their internal operation and manipulation.

Let the binary number is $(1011)_2$. This can be represented as: $1 \times 2^3 + 0 \times 2^2 + 1 \times 2^1 + 1 \times 2^0$

The weight of I^{st} digit 1 $= 1 \times 2^0$

The weight of IInd digit 1 $= 1 \times 2^1$

The weight of IIIrd digit 0 $= 0 \times 2^2$

The weight of IVth digit 1 $= 1 \times 2^3$.

So the weight of nth bit of the number considering from right hand side is

$$= n^{th} \text{ bit} \times (2)^{n-1}$$

$$= n^{th} \text{ bit} \times (\text{Base})^{n-1}$$

The weight of each bit depends upon the relative position of that bit in the number.

1.1.3 Octal Number System

The base of the octal number system is 8. It uses eight digits 0, 1, 2, 3, 4, 5, 6 and 7. Octal number system is also positional number system, the weight of each digit depends upon the relative position of that digit in the number.

Let the number is $(534)_8$. This can be represented as: $5 \times 8^2 + 3 \times 8^1 + 4 \times 8^0$

The weight of the I^{st} digit 4 $= 4 \times 8^0$

The weight of the IInd digit 3 $= 3 \times 8^1$

The weight of the IIIrd digit 5 $= 5 \times 8^2$.

This can be generalised as weight of nth digit of number from right hand side is

$$= n^{th} \text{ digit} \times (8)^{n-1}$$

The octal number system is the most popular number system in digital circuit. This system is also used in computer industry.

1.1.4 Hexadecimal Number System

Hexadecimal number system use 16 digits to represent a number. Its radix (base) is 16. Its digits 0 to 9 are same as decimal number system. The alphabets A, B, C, D, E, F are used to represent 10, 11, 12, 13, 14 and 15 respectively.

Let the number $(A49)_{16}$. This can be represented as: $A \times 16^2 + 4 \times 16^1 + 9 \times 16^0$

The weight of the I^{st} digit 9 $= 9 \times (16)^0$

The weight of the IInd digit 4 $= 4 \times (16)^1$

The weight of the IIIrd digit A $= A \times (16)^2$

So the weight of nth digit of a number can be represented as

$$= n^{th} \text{ digit} \times (16)^{n-1}$$

$$= n^{th} \text{ digit} \times (\text{Base})^{n-1}$$

Again hexadecimal number system is positional number system, weight of each digit depends upon the relative position of the digit in the number.

Table 1.1

Decimal Number	*Hexadecimal Number*
0	0
1	1
2	2
3	3
4	4
5	5
6	6
7	7
8	8
9	9
10	A
11	B
12	C
13	D
14	E
15	F

1.1.5 Conversions

Each and every positional number system is having its own application. There is requirement for converting a given number system into another number system for the internal processing of a computer system.

1.1.5.1 Decimal to Binary Conversion

A decimal number consists two parts: integer part and fraction part. So while converting a given decimal number into binary number first we will convert integer part into its equivalent binary number and then fraction part we will be converted into its binary equivalent. For converting the integer part, the number is divided by 2 progressively, until the quotient of zero is obtained. The binary equivalent is obtained by taking the remainder after each division in the reverse order. The binary equivalent of fraction part is obtained by multiplying the number continuously by 2, taking a carry in the integer position each time. The carries in the forward order provide required binary equivalent.

Example 1.1: *Convert the decimal number $(53.125)_{10}$ into an equivalent binary number.*

Solution. Step 1. Integer part : 53

Fraction part : 0.125

Step 2. Integer part conversion:

Division	Remainder
53 ÷ 2	1 (LSB)
26 ÷ 2	0
13 ÷ 2	1
6 ÷ 2	0
3 ÷ 2	1
1 ÷ 2	1 (MSB)
0	

Reading the remainder from bottom to top

$$(53)_{10} = (110101)_2$$

Step 3. Fractional part conversion:

Multiplication	Integer part	Fraction
.125 × 2 = 0. 250	0 (MSB)	.250
.250 × 2 = 0. 500	1	.500
.500 × 2 = 1.000	1 (LSB)	.000 (stop)

Now fraction is 0.

The binary equivalent of the fraction is written from top to bottom.

So $$(.125)_{10} = (.001)_2$$

On combining the solution of integer part and fractional part.

$$(53.\ 125)_{10} = (110101\ .\ 001)_2$$

Example 1.2: *Convert $(14.625)_{10}$ in its binary equivalent.*

Solution. Step 1. Integer part : 14

Fraction part : 0.625

Step 2. Integer part conversion:

Division	Remainder
14 ÷ 2	0 (LSB)
7 ÷ 2	1
3 ÷ 2	1
1 ÷ 2	1 (MSB)
0	

On reading the remainder from bottom to top

$$(14)_{10} = (1110)_2$$

Step 3. Fractional part conversion:

Multiplication	Integer part	Fraction
0. 625 × 2 = 1.250	1 (MSB)	.250
0.250 × 2 = 0.500	0	.500
0.500 × 2 = 1.000	1 (LSB)	.000 (stop)

$$(.625)_{10} = (.101)_2$$

On combining the solution of both the parts

$$(14.625)_{10} = (1110.101)_2$$

1.1.5.2 Decimal to Octal Conversion

The decimal to octal conversion is similar to decimal to binary conversion. First we will convert integer part into its octal equivalent and then fractional part is converted into its octal equivalent. The integer part is divided by 8 repeatedly until a quotient of 0 is obtained. The octal equivalent is obtained by taking the remainder after each division in the reverse order. The octal equivalent of fraction part is obtained by multiplying the number continuously by 8, taking the whole number in account every time.

Example 1.3: *Convert the decimal number $(159.456)_{10}$ into an equivalent octal number.*

Solution. Step 1. Integer part : 159

Fraction part : 0.456

Step 2. Integer part conversion:

Division	Remainder
159 ÷ 8	7 (LSB)
19 ÷ 8	3
2 ÷ 8	2 (MSB)
0	

So $(159)_{10} = (237)_8$

Step 3. Fractional part conversion:

Multiplication	Integer part	Fraction
0. 456 × 8 = 3.648	3 (MSB)	0.648
0.648 × 8 = 5.184	5	0.184

$0.184 \times 8 = 1.472$	1	0.472
$0.472 \times 8 = 3.776$	3	0.776
$0.776 \times 8 = 6.208$	6 (LSB)	0.208

The process is terminated when significant digits are obtained.

Thus the octal equivalent of $(159.456)_{10}$ is $(237.35136)_8$.

Example 1.4: *Convert $(274.23)_{10}$ in its binary equivalent.*

Solution. Step 1. Integer part : 274

Fraction part : 0.23

Step 2. Integer part conversion:

Division	Remainder
$274 \div 8$	2 (LSB)
$34 \div 8$	2
$4 \div 8$	4 (MSB)
0	

Reading the remainder from bottom to top

$$(274)_{10} = (422)_8$$

Step 3. Fractional part conversion:

Multiplication	Integer part	Fraction
$0.\ 23 \times 8 = 1.84$	1 (MSB)	0.84
$0.84 \times 8 = 6.72$	6	0.72
$0.72 \times 8 = 5.76$	5	0.76
$0.76 \times 8 = 6.08$	6 (LSB)	0.08

The octal equivalent of the fraction is written from top to bottom.

So $$(.23)_8 = (.1658)_8$$

On combining the solution of both the parts.

$$(274.23)_{10} = (422.1658)_8.$$

1.1.5.3 Decimal to Hexadecimal Conversion

The hexadecimal equivalent of a decimal number is obtained by dividing the integer part by 16 repeatedly, until a quotient of 0 is obtained. The fraction part is multiplied by 16 and integer part is taken into account at every step.

Example 1.5: *Convert the decimal number $(234.14)_{10}$ into an equivalent hexadecimal number.*

Solution. Step 1. Integer part : 234

Fraction part : 0.14

Step 2. Integer part conversion:

Division	Remainder
$234 \div 16$	$10 \leftarrow$ A (LSB)

14 ÷ 16	14 ← E (MSB)
0	

On reading the remainder from bottom to top

$$(234)_{10} = (EA)_{16}$$

Step 3. Fractional part conversion:

Multiplication	Integer part	Fraction
0. 14 × 16 = 2.24	2 (LSB)	0.24
0.24 × 16 = 3.84	3	0.84
0.84 × 16 = 13.44	13 = D	0.44
0.44 × 16 = 7.04	7 (MSB)	0.04

This multiplication can be performed upto some significant bits.

So $$(0.14)_{10} = (.23\ D7)_{16}$$

Combining the solution of integer and fractional part. The equivalent hexadecimal number is $(EA.\ 23\ D7)_{16}$

$$(234.14)_{10} = (EA.\ 23\ D7)_{16}.$$

Example 1.6: *Convert $(2162.675)_{10}$ in its hexadecimal equivalent.*

Solution. Step 1. Integer part : 2162

Fraction part : 0.675

Step 2. Integer part conversion:

Division	Remainder
2162 ÷ 16	2 (LSB)
135 ÷ 16	7
8 ÷ 16	8 (MSB)
0	

$$(2162)_{10} = (872)_{16}.$$

Step 3. Fractional part conversion:

Multiplication	Integer part	Fraction
0. 675 × 16 = 10.80	10 = A (MSB)	0.80
0.80 × 16 = 12.80	12 = B	0.80
.80 × 16 = 12.80	12 = A (LSB)	0.80

So $$(2162.675)_{10} = (872.ABB)_{16}.$$

1.1.5.4 Binary to Decimal Conversion

The conversion of the binary number into decimal number is carried out by multiplying each binary bit by its positional weight and then adding all the product of binary bit and positional weight. The binary number has two parts *i.e.,* whole number and fraction.

Let decimal number is written as $b_{m-1}, b_{m-2}, b_{m-3}.... b_0, b_{-1}, b_{-2}....b_{-n}$ then binary equivalent can be obtained from the following expression:

$$b_{m-1}\,(2)^{m-1} + b_{m-2}\,(2)^{m-2} + ... b_0\,(2)^0 + b_{-1}\,(2)^{-1} + b_{-2}\,(2)^{-2} + ... + b_{-n}\,(2)^{-n} \quad ...(1.1)$$

This equation represents the weights of the binary number.

Example 1.7: *Convert the binary number $(101101)_2$ into its decimal equivalent.*

Solution. By referring to the equation (1.1), this binary number can be converted into equivalent decimal by multiplying each bit by its positional weight.

So
$$\begin{aligned}(101101)_2 &= 1 \times 2^5 + 0 \times 2^4 + 1 \times 2^3 + 1 \times 2^2 + 0 \times 2^1 + 1 \times 2^0\\ &= 32 + 8 + 4 + 1\\ &= (45)_{10}.\end{aligned}$$

Example 1.8: *Convert $(110110.101)_2$ into decimal equivalent.*

Solution.
$$\begin{aligned}(110110.101)_2 &= (1 \times 2^5 + 1 \times 2^4 + 0 \times 2^3 + 1 \times 2^2 + 1 \times 2^1 + 0 \times 2^0)\\ &\quad + (1 \times 2^{-1} + 1 \times 2^{-2} + 1 \times 2^{-3})\\ &= (32 + 16 + 0 + 4 + 2 + 0) + (0.50 + 0 + 0.125)\\ &= (54.625)_{10}\end{aligned}$$

The decimal equivalent of given binary number $(110110.101)_2$ is $(54.625)_{10}$.

Example 1.9: *Convert $(1001.1101)_2$ into decimal equivalent:*

Solution.
$$\begin{aligned}(1001.1101)_2 &= (1 \times 2^3 + 0 \times 2^2 + 0 \times 2^1 + 1 \times 2^0)\\ &\quad + (1 \times 2^{-1} + 1 \times 2^{-2} + 0 \times 2^{-3} + 1 \times 2^{-4})\\ &= (8 + 0 + 0 + 1) + (0.50000 + 0.2500 + 0.0000 + 0.0625)\\ &= (9.8125)_{10}\end{aligned}$$

Therefore $(1001.1101)_2$ is equal to $(9.8125)_{10}$.

1.1.5.5 Binary to Octal Conversion

For converting a given binary number into its equivalent octal number, starting from the least significant bit, each group of 3 bits is replaced by its decimal equivalent. If less than 3 bits remain in grouping then the zeros are placed to make a group of 3 bits.

Table 1.2

Octal Number	*Binary Equivalent*
0	000
1	001
2	010
3	011
4	100
5	101
6	110
7	111

Example 1.10: *Convert $(101\ 110\ 101)_2$ into its octal equivalent.*

Solution. Given binary number 101 110 101.

Making the group of 3 bits from right to left.

$$\underbrace{101}_{\downarrow\ 5}\qquad \underbrace{110}_{\downarrow\ 6}\qquad \underbrace{101}_{\downarrow\ 5}$$

Then the decimal equivalent of each group is written *i.e.,* the octal equivalent of the given number will be

$$(101\ 110\ 101)_2 = (565)_8.$$

Example 1.11: *Convert the following binary number into its octal equivalent.*

$$(100\ 1011\ 001\ .\ 10101)_2 = (?)_8.$$

Solution. The given binary number has fraction part also. The integer part will be converted into octal equivalent by grouping of 3 bits from right to left and fraction part will be converted by grouping of 3 bits from left to right.

$$\underbrace{001}_{\downarrow\ 1}\quad \underbrace{001}_{\downarrow\ 1}\quad \underbrace{011}_{\downarrow\ 3}\quad \underbrace{001}_{\downarrow\ 1}\quad .\quad \underbrace{101}_{\downarrow\ 5}\quad \underbrace{010}_{\downarrow\ 2}$$

So the octal equivalent of the given number is $(1131.52)_8$.

1.1.5.6 Binary to Hexadecimal Conversion

To convert a given binary number into its equivalent hexadecimal number, we start from least significant bit, each group of 4 bits is replaced by its decimal equivalent. If less than 4 bits remain in grouping then the zeros are placed to make a group of 4 bits.

Table 1.3

Hexadecimal Number	*Binary Equivalent*
0	0000
1	0001
2	0010
3	0011
4	0100
5	0101
6	0110
7	0111
8	1000

9	1001
A	1010
B	1011
C	1100
D	1101
E	1110
F	1111

Example 1.12: *Convert $(1011001011111000)_2$ into its hexadecimal equivalent.*

Solution. Forming the groups of 4 bits from right to left.

1011	0010	1111	1000
↓	↓	↓	↓
B	2	F	8

Then the hexadecimal equivalent is written. The hexadecimal equivalent of the given number will be

$$(1011\ 0010\ 1111\ 1000)_2 = (B2F8)_{16}.$$

Example 1.13: *Convert $(0110110111101010.\ 10110101)_2$ into hexadecimal equivalent.*

Solution.

0110	1101	1110	1010	.	1011	0101
↓	↓	↓	↓		↓	↓
6	D	E	A	.	B	5

So $(0110\ 1101\ 1110\ 1010\ .\ 1011\ 0101)_2$

$$= (6\ D\ E\ A\ .\ B\ 5)_{16}.$$

1.1.5.7 Octal Decimal Conversion

The conversion of the octal number into decimal number is carried out by multiplying each bit of the octal number by its positional weight and then adding all the product of octal bits and positional weights.

Let decimal number is written as $b_{m-1}\ b_{m-2}\ b_{m-3}......\ b_0.\ b_{-1}\ b_{-2}\ b_{-3}.....\ b_{-n}$ then octal equivalent can be obtained from the following expression:

$$b_{m-1}\ (8)^{m-1} + b_{m-2}\ (8)^{m-2} +...+ b_0\ (8)^0 + b_{-1}\ (8)^{-1} + b_{-2}\ (8)^{-2} +...+ b_{-n}\ (8)^{-n} \quad ...(1.2)$$

This equation represents the weights of the octal number.

Example 1.14: *Convert $(42.10)_8$ into decimal equivalent.*

Solution. By referring the equation (1.2) this octal number can be converted into equivalent decimal by multiplying each bit by its positional weight.

So

$$(42.10)_8 = (4 \times 8^1 + 2 \times 8^0) + (1 \times 8^{-1} + 0 \times 8^{-2})$$
$$= (32 + 2) + (0.125 + 0)$$
$$= (34.125)_{10}.$$

Example 1.15: *Convert $(117.33)_8$ into decimal.*

Solution.
$$\begin{aligned}(117.33)_8 &= (1 + 8^2 + 1 \times 8^1 + 7 \times 8^0) + (3 \times 8^{-1} + 3 \times 8^{-2})\\ &= (16 + 8 + 7) + (.375 + .046)\\ &= (320) + (.421)\\ &= (320.421)_{10}.\end{aligned}$$

1.1.5.8 Octal to Binary Conversion

The conversion from octal to binary number can be performed by two methods. First the number can be converted into decimal and then decimal number is converted into equivalent binary number. In the second method each digit in the octal number can be replaced by its 3 bit binary equivalent. [Refer to Table 1.2]

Example 1.16: *Convert $(7516)_8$ into its binary equivalent.*

Solution.

7	5	1	6
↓	↓	↓	↓
111	101	001	110

So $(7516)_8 = (111\ 101\ 001\ 110)_2.$

Example 1.17: *Perform the following conversion and find (X)*

$(4057.06)_8 = (X)_{10}$ [Raj. Univ 2004]

Solution. To findout the value of X we have to perform conversion from octal number to decimal number.

$$\begin{aligned}(4057.06)_8 &= (4 \times 8^3 + 0 \times 8^2 + 5 \times 8^1 + 7 \times 8^0) + (0 \times 8^{-1} + 6 \times 8^{-2})\\ &= (2048 + 0 + 40 + 7) + (0 + 0.09375)\\ &= (2095.09375)_{10}\end{aligned}$$

So the value of X is 2095.09375.

1.1.5.9 Octal Hexadecimal Conversion

The conversion from octal number to hexadecimal number is performed in two steps:

Step 1. Convert the given octal number into its binary equivalent.

Step 2. Convert the binary equivalent into equivalent hexadecimal number.

This is illustrates by following examples.

Example 1.18: *Convert the octal number 736 to its equivalent hexadecimal number.*

Solution. Step 1. Convert the given number in binary number.

$$\begin{aligned}(736)_8 &= (111)\ (011)\ (110)\\ &= (111\ 011\ 110)_2\end{aligned}$$

Step 2. Now forming the groups of 4 binary bits to obtain its hexadecimal equivalent

$(111011\ 110)_2$ = 0001 1101 1110

0001	1101	1110
↓	↓	↓
1	D	E

$= (1\ D\ E)_{16}.$

Example 1.19: *Convert $(1736.57)_{16}$ to its equivalent hexadecimal number.*

Solution. Step 1. $(1736)_8 = (001)\ (111)\ (011)\ (110)$

$= (001111\ 011\ 110)_2$ [for integer part]

For fraction part

$(.57)_8 = (101)\ (111)$

$= (101111)_2$

So $(1736.57)_8 = (001111\ 011\ 110.\ 101111)_2$

Step 2. Now forming the groups of 4 binary bits. We get

0011	1101	1110	.	1011	1100
↓	↓	↓		↓	↓
3	D	E		B	C

So $(3\ D\ E\ .\ B\ C)_{16}$.

This is hexadecimal equivalent.

1.1.5.10 Hexadecimal Decimal Conversion

The conversion of the hexadecimal number into decimal number is carried out by multiplying each digit by its positional weight and then adding all the product of digits and positional weight.

Let decimal number is represented in the following form:

$b_{m-1}\ b_{m-2}......b_0,\ b_{-1}\ b_{-2}\ b_{-3}$

Then hexadecimal equivalent can be obtained from the following expression:

$$b_{m-1}\ (16)^{m-1} + b_{m-2}\ (16)^{m-2} + ... + b_0\ (16)^0 + b_{-1}\ (16)^{-1} + b_{-2}\ (16)^{-2} + ...\ b_{-n}\ (2)^{-n} \qquad ....(1.3)$$

This equation represents the weights of hexadecimal digits.

Example 1.20: *Convert the hexadecimal number 2B6D to its equivalent decimal number.*

Solution. $2B6D = 2 \times 16^3 + B \times 16^2 + 6 \times 16^1 + D \times 16^0$

$= 2 \times 4096 + 11 \times 256 + 6 \times 16 + 13 \times 1$

$= 8192 + 2816 + 96 + 13$

$= (11117)^{10}.$

Example 1.21: *Convert $(8A3.D)_{16}$ into decimal equivalent.*

Solution. The given hexadecimal number is $(8A3.D)_{16}$.

8	A	3	.	D
↓	↓	↓		↓
8	10	3		13

These decimal equivalents are multiplied by positional weights.

$= (8 \times 16^2 + 10 \times 16^1 + 3 \times 16^0) + (13 \times 16^{-1})$

$= (2048 + 160 + 3) + (.8125)$

$= (2211.\ 8125)_{10}.$

1.1.5.11 *Hexadecimal Binary Conversion*

A binary number has a base of 2 while a hexadecimal number has a base of $2^4 = 16$. The conversion from hexadecimal number into binary number can be obtained by replacing each digit of hexadecimal number into its 4 bit binary equivalent. It is very easy method. [Refer to Table 1.3]

Let us take the following examples.

Example 1.22: *Convert $(A2F9)_{16}$ into its binary equivalent.*

Solution. The given hexadecimal number is $(A2F9)_{16}$ each digit is replaced by its corresponding

A	2	F	9
↓	↓	↓	↓
1010	0010	1111	1001

$$(A2F9)_{16} = (1010\ 0010\ 1111\ 1001)_2.$$

Example 1.23: *Convert hexadecimal number 6DEA.B5 to binary.*

Solution. The given hexadecimal number is

6	D	E	A	.	B	5
↓	↓	↓	↓		↓	↓
0110	1101	1110	1010		1011	0101

The equivalent binary number is

$(0110\ 1101\ 1110\ 1010\ .\ 1011\ 0101)_2$.

1.1.5.12 *Hexadecimal Octal Conversion*

This conversion is performed in two steps.

Step 1. Convert the given hexadecimal number into equivalent binary number.

Step 2. Then this binary number is grouped in 3 bits starting from right to left for integer part and from left to right for the fractional part. Then these 3 bit groups are converted into their decimal equivalent and we will get equivalent octal number.

Example 1.24: *Convert $(BEC2)_{16}$ into octal.*

Solution. Step 1. Convert the number into its equivalent binary number.

B	E	C	2
↓	↓	↓	↓
1011	1110	1100	0010

$$= (1011\ 1110\ 1100\ 0010)_2.$$

Step 2. Now this binary equivalent is converted into octal by grouping of 3 bits.

001	011	111	011	000	010
└┘	└┘	└┘	└┘	└┘	└┘
10	3	7	3	0	2

So the equivalent octal number is

$(10\ 3\ 7\ 3\ 0\ 2)_8$.

Example 1.25: *Convert the real hexadecimal number 5B.3A to its equivalent octal number.*

Solution. Step 1. (5B . 3A) is converted into binary form

$$5B.3A = (0101)\ (1011)\ .\ (0011)\ (1010)$$
$$= (01011011\ .\ 00111010)_2$$

Step 2. Now forming the groups of 3 binary bits to obtain equivalent octal number.

$$(01011011.\ 00111010)_2$$
$$= (01)\ (011)\ (011)\ .\ (001)\ (110)\ (10)$$
$$= (001)\ (011)\ (011)\ .\ (001)\ (110)\ (100)$$
$$= (133.\ 164)_8.$$

1.2 COMPLEMENTS

In digital computer complements are used to simplify the operation of subtraction and for logical manipulation. For each base system *r* two types of complements are defined.

1. *r*'s Complement
2. (*r*–1)'s Complement.

When the value of base *r* is 2 then 2's complement and 1's complement are defined. When the value of *r* is 10 then 10's complement and 9's complement are defined.

1.2.1 (r–1)'s Complement

Given a number N having base *r* and *n* digit, the (r–1)'s complement of N is defined as $(r^n-1) - N$.

1.2.1.1 1's Complement

It is defined for binary number system. The 1's complement of any given number N is $(2^n - 1) - N$. 2^n represents a binary number whose MSB is 1 and all other bits are zero. For example if N = 1001 then

$$2^n = 2^4\ (16)_{10} = (10000)_2$$

and

$$2^n-1 = 10000 - 1 = (1111)_2$$

Then 1's complement of $(1001)_2$ is

$$= [2^n-1] - N = 1111 - 1001 = 0110.$$

$(2^n - 1)$ has n 1's, so 1's complement of a given number can be obtained when each bit of N is subtracted from 1. Bits are only two either 0 or 1.

So

$$1 - 0 = 1$$
$$1 - 1 = 0$$

Implies 0 is got converted into 1 and 1 is converted into 0.

Therefore the 1's complement of a given number can be obtained by replacing each bit of the number *i.e.*, '1' into '0' and '0' into 1. It is direct method by which easily we can get 1's complement of a given binary number.

1.2.1.2 9's Complement

9's complement of a given number is defined as $[10^n-1] - N$

where n = No. of digits in number

N = Given decimal number

10^n represents a number that consists a single 1 followed by n 0's. $[10^n -1]$ will represent a number having n 9's. For example,

$$N = (1234)_{10}$$

then $10^n-1 = 10^4 -1 = 10000 -1 = 9999$

9's complement of $(1234)_{10}$ is

$$= [10^n -1] - N$$
$$= 9999 - 1234$$
$$= 8765$$

So 9's complement of a given number N can be obtained by subtracting each digit of given number by 9. It is very easy and direct method.

Example 1.26: *Find out 1's complement of* $(10\ 101.\ 1011)_2$.

Solution.

1	0	1	0	1	.	1	0	1	1
↓	↓	↓	↓	↓		↓	↓	↓	↓
0	1	0	1	0	.	0	1	0	0

It is obtained by replacing each binary bit '0' by '1' and '1' by '0'.

Example 1.27: *Find out the 9's complement of* $(413052)_{10}$.

Solution. 9's complement is

$$= [10^6 -1] - 413052$$
$$= 999999 - 413052$$
$$= 586947.$$

1.2.2 r's Complement

It is radix complement. The r's complement of a given number N having n digits and base r is defined as

$$= r^n - N \qquad \text{for } N \neq 0$$
$$= 0 \qquad \text{for } N = 0$$

r's complement = $r^n - N$

$$= [(r^n - 1) - N] + 1$$
$$= (r - 1)\text{'s complement} + 1$$

So adding 1 to $(r - 1)$'s complement, we get r's complement of a number.

1.2.2.1 2's Complement

It is defined for binary number system. The 2's complement of a given number N is defined as

$$2^n - N$$

where n = no. of bits in number

2's complement can be findout using two method.

Method 1. (*i*) Findout the 1's complement of the given number by changing 1 into 0 and 0 into 1.

(*ii*) Add 1 to 1's complement to get 2's complement of the number.

Method 2. (*i*) Start from the LSB of the given number

(*ii*) The first 1 occurs will remain unchanged.

(*iii*) After the first 1 change all significant bits 0 by 1 and 1 by 0.

1.2.2.2 10's Complement

10's complement is defined for decimal number system. 10's complement is defined as

$$= 10^n - N$$

where N = Given number

n = number of digits

10's complement can be written as

$$= [10^n - 1] - N + 1$$

$$= 9\text{'s complement} + 1$$

So 10's complement of a given number can be obtained by adding 1 to 9's complement.

Example 1.28: *Find out 2's complement of* $(100101.11)_2$.

Solution. Direct Method. Scan the number starting from LSB. LSB is 1 so it will remain unchanged and all other bits will change from 0 to 1 and 1 to 0.

So	1	0	0	1	0	1	.	1	1
	↓	↓	↓	↓	↓	↓		↓	↓
	0	1	1	0	1	0		0	1

Decimal point is placed at the same place so 2's complement is 011010.01.

Example 1.29: *Find out 10's complement of 232140.*

Solution. Here N = 232140

n = 6

So 10's complement is

$$= 10^6 - 232140$$

$$= 1000000 - 232140$$

$$= 767860$$

1.2.3 Subtraction Using 2's Complement

The subtraction of two binary number can be obtained using 2's complement. 2's complement of number can be directly obtained by adding 1 to 1's complement.

Let we have to perform (A – B) then using 2's complement method we have to follow the following steps:

(*i*) Findout the 2's complement of B.

(*ii*) Add A + B.

(*iii*) If carry is generated then ignore it. If there is no carry then take 2's complement of the result and change the sign of result.

Example 1.30: *Subtract $(1010)_2$ from $(1111)_2$ using 2's complement method.*

Solution.

$$B = (1010)_2$$

$$A = (1111)_2$$

2's complement of B = 0101 + 1 = 0110

Addition of A and B = 1111 + 0110

= 10101

↑

carry generation

The addition operation is generating carry.

So after ignoring carry bit we will get answer is $(0101)_2$.

Example 1.31: *Subtract 5 from 3 using 2's complement method.*

Solution.

$$(A) = (3)_{10} = (0011)_2$$

$$(B) = (5)_{10} = (0101)_2$$

2's complement of 5 = 1010 + 1

= 1011

Adding A and B

$$\begin{array}{r} 0\,0\,1\,1 \\ 1\,0\,1\,1 \\ \hline 1\,1\,1\,0 \end{array}$$

There is no carry so we take 2's complement of the result and will change the sign of the result.

2's complement of 1110 is

$$\begin{array}{r} 0\,0\,0\,1 \\ +\ 1 \\ \hline 0\,0\,1\,0 \end{array}$$

$(0010)_2 = (2)_{10} = (-2)_{10}$ [after changing the sign].

1.3 LOGIC GATES

A logic gate is an electronics circuit which takes some logical decision based on some condition. When the given condition is satisfied a gate allows a signal to pass. Logic gates consists of transistors, diodes etc. Logic gates are switching devices which change from one position to another. The manipulation of binary information is done by logic gates. The knowledge of logic gates is essential to understand the important digits circuits that are used in computers.

The most common logic gates used are OR, AND, NOT, NAND and NOR gates. The NAND and NOR gates are known as Universal gates. The exclusive OR gate is another logic gate that can be constructed using basis logic gates AND, OR and NOT gates.

Except the NOT gate, all other logic gates have two or more inputs and only one output. The output signal is high certain combination of input signals. The operation of these logic gates can be described by means of an algebraic function. The tabular representation of relationship between input signal and output signal is known as truth table.

1.3.1 OR Gate

OR gate has two or more inputs and only one output. The output of OR gate will be high if any of the input signal is high. When all the inputs are in low state then output will be low. OR gate performs logical sum of two or more inputs.

If A and B are the input variables and y is the output variable then

$$y = A + B$$

If there are more than two variables then output can be expressed as

$$y = A + B + C + D + \ldots\ldots$$

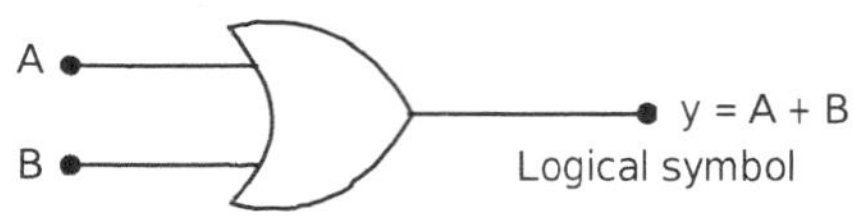

Fig. 1.1 Two input OR gate

The logical symbol of two inputs OR gate is shown in Fig. 1.1. Input variables A and B are applied to OR gate, output y is equivalent to sum of input variables.

The logical operation of two input OR gate is described in the truth table shown in Table 1.4.

Table 1.4 Truth table of two input OR gate

Inputs		*Output*
A	*B*	*y*
0	0	0
0	1	1
1	0	1
1	1	1

In the I[st] case both the input variables are low so output will be low. In second and third case only one input is high so output will be high if any one of the input variable is high. In forth case both the input variables are high so output will be high.

Table 1.5 Truth table for three input OR gate

Inputs			*Output*
A	*B*	*C*	*y*
0	0	0	0
0	0	1	1
0	1	0	1
0	1	1	1
1	0	0	1
1	0	1	1
1	1	0	1
1	1	1	1

1.3.2 AND Gate

An AND gate has two or more inputs but it has only one output. The output of AND gate will be high if all input signals are in high state. If any of the input variable is low then output will be low. AND gate performs logical multiplication of two or more inputs.

If A and B are input variables and y is the output variable then

$$y = A . B$$

where denotes the AND operation.

If there are more than two variables then output can be expressed as

$$y = A . B . C . D.......$$

The logical symbol of two inputs AND gate is shown in Fig. 1.2.

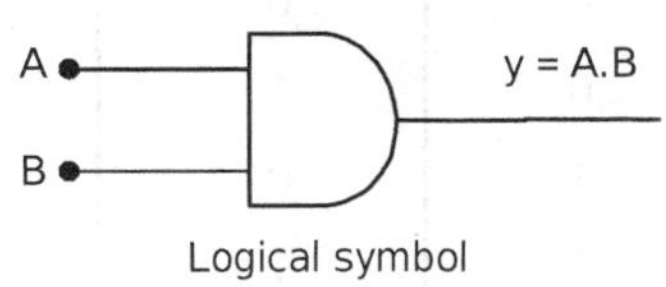

Fig. 1.2 Two input AND gate

Input variables A and B are applied to AND gate, output y is equivalent to multiplication of input variables.

The logical operation of two input AND gate is described in the truth table shown in Table 1.6.

Table 1.6 Truth table of two input AND gate

Inputs		*Output*
A	*B*	*y*
0	0	0
0	1	0
1	0	0
1	1	1

Case 1: A = 0, B = 0

So y = 0. 0 = 0. So output will be low.

Case 2: A = 0, B = 1 So y = 0, first input variable is low so output will be low.

Case 3: A = 1, B = 0 one of the input variable is low so output y will be low.

Case 4: A = 1, B = 1, Both the input variables are high so output will be in high state.

Output will be high when all the input variables are high.

Table 1.7 represents three input AND gate.

Table 1.7 Truth table for three input AND gate

Inputs			*Output*
A	*B*	*C*	*y*
0	0	0	0
0	0	1	0
0	1	0	0
0	1	1	0
1	0	0	0
1	0	1	0
1	1	0	0
1	1	1	1

1.3.3 NOT Gate

It is also known as Inverter or complementer. It is single input gate. There is one input variable and one output variable. If input variable is in high state then output will be low and when input variable is in low state output will be high.

The output y can be expressed in terms of input variable A as

$$y = \bar{A}$$

where $\bar{A}$ represent the NOT operation

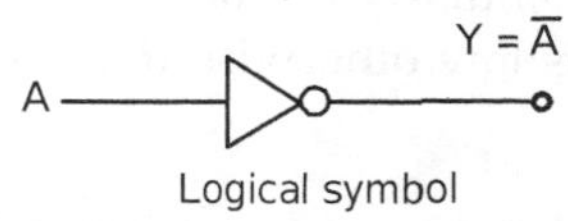

Fig. 1.3 NOT gate

The purpose of this gate is to convert one logical level into the opposite logic level.

Table 1.8 Truth table of NOT gate

Input *A*	*Output* $y = \bar{A}$
0	1
1	0

1.3.4 NAND Gate

NAND gate is a contraction of the NOT-AND gates. It has two or more inputs and only output. Universal gates are the logic gates by which any combinational circuit or digital system can be implemented with a collection of just one of these gates. This gate performs NOT-AND operation. It is also a complement of AND gate.

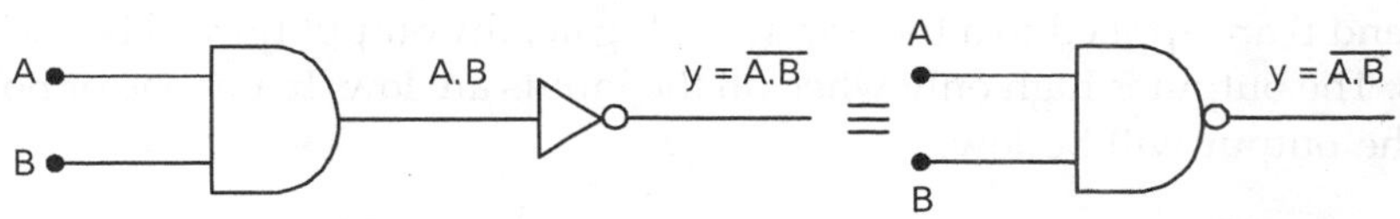

Fig. 1.4 Symbol of NAND gate

Fig. 1.4 shows symbolic representation of NAND gate. The bubble is placed to represent the NOT operation. The output y is expressed as

$$y = \overline{A . B}.$$

If two inputs A and B are applied to NAND gate, output (y) is the complement of the product of the inputs. When all of the input variables are high, the output is low. If any one or both the input are low then the output is high.

Table 1.9 Truth table of two input NAND gate

Inputs		*Output*
A	*B*	*y*
0	0	1
0	1	1
1	0	1
1	1	0

NAND gate is an universal gate. Similarly in Table 1.10, three input NAND operation, if all three inputs are high then the output is low otherwise if any one of the inputs is low, the output is high.

Table 1.10 Truth table of three input NAND gate

Inputs			*Output*
A	*B*	*C*	*y*
0	0	0	1
0	0	1	1
0	1	0	1
0	1	1	1
1	0	0	1
1	0	1	1
1	1	0	1
1	1	1	0

1.3.5 NOR Gate

The NOR gate is a combination of OR and NOT gate. It represents complement of OR gate. If two inputs A and B are applied to a two input NOR gate, the output (y) will be the complement of sum of inputs. The output is high only when all the inputs are low. It any one or both the inputs are high, then the output will be low.

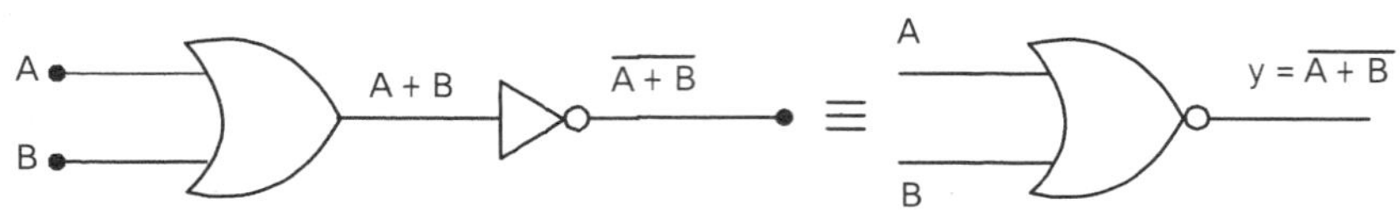

Fig. 1.5 Logical symbol NOR gate

The output y can be expressed as

$$y = \overline{A + B}$$

Table 1.11 Truth table for two input NOR gate

Inputs		*Output*
A	*B*	*y*
0	0	1
0	1	0
1	0	0
1	1	0

From truth table we can observe that when either input is 1, output (y) will be 0. When both the inputs are zero. Output will be high.

Table 1.12 Truth table for three input NOR gate

Inputs			*Output*
A	*B*	*C*	*y*
0	0	0	1
0	0	1	0
0	1	0	0
0	1	1	0
1	0	0	0
1	0	1	0
1	1	0	0
1	1	1	0

1.3.6 Exclusive OR Gate

It is written as Ex-OR or XOR gate. Normally Ex-OR gate has two input variables and one output variable. The output of the Ex-OR gate will be high when both the input variables are having different states. That output of two input Ex-OR gate assumes a high state if one and only one input assumes a high state.

If A and B are two input variables and y is the output variable then

$$y = A\overline{B} + \overline{A}B = A \oplus B$$

The symbol $\oplus$ represents the Ex-OR logical operation of inputs.

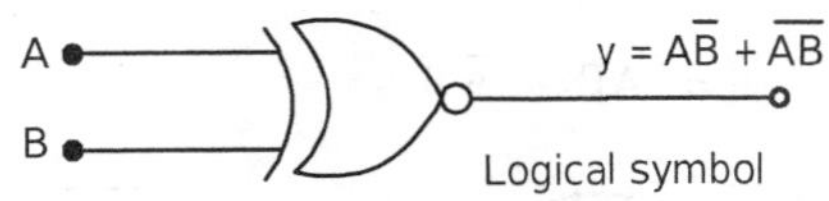

Fig. 1.6 Two input Ex-OR gate

The logical symbol of two inputs Ex-OR gate is shown in Fig. 1.6. The Ex-OR gate produces high output when an odd number of inputs are high. If an even number of inputs are high then the output will be low.

Table 1.13 represents truth table for two input Ex-OR gate

Table 1.13 Truth table for two input Ex-OR gate

Inputs		*Output*
A	*B*	*y*
0	0	0
0	1	1
1	0	1
1	1	0

Similarly we can represent truth table for three input variables.

Table 1.14 Truth table for three input Ex-OR gate

Inputs			*Output*
A	*B*	*C*	*y*
0	0	0	0
0	0	1	1
0	1	0	1
0	1	1	0
1	0	0	1
1	0	1	0
1	1	0	0
1	1	1	1

1.3.7 Exclusive NOR Gate

It is written as XNOR gate. The gate represents the complement of XOR operation. The output of this gate is high only when both the input variables are in the same state either both are low or both are in high state. When one is low and other variable is high then the output will be in low state.

When A and B are two input variable then output variable y can be written as

$$y = \overline{A \oplus B}$$

$$= AB + \bar{A}\bar{B}$$

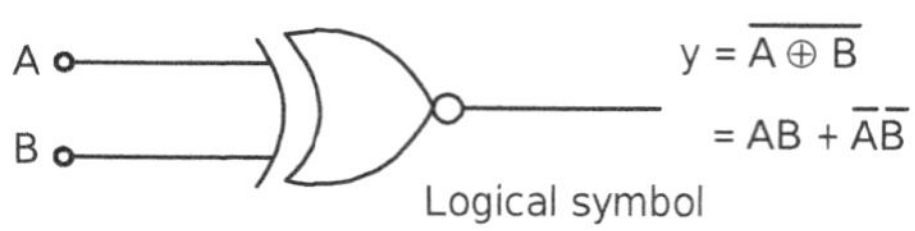

Fig. 1.7 Two input XNOR gate

The logical symbol of two inputs XNOR gate is shown in Fig. 1.7. Ex-NOR gate can be used for bit comparison. The output of an Ex-NOR gate is 1, if both the inputs are similar so it can be used as a one bit comparator. The output of Ex-NOR gate is 1, if the number of 1's is even in input. If the number of 1's is odd, then the output is 0. So it can be used for even/odd parity checker.

Table 1.15 represents truth table for two input Ex-NOR gate.

Table 1.15 Truth table for two input XNOR gate

Inputs		*Output*
A	*B*	$y = \overline{A \oplus B}$
0	0	1
0	1	0
1	0	0
1	1	1

1.4 COMPUTER CODES

A digital computer has only two states high and low. These two states are represented by 1 and 0. Computer system can take data in decimal form alphabets or special characters but information is handled and manipulated in digital form only and then the output is again in the form of decimal, alphabets, special characters etc. A code is used to enable an operator to feed data into a computer in any form. The computer converts these data into binary codes and after computation again the result is supplied into its original form. So computers codes are symbolic representation of discrete information. These computer codes are used for communicating information to a digital computer and retrieve the messages from it.

Computer codes are classified as weighted binary codes, non weighted codes, alphanumeric codes etc.

1.4.1 Weighted Binary Codes

Weighted binary codes are based on their positional weighting principles. Each digit in the given number has a specific weight that depends upon the position of the digit. In weighted binary codes each bit is multiplied by the weights, the sum of these weighted bits provide equivalent decimal digit. There are many weighted codes. For example 8421, 5421 and 2421 are weighted binary codes. These all come under Binary Coded Decimal (BCD) numbers. Each decimal digit is represented by a four bit binary word.

1.4.1.1 BCD or 8421 Codes

The Binary Coded Decimal (BCD) use binary number system to specify decimal numbers 0 to 9. It has four bits. The weights are according to the position. The weight of first position is 2° from right most side.

The weight of second position is 2^1, third position 2^2 and fourth position weight is 2^3. Reading from left to right weights are 8, 4, 2, and 1 so BCD codes are known as 8421 codes. In BCD scheme each digit is represented by four binary bits like 5 will be represented as $[0101]_2$. 0 to 9 this representation is followed but after 9 we write four binary bits corresponding to each digit of the number like we have to write BCD equivalent for 13 then we will write four binary bits for 1 and four binary bits for 3. So 13 will be represented as [0001 0011] in BCD.

BCD codes are used where the decimal number is directly transferred into or out of a digital system. Electronic calculators, digital voltmeters, digital clock etc., work with BCD numbers.

Example 1.32: *Give BCD code for the decimal number 789.*

Solution. Decimal number = 789

We have to write four bits corresponding to each digit.

$$7 \rightarrow 0111$$
$$8 \rightarrow 1000$$
$$9 \rightarrow 1001$$

So BCD equivalent is (0111 1000 1001) BCD.

Table 1.16 represents some standard BCD codes.

Table 1.16 BCD codes

Decimal Number	*Standard BCD Codes*
0	0000
1	0001
2	0010
3	0011
4	0100
5	0101
6	0110
7	0111
8	1000
9	1001
10	0001 0000
11	0001 0001
12	0001 0010
13	0001 0011
56	0101 0110
84	1000 0100
99	1001 1001

1.4.2 Non Weighted Codes

The codes that are not positionally weighted are known as non weighted codes. Each position is not assigned and fixed weight. Examples of non weighted codes are excess-3 codes and gray codes.

1.4.2.1 *Excess-3 Codes*

The excess-3 represents a decimal number in binary form as a number greater than 3. An excess-3 code is obtained by adding 3 to a decimal number. Like when we have to write excess-3 code for 4 then

$$= 0100 + (3)_{10}$$
$$= 0100 + 0011$$
$$= 0111$$
$$= (7)_{10}.$$

So excess code is obtained by adding 3 to BCD equivalent. When we have to write excess-3 code for numbers greater than 9 then each digit is added by 3 and then write the binary equivalent for each digit.

The excess-3 code is shown in Table 1.17.

Table 1.17 Excess-3 code

Decimal Number	*Excess-3 Code*
0	0011
1	0100
2	0101
3	0110
4	0111
5	1000
6	1001
7	1010
8	1011
9	1100

Example 1.33: *Convert the following excess-3 code into decimal: 0011 0101 1010 0100.*

Solution. First we group the number in 4-bits form

0011	0101	1010	0100
↓	↓	↓	↓
3	5	10	4

Now subtracting 3 from each group

$$\begin{array}{rrrrr} & 3 & 5 & 10 & 4 \\ - & 3 & 3 & 3 & 3 \\ \hline & 0 & 2 & 7 & 1 \end{array}$$

So the decimal equivalent will be 0271.

1.4.2.2 Gray Code

In gray code the binary bits are arranged in such a way that only one binary bit changes at a time when we make a change from any number to the next. The gray code is also known as unit distance code or minimum change code because only 1-bit changes from any number to the next. It is a non weighted code because there are not positionally weighted. It is not a self complementing code. The gray code is shown in Table 1.18.

Table 1.18 Gray code

Decimal Number	*Binary Code*	*Gray Code*
0	0000	0000
1	0001	0001
2	0010	0011
3	0011	0010
4	0100	0110
5	0101	0111
6	0110	0101
7	0111	0100
8	1000	1100
9	1001	1101
10	1010	1111
11	1011	1110
12	1100	1010
13	1101	1011
14	1110	1001
15	1111	1000

Gray code can be used in a shaft encoder in which the position of a shaft is an analog quantity is represented digitally. Gray code avoids errors in reading the information.

1.4.3 Alphanumeric Codes

A code that represents numbers, alphabets, special symbols and characters. A complete set includes:

(*a*) 26 lower case alphabets

(*b*) 26 upper case alphabets

(*c*) 10 numeric digits

(*d*) About 25 special characters such as +, /, ≠ % etc.

Total up to 87 symbols. For these symbol's representation we require at least 7-bits. Each character is represented by a 7-bit code, 8-bit is inserted for parity. Using 7-bit, there are 128 combinations (2^7) are possible. 87 symbols represent this set. Now 41 combinations are left 8 characters represent graphic symbols, 23 characters represent formal effectors which are functional characters for controlling the layout of printing and display devices such as carriage return. Other 10 characters are used to direct the data communication flow and report its status.

The most used alphanumeric codes are ASCII codes and EBCDIC codes.

1.4.3.1 ASCII Code

ASCII stands for American Standard Code for Information Interchange. It is used extensively in small computers, peripherals, instruments and communication devices. It is a 7-bit code. The 8th bit can be used for parity or it can be permanently 1 or 0. Using 7-bits 128 characters can be coded. It includes upper and lower case alphabets, numbers, punctuation marks, special characters and control characters. ASCII codes are shown in Table 1.19.

ISCII stands for Indian Standard Code for Information Interchange. It is 8-bit code that is used for Indian languages. Using 8-bits total 256 characters can be coded.

Table 1.20 definition of control characters.

Table 1.19 ASCII codes

Characters or Abbreviation	*Hex Codes for 7-bit ASCII*	*Characters or Abbreviations*	*Hex Codes for 7-bit ASCII*
NUL	00	&	26
SOH	01	'	27
STX	02	(	28
ETX	03	)	29
EOT	04	*	2A
ENQ	05	+	2B
ACK	06	,	2C
BEL	07	-	2D
BS	08	.	2E
HT	09	/	2F
LF	0A	‘	60
VT	0B	:	3A
FF	0C	;	3B
CR	0D	<	3C
SO	0E	=	3D
SI	0F	>	3E
DLE	10	?	3F

DC1	11	@	40
DC2	12	[	5B
DC3	13	\	5C
DC4	14	]	5D
NAK	15	^	5E
SYN	16	—	5F
ETB	17	{	7B
CAN	18	|	7C
EM	19	}	7D
SUB	1A	~	7E
ESC	1B	DEL	7F
FS	1C	a	61
GS	1D	b	62
RS	1E	c	63
US	1F	d	64
SP	20	e	65
!	21	f	66
″	22	g	67
#	23	h	68
$	24	i	69
%	25	j	6A
k	6B	K	4B
l	6C	L	4C
m	6D	M	4D
n	6E	N	4E
o	6F	O	4F
p	70	P	50
q	71	Q	51
r	72	R	52
s	73	S	53
t	74	T	54
u	75	U	55
v	76	V	56
w	77	W	57

x	78	X	58
y	79	Y	59
z	7A	Z	5A
A	41	0	30
B	42	1	31
C	43	2	32
D	44	3	33
E	45	4	34
F	46	5	35
G	47	6	36
H	48	7	37
I	49	8	38
J	4A	9	39

Table 1.20 Definition of control structures

NUL	Null	DC2	Direct Control 2
SOH	Start of Heading	DC3	Direct Control 3
STX	Start Text	DC4	Direct Control 4
ETX	End Text	NAK	Negative Acknowledge
EOT	End of Transmission	SYN	Synchronous Idle
ENQ	Enquiry	ETB	End Transmission Block
ACK	Acknowledge	CAN	Cancel
BEL	Bell	EM	End of Medium
BS	Backspace	SUB	Substitute
HT	Horizontal Tab	ESC	Escape
LF	Line Feed	FS	Form Separator
VT	Vertical Tab	GS	Group Separator
FF	Form Feed	RS	Record Separator
CR	Carriage Return	US	Unit Separator
SO	Shift Out		
SI	Shift In		
DLE	Data Link Escape		
DC1	Direct Control 1		

1.4.3.2 EBCDIC Codes

EBCDIC stands for Extended Binary Coded Decimal Interchange code. It is an 8-bit code with out parity. A 9th bit can be used for parity. With 8-bits a total of 256 characters can be coded. First 4-bits are known as zone bits and remaining 4-bits represent digit values. It differs from ASCII only in its code grouping for the different alphanumeric characters.

Table 1.21 represents EBCDIC codes.

Table 1.21 EBCDIC codes

Characters or Control Characters	*Hex Codes for EBCDIC*	*Characters of Control Characters*	*Hex Codes for EBCDIC*
NUL	00	¢	4A
SOH	01	.	4B
STH	02	,	6B
ETS	03	?	6F
HT	05	:	7A
DEL	07	;	5E
VT	0B	!	5A
FF	0C	'	7D
CR	0D	"	7F
SO	0E	+	4E
SI	0F	–	60
DLE	10	—	6D
DC1	11	*	5C
DC2	12	/	61
DC3	13	=	7E
RES	14	<	4C
NL	15	>	6E
BS	16	(	4D
CAN	18	)	5D
EM	19	{	8B
FLS	1C	}	9B
GS	1D	[	AD
RDS	1E	]	DD
US	1F	|	4F
BYP	24	&	50

LF	25	$	5B
EOB	26	¬	5F
ENQ	2D	%	6C
ACK	2E	#	7B
BEL	2F	@	7C
SYN	32	a	81
DC4	35	b	82
EOT	37	c	83
NAK	3D	d	84
SUB	3F	e	85
SP	40	f	86
BLANK	E0	g	87
h	88	J	D1
i	89	K	D2
j	91	L	D3
k	92	M	D4
l	93	N	D5
m	94	O	D6
n	95	P	D7
o	96	Q	D8
p	97	R	D9
q	98	S	E2
r	99	T	E3
s	A2	U	E4
t	A3	V	E5
u	A4	W	E6
v	A5	X	E7
w	A6	Y	E8
x	A7	Z	E9
y	A8	0	F0
z	A9	1	F1
A	C1	2	F2
B	C2	3	F3
C	C3	4	F4

D	C4	5	F5
E	C5	6	F6
F	C6	7	F7
G	C7	8	F8
H	C8	9	F9
I	C9		

1.5 COMBINATIONAL CIRCUITS

A combinational circuit consists of logic gates whose outputs at any time are determined from the present combination of inputs. A combinational circuit performs an operation that can be specified logically by a set of Boolean functions.

A combinational circuit consists of input variables, logic gates, and output variables. The logic gates accept signals from the inputs and generate signals to the outputs. This process transforms binary information from the given input data to a required output data.

The block diagram of a combinational circuit is shown as follows:

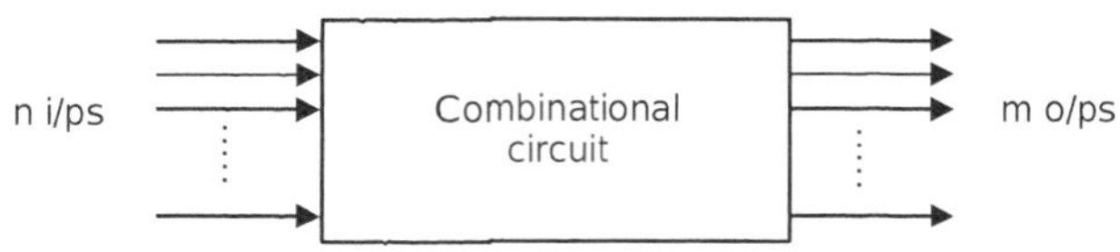

Fig. 1.8 Block diagram of combinational circuit

The n input variables come from an external source; the m output variables go to an external destination. Each input and output variable exists as a binary signal that represents logic 1 and logic 0.

For n input variables, there are 2^n possible binary *i/p* combinations. For each possible input combination, there is one possible output value. Thus, a combinational circuit can be specified with a truth table that lists the output values for each combination of input variables.

1.5.1 Half Adder

A combinational circuit that performs the addition of two bits is called a half adder. This circuit needs two binary inputs and two binary outputs. The input variables designate the augend and addend bits; the output variable produce the sum and carry.

We assign symbols x and y to the two inputs and S (for sum) and C (for carry) to the outputs.

1. **Block Diagram of Half Adder:**

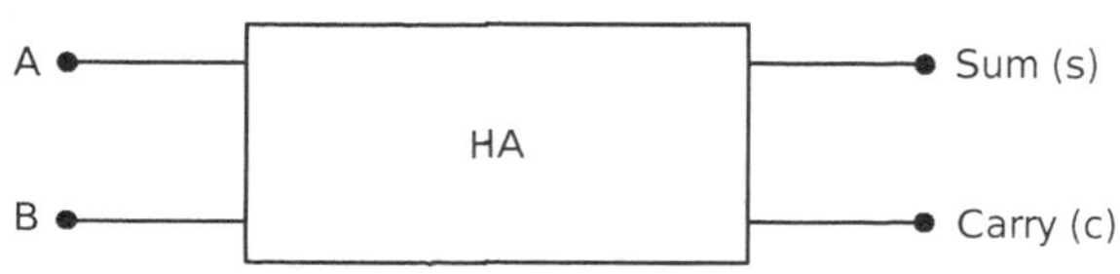

Fig. 1.9 Half adder block diagram

2. **Truth Table for Half Adder:** The truth table for half adder is listed in the table:

Table 1.22 Half adder

x	*y*	*C*	*S*
0	0	0	0
0	1	0	1
1	0	0	1
1	1	1	0

From the truth table of half adder, we have seen that the C output is 1 only when both inputs are 1. The S output represents the least significant bit of the sum.

The simplified boolean expressions for the two outputs can be obtained directly from the truth table. The simplified sum of products expressions are.

$$S = x'y + xy'$$
$$C = xy$$

The expressions for half adder can also be modified as:

$$S = \bar{X}\,Y + X\,\bar{Y} \qquad C = X\,.\,Y$$

$$S = \overline{X\,Y + \bar{X}\,\bar{Y}} \qquad \bar{C} = \overline{X\,.\,Y}$$

$$= \overline{\overline{(X + Y)\,.\,(\bar{X} + \bar{Y})}} \quad = \left(\overline{\overline{\bar{X} + \bar{Y}}}\right)$$

$$= (X + Y)\,.\,(\bar{X} + \bar{Y}) \quad = \bar{X} + \bar{Y}$$

3. **Implementation of Half Adder:** The logic diagram of the half adder is implemented in sum of products. It can also be implemented with an exclusive-OR and an AND Gate.

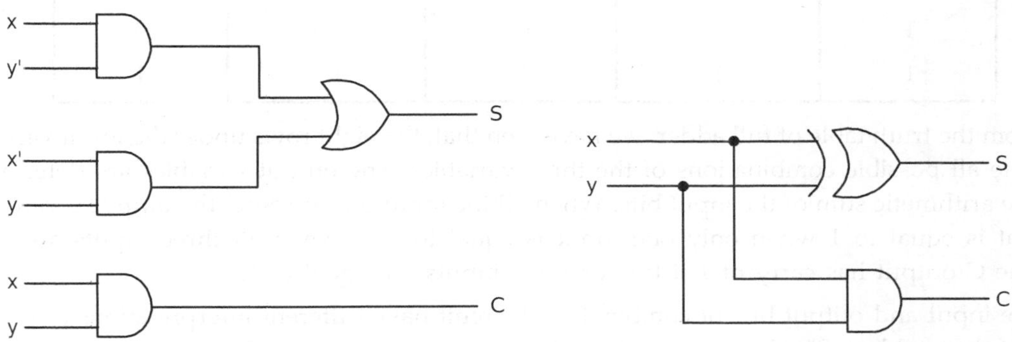

(a) S = xy′ + x′y
C = xy

(b) S = x ⊕ y
C = xy

Fig. 1.10 Implementation of half adder

1.5.2 Full Adder

A full adder is a combinational circuit that forms the arithmetic sum of three bits. It consists of three inputs and two outputs. Two of the input variables, denoted by *x* and *y*, represent the two significant bits to be added. The third input *z*, represents the carry from the previous lower significant position.

Two outputs are necessary because the arithmetic sum of three binary digits ranges in value from 0 to 3, and binary 2 or 3 needs two digits. The two outputs are designated by the symbol S for sum and C for carry. The binary variable S gives the value of the least significant bit of the sum.

1. **Block Diagram of Full Adder:**

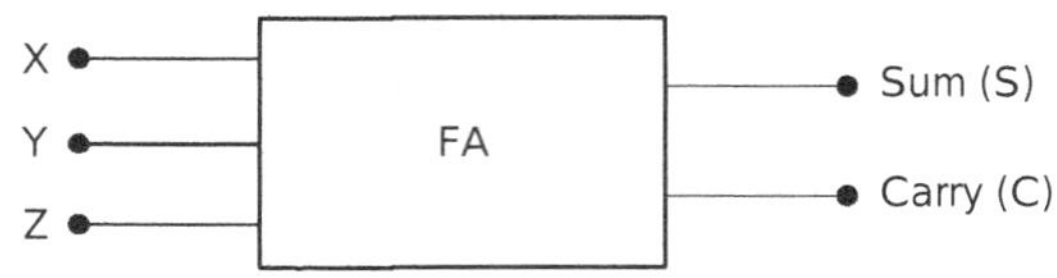

Fig. 1.11 Block diagram of half adder

2. **Truth Table for Full Adder:**

Table 1.23 Full adder

x	*y*	*z*	*C*	*S*
0	0	0	0	0
0	0	1	0	1
0	1	0	0	1
0	1	1	1	0
1	0	0	0	1
1	0	1	1	0
1	1	0	1	0
1	1	1	1	1

From the truth table of full adder, we have seen that, the eight rows under the input variables designate all possible combinations of the three variables. The output variables are determined from the arithmetic sum of the input bits. When all the input bits are zero, the output is zero. The S output is equal to 1 when only one input is equal to 1 or when all three inputs are equal to 1. The C output has carry of 1 if two or three inputs are equal to 1.

The input and output bits of combinational circuit have different interpretations at various stages of the problem. The binary signals of the inputs are considered binary digits to be added arithmetically to form a two-digit sum at the output. On the other hand, the same binary values are considered as variables of boolean functions when expressed in the truth table or when the circuit is implemented with logic-gates.

3. **Maps for Full Adder:**

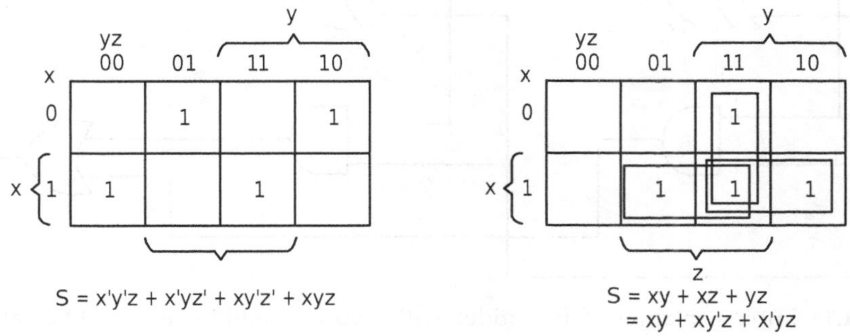

Fig. 1.12 Maps for full adder

The maps for the outputs of the full adder are shown in the above Fig. 1.12. The simplified expressions are:

$$S = x'y'z + x'yz' + xy'z' + xyz$$

$$C = xy + xz + yz$$

The logic diagram for the full adder implemented in sum of products is shown in Fig. 1.13. It can also be implemented with two half adders and one OR gate.

4. **Implementation of Full Adder:** The S output from the second half adder is the exclusive-OR of Z and the output of the first half adder, giving

$$\begin{aligned} S &= z \oplus (x \oplus y) \\ &= z' (xy' + x'y) + z (xy' + x'y') \\ &= z' (xy' + x'y) + z (xy + x'y') \\ &= xy'z' + x'yz' + xyz + x'y'z \end{aligned}$$

The carry output is

$$\begin{aligned} C &= z (xy' + x'y) + xy \\ &= xy'z + x'yz + xy \end{aligned}$$

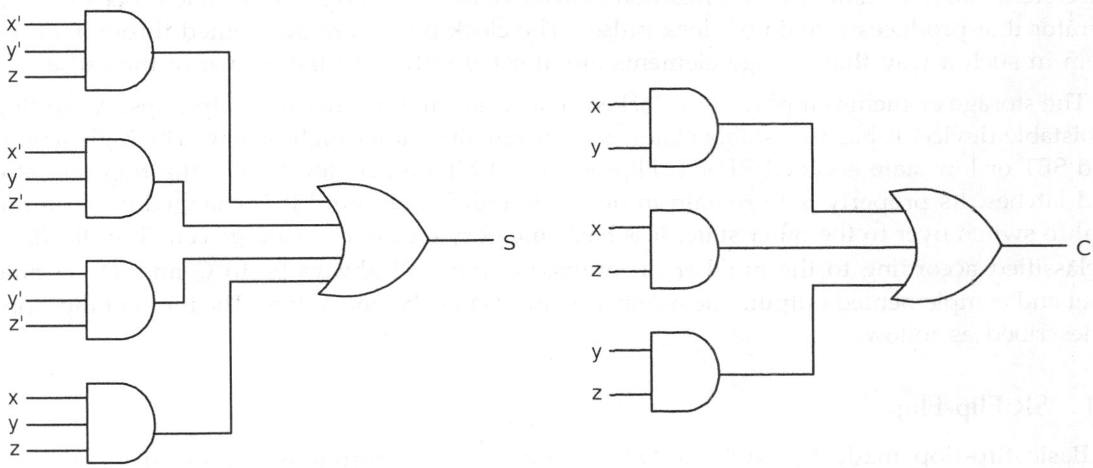

Fig. 1.13 Implementation of full adder in sum of products

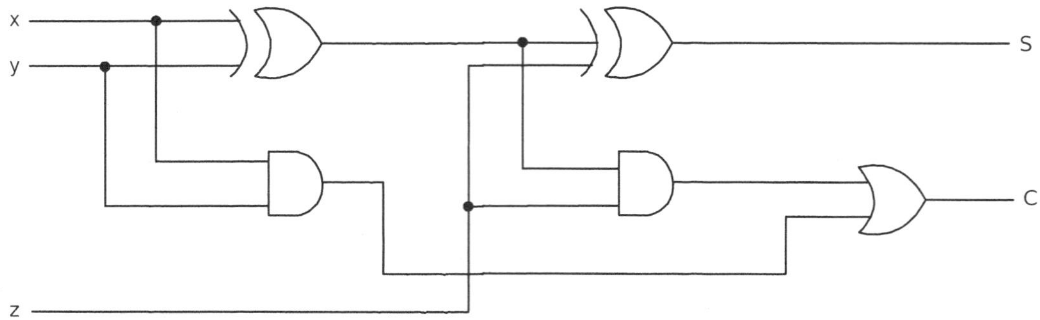

Fig. 1.14 Implementation of full adder with two half adders and an OR gate

1.6 SEQUENTIAL CIRCUITS

Basically a sequential circuit is a combinational circuit along with a memory unit. Thus the output of the sequential circuit does not depends upon the present state of the input, it also depends upon the previous state of the input variable. Previous state is stand in the memory unit.

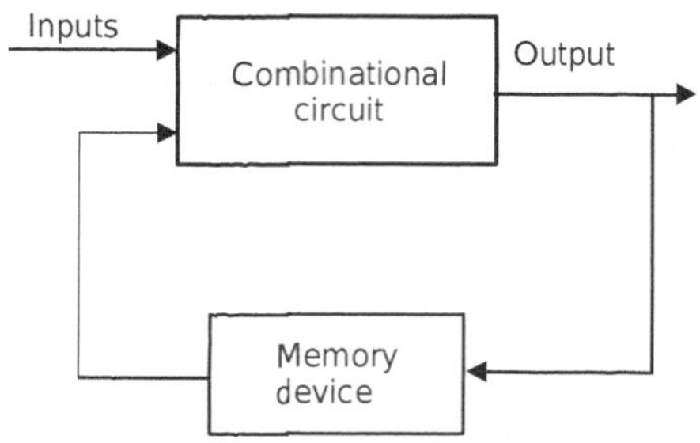

Fig. 1.15 Block diagram of sequential circuit

Fig. 1.15 depicts block diagram of sequential circuit. The most common type of sequential circuit is the synchronous type. Synchronous sequential circuits affect the storage element only at discrete instants of time. Synchronization is achieved by a timing device called a clock pulse generator that produces a chain of clock pulses. The clock pulses are distributed throughout the system in such a way that storage elements are affected only with the arrival of the pulse.

The storage elements employed in clocked sequential circuits are called flip-flops. A flip-flop is a bistable device. It has two stable states, output remains either high or low. The high state is called SET or low state is called RESET. Flip-flop is a 1 bit storage device. The flip-flops are also called latches. Its property is to remain in one state indefinitely until it is changed by an input signal to switch over to the other state. It is basic memory element or storage cell. The flip-flops are classified according to the number of inputs. Output will always be to Q and $\bar{Q}$, normal output and complemented output. The number of inputs may be one or two. The types of flip-flops are described as follows.

1.6.1 SR Flip-Flop

Basic flip-flop made by NOR or NAND gate are asynchronous. To make flip-flop as synchronous a clock is used. So that input R and S reached to the flip-flop ON when clock is high and output changed only, during clock is high. The clocked S-R flip-flop consists of a basic NOR flip-flop and two AND gates.

When the CLK input is low (0) output of AND gates will be 0 and, thus input to NOR gates are 0. When the CLK input becomes high (1). The AND gate will enabled and passed R and S to R′ and S′ respectively. The set state is reached with S = 1, R = 0 and CP = 1. To change to the clear state, the inputs must be S = 0, R = 1 and CP = 1. With both S = 1 and R = 1 the occurrence of a clock pulse causes both outputs to momentarily go to 0. The Q will hold this information when the CLK is low. The clocked S-R flip-flop is shown in Fig. 1.16.

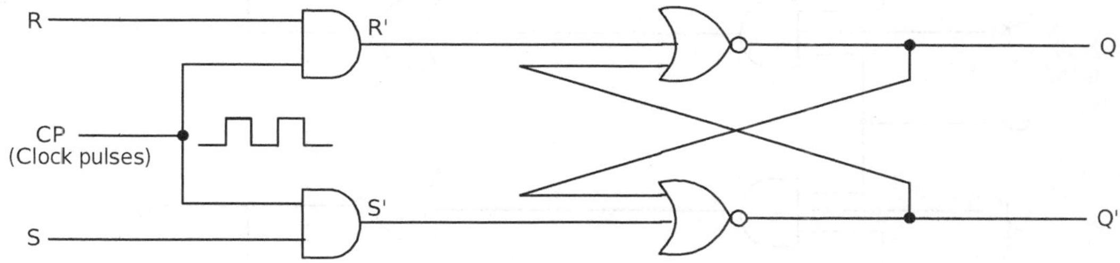

(a) Logic diagram

Table 1.24 Characteristic table

Q	S	R	Q (t + 1)
0	0	0	0
0	0	1	0
0	1	0	1
0	1	1	Indetermine
1	0	0	1
1	0	1	0
1	1	0	1
1	1	1	indetermine

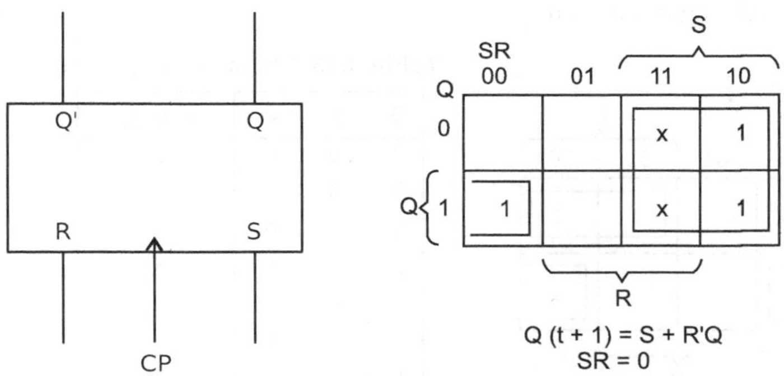

(*b*) Graphic symbol (*c*) Characteristic equation

Fig. 1.16 Clocked S-R flip-flop

The graphic symbol for the clocked S-R flip-flop is shown in Fig 1.16(*b*). It has three inputs: S, R and CP. The CP input is recognized from the marked small triangle. It denotes the fact that the flip-flop responds to an input clock transition from a low-level (binary 0) to a high-level (binary 1) signal. The outputs of the flip-flop are marked with Q and Q′ within the box. The state of the flip-flop is determined from the value of its normal output Q and its complement Q′.

The characteristic table for the flip-flop is shown in Table 1.24. This table summarizes the operation of the flip-flop in a tabular form. Q is the binary state of the flip-flop at a given time, the S and R columns give the possible values of the inputs, and Q (t +1) is the state of the flip-flop after the occurrence of a clock pulse (referred to as next state).

The characteristic equation of the flip-flop is derived in the map of Table 1.24. The equation specifies the value of the next state as a function of the present state and the inputs. The characteristic equation is an algebraic expression for the binary information of the characteristic table.

1.6.2 J-K Flip-Flop

A J-K flip-flop is a refinement of the S-R flip-flop in that the indetermine state of the S-R type is defined in the J-K type. Inputs J and K behaves like inputs S and R to set and clear the flip-flop. When inputs are applied to both J and K simultaneously, the flip-flop switches to its complement state, that is, if Q = 1, it switches to Q = 0; and vice versa.

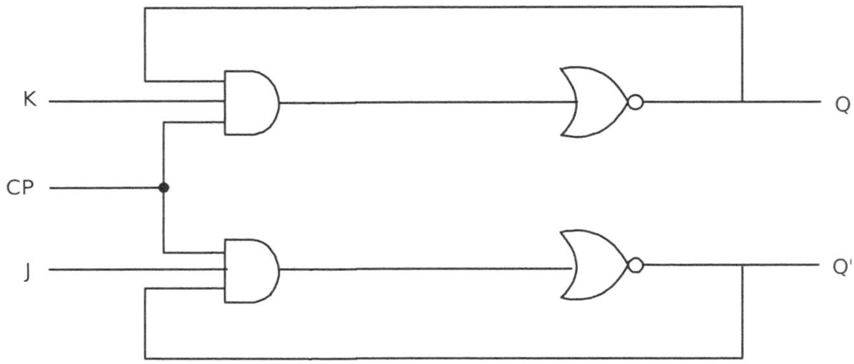

(*a*) Logic diagram

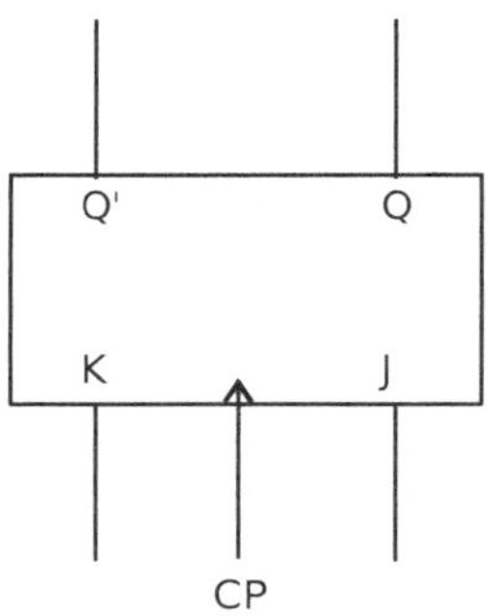

(*b*) Graphic symbol

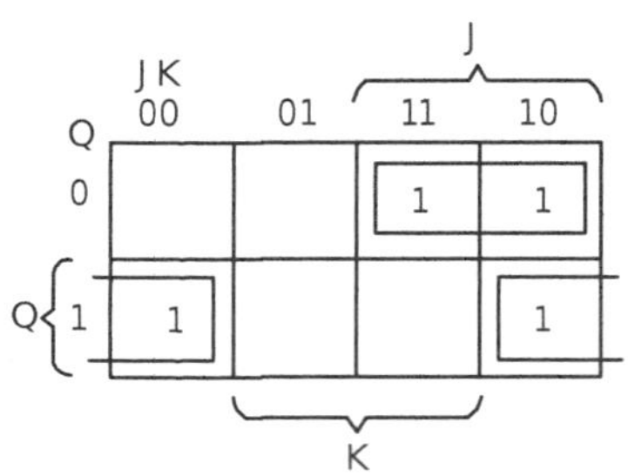

Q (t + 1) = J Q' + K'Q

(*c*) Characteristic equation

Table 1.15 Characteristic table

Q	*J*	*K*	*Q (t+1)*
0	0	0	0
0	0	1	0
0	1	0	1
0	1	1	1
1	0	0	1
1	0	1	0
1	1	0	1
1	1	1	0

Fig. 1.17 Clocked J-K flip-flop

A clocked J-K flip-flop is shown in Fig. 1.17. Output Q is ANDed with K and CP inputs so that the flip-flop is cleared during a clock pulse only if Q was previously 1. Similarly, output Q′ is ANDed with J and CP inputs so that the flip-flop is set with a clock pulse only if Q′ was previously 1.

The characteristic table shown in Table 1.25, the J-K flip-flop behaves like an S-R flip flop, except when both J and K are equal to 1. When both J and K are 1, the clock pulse is transmitted through one AND gate only-the one whose input is connected to the flip-flop output which is presently equal to 1. Thus, if Q = 1, the output of the upper AND gate becomes 1 upon application of a clock pulse, and flip-flop is cleared. If Q′ = 1, the output of the lower AND gate becomes a 1 and the flip-flop is set. In either case, the output state of the flip-flop is complemented.

The characteristic equation is given in Table 1.25 and is derived from the map of the characteristic table.

1.6.3 D Flip-Flop

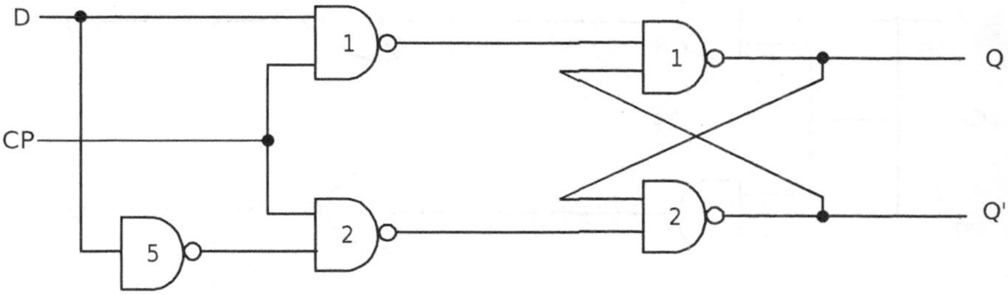

(*a*) Logic diagram with NAND gates

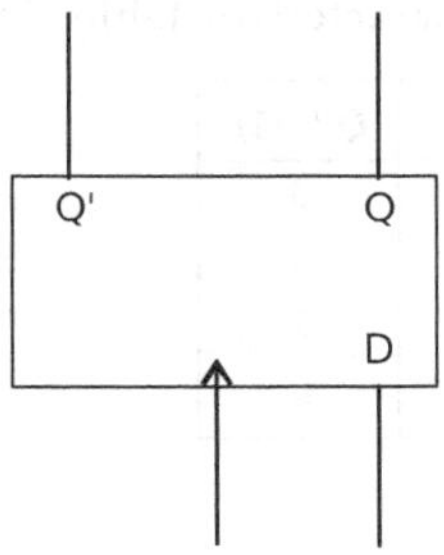

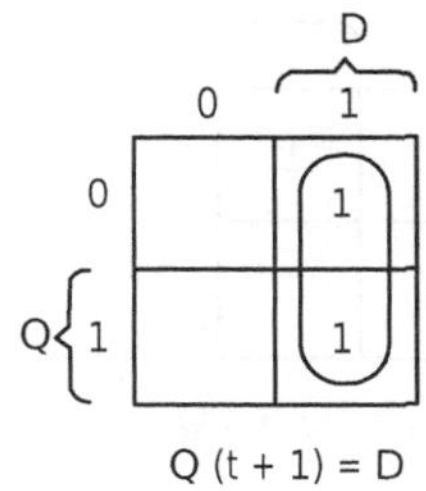

Table 1.26 Characteristic table

Q	D	Q (t+1)
0	0	0
0	1	1
1	0	0
1	1	1

(*b*) Graphic symbol 1.18 D flip-flop (*c*) Characteristic equation

Fig. 1.18 Clocked D flip-flop

The D flip-flop shown in Fig. 1.18 is a modification of the clocked S-R flip-flop. NAND gates 1 and 2 from a basic flip-flop and gates 3 and 4 modify if into a clocked S-R flip-flop. The D input goes directly to the S input, and its complement, through gate 5, is applied to the R input. As long as the clock pulse is at 0, gates 3 and 4 have a 1 in their outputs, regardless of the value of the other inputs. The D input is sampled during the occurrence of a clock pulse. If it is 1, the output of gate 3 goes to 0, switching the flip-flop to the set state. If it is 0, the output of gate 4 goes to 0, switching the flip-flop to the clear state.

The symbol for a clocked D flip-flop is shown in Fig. 1.18 (*b*)

The characteristics table is listed in Table 1.26 and the characteristics equation is derived in Fig. 1.18(c). The characteristics equation shows that the next state of the flip-flop is the same as the D input and is independent of the value of the present state.

1.6.4 T Flip-Flop

The T flip-flop is a single input version of the J-K flip-flop. As shown in Fig. 1.19, the T flip-flop is obtained from a J-K type if both input are tied together. The designation T comes from the ability of the flip-flop to "toggle" or change state. Regardless of the present state of the flip-flop, it assumes the complement state when the clock pulse occurs while input T is logic 1.

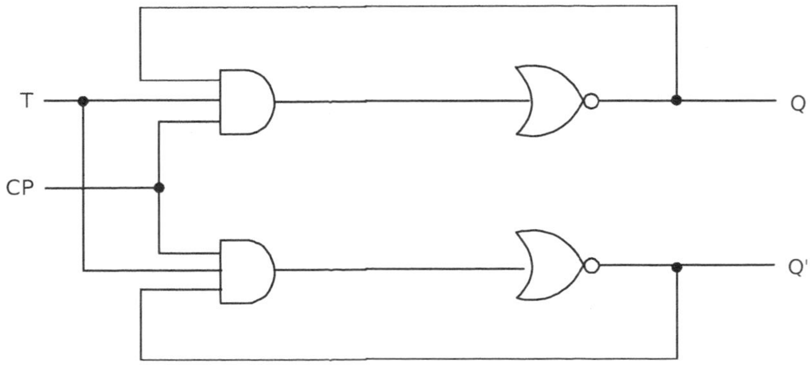

(*a*) Logic diagram

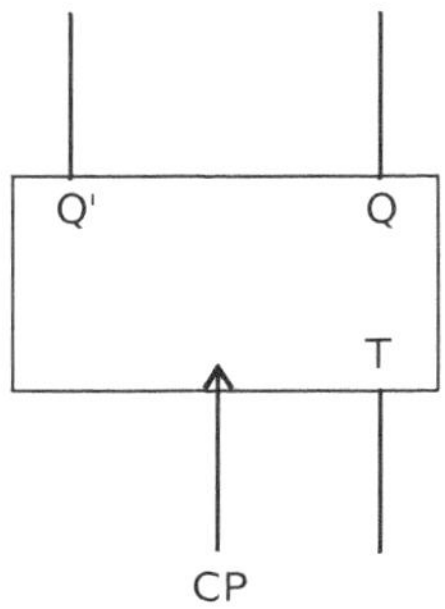

(*b*) Graphic symbol

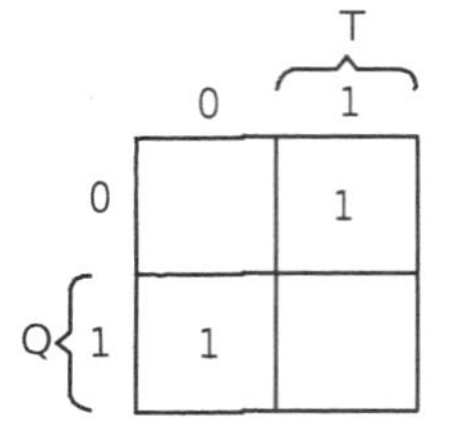

Q (t + 1) = TQ' + T'Q

(*c*) Characteristic equation

Table 1.27 Characteristic table

Q	*T*	*Q (t+1)*
0	0	0
0	1	1
1	0	1
1	1	0

Fig. 1.19 Clocked T flip-flop

The symbol characteristic table and characteristic equation of the T flip-flop are shown in Table 1.27.

1.7 DIGITAL COMPONENTS

The following are the most important combinational circuit type MSI components that are readily available in IC package.

1. Multiplexer
2. De-Multiplexer
3. Encoder
4. Decoder
5. Register

1.7.1 Digital Multiplexer

Multiplex means "many into one". It means transmitting large information or inputs to single output. The device which is used to convert many inputs into a single output is called a multiplexer. A digital multiplexer (MUX) is a combinational circuit that selects digital information from various input lines and transmits the selected information to a single output. The selection of particular input line is controlled by a set of selection lines.

Generally, there are 2^n *i/p* lines and n selection lines whose bit combination decides which *i/p* is to be selected. For example, if four *i/p* lines are used for one output then two selection lines are required (*i.e.*, $2^2 = 4$, so $n = 2$) or to select one of eight *i/p* lines, then three selection lines are required (*i.e.*, $2^3 = 8$ so, $n = 3$).

The block diagram of multiplexer ($m = 2^n$) m i/p lines, n selection lines and 1 o/p is shown in Fig. 1.20.

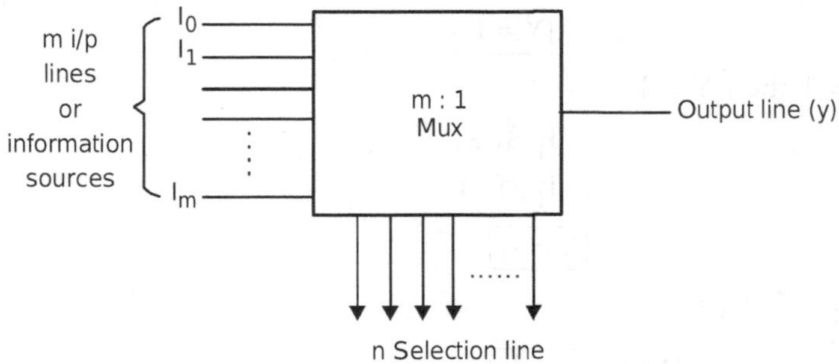

Fig. 1.20 Block diagram of *m*:1 MUX

1.7.1.1 4 × 1 Multiplexer

The 4:1 Mux is shown in Fig. 1.21.

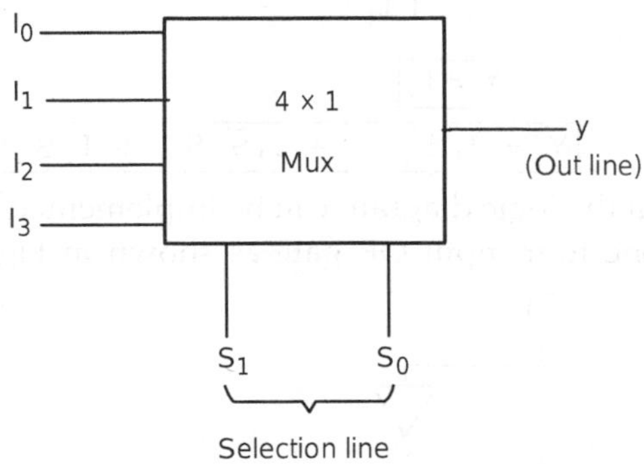

Fig. 1.21 Block diagram

The four inputs I_0 to I_3, a single output y and two selection lines S_0 and S_1 are used to select one output of four input lines.

The truth table of 4:1 Mux is shown in Table 1.28.

Table 1.28 Truth table

Selection Inputs		*Output*
S_1	S_0	y_0
0	0	I_0
0	1	I_1
1	0	I_2
1	1	I_3

According to truth table, (1) If $S_1 = 0, S_0 = 0$

Then output $Y = I_0$

$$Y = I_0 \bar{S}_1 \bar{S}_0$$

$$Y = I_0 \bar{0}\ \bar{0}$$

$$Y = I_0\ 1 \cdot 1$$

$$\boxed{Y = I_0}$$

2. If $S_1 = 0$, $S_o = 1$ then $Y = I_1$

$$Y = I_1 \bar{S}_1 \bar{S}_0$$

$$Y = I_1\ \bar{0} \cdot 1$$

$$\boxed{Y = I_1}$$

3. Similarly if $S_1 = 1$, $S_0 = 0$

Then $\boxed{Y = I_2}$

4. If $S_1 = 1$, $S_0 = 1$

Then

$$Y = I_3$$

$$Y = S_1 S_0 I_3$$

$$Y = 1 \cdot 1\ I_3$$

$$\boxed{Y = I_3}$$

$$\boxed{Y = I_0 \bar{S}_1 \bar{S}_0 + I_1 \bar{S}_1 S_0 + I_2 S_1 \bar{S}_0 + I_3 S_1 S_0}$$

By using above expression the logic diagram can be implemented using two NOT gates, four three input AND gates and one four input OR gate as shown in Fig. 1.22.

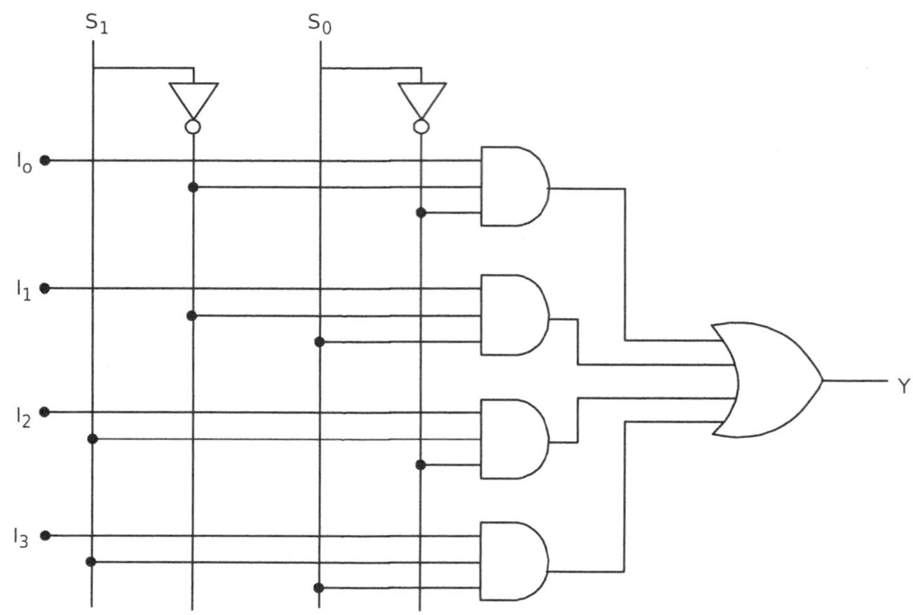

Fig. 1.22 Logic diagram

The operation of the circuit can be understood as follows. If we consider the case when S_1S_0 = 00, it means s_1s_0 = 00 is applied to the select lines, then AND Gate associated with I_0, $\bar{S}_1$ will have two inputs equal to 1 and third *i/p* will be I_0. For the other three AND gates, the output will be equal to *0* because atleast one input will have zero value in all the three AND gates.

1.7.1.2 *Applications of Multiplexer*

Multiplexer circuits find numerous applications in digital systems as follows.

1. **Data Routing.** Multiplexers can be used to route data from one of several source to one destination.
2. **Logic Function Generator.** It is used to implement the logic functions in sum of products form directly from a truth table. The logic variables are used as the select inputs and each data inputs is connected permanently high or low.
3. **Control Sequencer.** It is used as a part of control sequencer.

1.7.2 Demultiplexer (Data Distributors)

The word "demultiplex" means one to many. Demultiplexing in the process of talking information frame one input and transmitting the same over one of the several outputs.

A demultiplexer is a logic circuit that receives information on a single input and transmits the same information over one of several (2^n) output lines.

The circuit has one input signal, *m* select signals and *n* output signals. The select input determine to which output the data input will be connected this is also called a serial-to parallel converter.

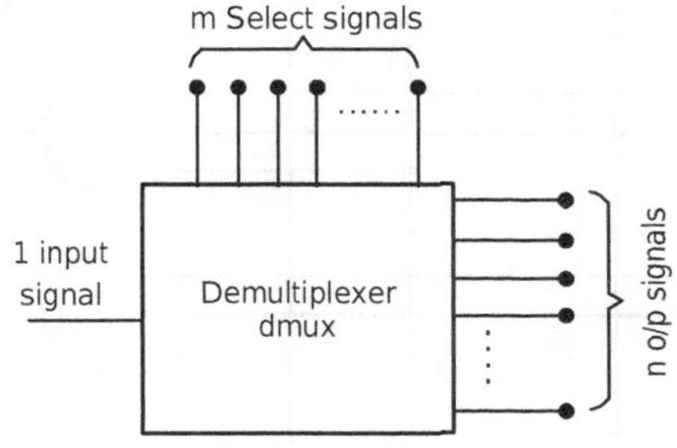

Fig. 1.23 Block diagram of demultiplexer

1.7.2.1 *2.D 1 : 4 Demultiplexer*

A 1 to 4 demultiplexer has a single input (D), four outputs (Y_0 to Y_3) and two select inputs (S_1 and S_0). The truth table is shown in Table 1.29.

Truth table of 1 : 4 demultiplexer.

Table 1.29

Data Input	*Select Inputs*		*Outputs*			
D	S_1	S_0	Y_3	Y_2	Y_1	Y_0
D	0	0	0	0	0	D
D	0	1	0	0	D	0
D	1	0	0	D	0	0
D	1	1	D	0	0	0

$$Y_0 = \overline{S_1 S_0}\, D \qquad Y_2 = S_2 \overline{S}_0 D$$

$$Y_1 = \overline{S}_1 S_0 D \qquad Y_3 = S_1 S_0 D$$

1.7.2.2 1 : 4 Demultiplexer Logic Diagram

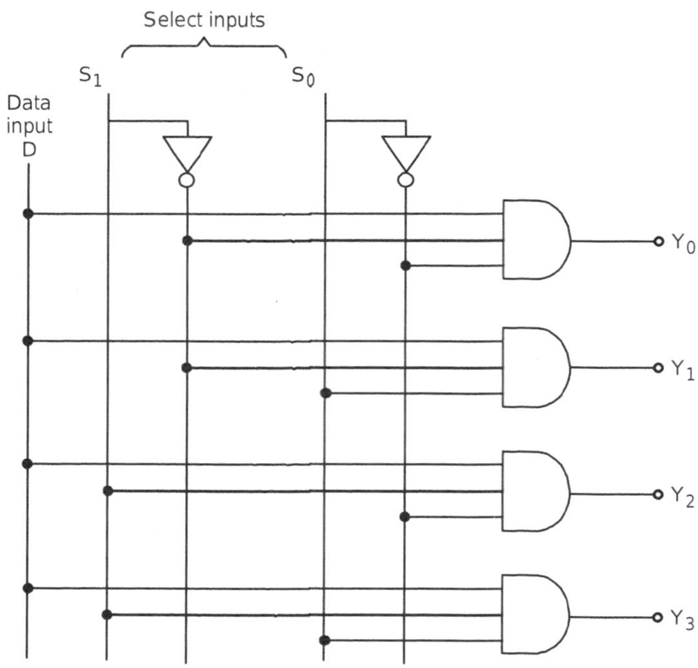

Fig. 1.24 Logic diagram of 1 : 4 demultiplexer

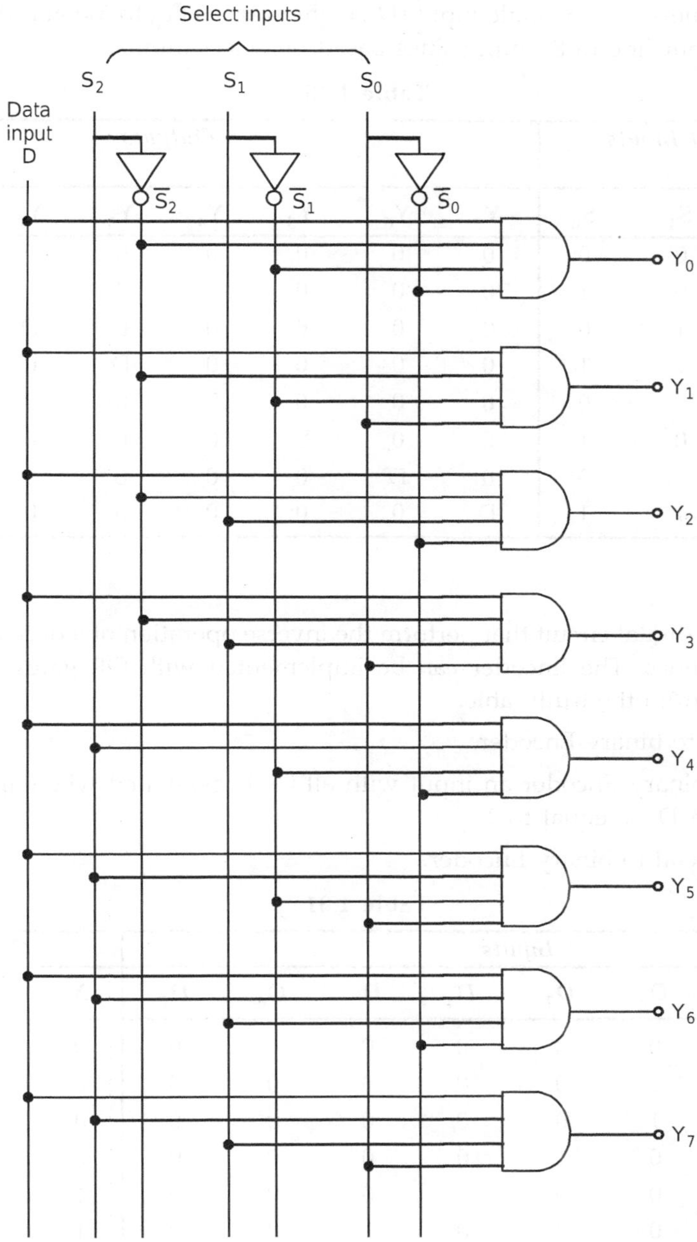

Fig. 1.25 Logic diagram of 1 : 8 demultiplexer

1.7.2.3 1 : 8 Demultiplexer

A 1 : 8 demultiplexer has a single input (D), eight outputs (Y_0 to Y_7) and three select inputs. It distributes one input line to 8 output lines based on select inputs.

Table 1.30

Data Input	*Select Inputs*			*Outputs*							
D	S_2	S_1	S_0	Y_7	Y_6	Y_5	Y_4	Y_3	Y_2	Y_1	Y_0
D	0	0	0	0	0	0	0	0	0	0	D
D	0	0	1	0	0	0	0	0	0	D	0
D	0	1	0	0	0	0	0	0	D	0	0
D	0	1	1	0	0	0	0	D	0	0	0
D	1	0	0	0	0	0	D	0	0	0	0
D	1	0	1	0	0	D	0	0	0	0	0
D	1	1	0	0	D	0	0	0	0	0	0
D	1	1	1	D	0	0	0	0	0	0	0

1.7.3 Encoders

An Encoder is a digital circuit that perform the inverse operation of a decoder. It has 2^n input lines and n output lines. The Encoder can be implemented with OR gates whose inputs are determined directly from the truth table.

Example: Octal to binary Encoder.

In the octal to binary Encoder an input with all 0's is generated when all the inputs are 0 this is same as when D_0 is equal to 1.

Truth table of octal to binary Encoder.

Table 1.31

Inputs								*Outputs*		
D_0	D_1	D_2	D_3	D_4	D_5	D_6	D_7	X	Y	Z
1	0	0	0	0	0	0	0	0	0	0
0	1	0	0	0	0	0	0	0	0	1
0	0	1	0	0	0	0	0	0	1	0
0	0	0	1	0	0	0	0	0	1	1
0	0	0	0	1	0	0	0	1	0	0
0	0	0	0	0	1	0	0	1	0	1
0	0	0	0	0	0	1	0	1	1	0
0	0	0	0	0	0	0	1	1	1	1

1.7.3.1 Priority Encoder

A priority Encoder is an Encoder circuit that includes the priority function. In this Encoder if two or more inputs are equal to 1, the input having the highest priority will take precedence, in addition to the two outputs x and y. The circuit has a third output designated by *av*: this is a valid bit indicator *i.e.*, set to 1. When one or more inputs are equal to 1.

If all inputs are *o*, there is no valid input v is equal to *o*. Two outputs are not inspected when v equal to *o* are not specified as don't care conditions.

Truth table of a priority Encoder.

Inputs				*Outputs*		
D_0	D_1	D_2	D_3	X	Y	V
0	0	0	0	X	X	0
1	0	0	0	0	0	1
X	1	0	0	0	1	1
X	X	1	0	1	0	1
X	X	X	1	1	1	1

Maps for a Priority Encoder

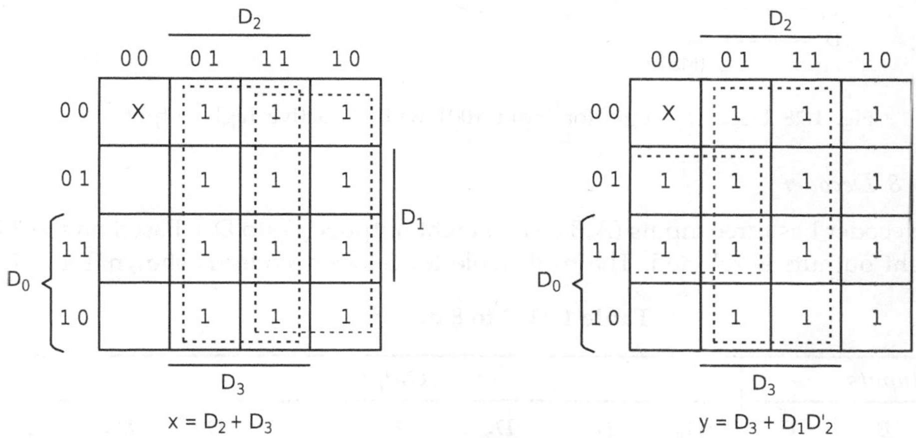

Fig. 1.26 K-Map

4-Input Priority Encoder

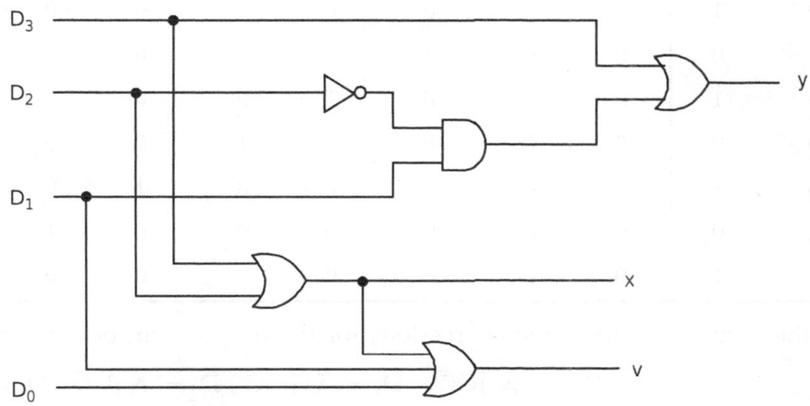

$X = D_2 + D_3$ $Y = D_3 + D, D'_2$ $Z = D_0 + D_1 + D_2 + D_3$

Fig. 1.27 Input priority encoder

1.7.4 Decoders

A decoder is similar to demultiplexer but without any data input. A decoder is a logic circuit that converts an *n*-bit binary input code (data) into 2^n output lines, such that each output line will be activated for only one of the possible combination of inputs.

In a decoder, the number of output is greater than the number of inputs. Here, it is important to note that if the number of inputs and outputs are equal in a digital system then it can be called converters, for example BCD to Excess-3 code, Binary to Gray and Gray to Binary code converters.

1.7.4.1 Basic Binary Decoder

An AND gate can be used as the basic decoding element because its output is high only when all the inputs are high.

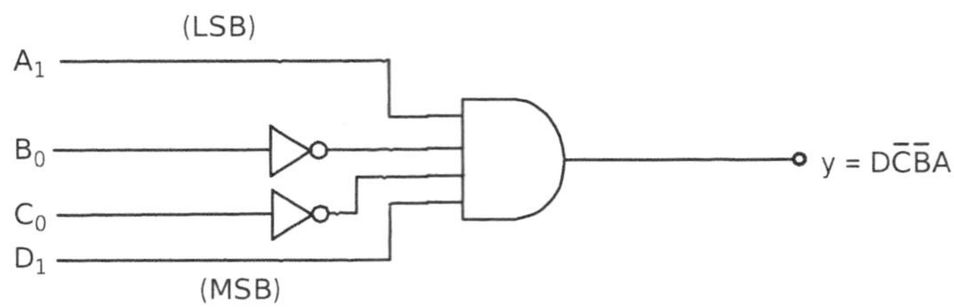

Fig. 1.28 Decoding logic for input 1001 with an active high output

1.7.4.2 3 to 8 Decoder

A 3 to 8 decoder has three inputs (A,B,C) and eight outputs (D_o to D_7). Based on the 3 inputs, one of the eight outputs is selected. The truth table for 3-to-8 decoder is shown Table 1.32.

Table 1.32 3 to 8 decoder

Inputs			*Outputs*							
A	*B*	*C*	D_0	D_1	D_2	D_3	D_4	D_5	D_6	D_7
0	0	0	1	0	0	0	0	0	0	0
0	0	1	0	1	0	0	0	0	0	0
0	1	0	0	0	1	0	0	0	0	0
0	1	1	0	0	0	1	0	0	0	0
1	0	0	0	0	0	0	1	0	0	0
1	0	1	0	0	0	0	0	1	0	0
1	1	0	0	0	0	0	0	0	1	0
1	1	1	0	0	0	0	0	0	0	1

Also, from the truth table, the logic expressions for the outputs can be written as follows:

$$D_0 = \bar{A}\,\bar{B}\,\bar{C},\ D_1 = \bar{A}\,\bar{B}\,C,\ D_2 = \bar{A}\,B\,\bar{C},\ D_3 = \bar{A}\,BC$$

$$D_4 = A\,\bar{B}\,\bar{C},\ D_5 = A\,\bar{B}\,C,\ D_6 = AB\bar{C},\ D_7 = ABC$$

1.7.4.3 Enable Inputs

Decoders have one or more enable inputs which are used to control the operation of the decoder. With the enable line held HIGH, the decoder functions normally and the input code, A,B and C will determine which output is HIGH. Hence, the decoder is enabled only if the enable line is HIGH.

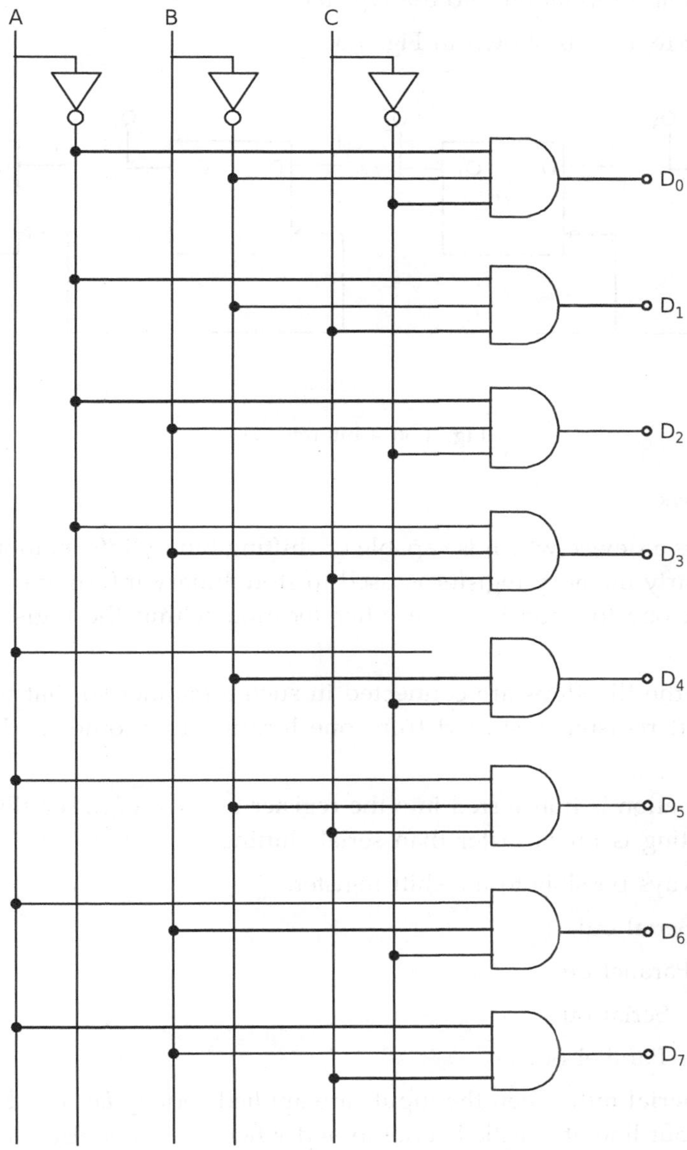

Fig. 1.29 Logic diagram of 3 to 8 decoder

1.7.5 Registers

A register is a group of flip-flops or binary cells which holds the binary information. Since a binary cell stores a bit of information, an n-bit binary register has a n-flip-flops and capable of storing any information of n-bits.

The register has logic gates and flip-flop. The flip-flops store the binary information and gates control the transition of information into the register.

The simple 4-bit register is shown in Fig. 1.30.

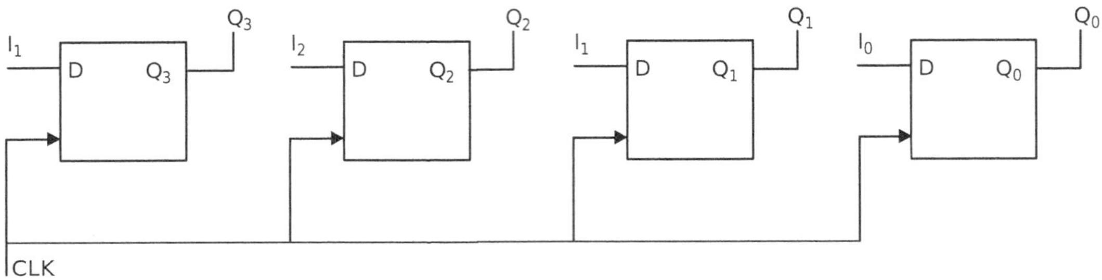

Fig. 1.30 4-bit register

1.7.5.1 Shift Registers

A shift register is a device which is capable of shifting binary information either to the left or to the right. Similarly memory register is used to store binary information. This stored data may be moved from one location to some other location within the register by use of shift register.

In shift register the flip-flops are connected in such a manner so that the entered binary number into the shift register is shifted from one location to another and then shifted out finally.

When the information is transferred into the register bit by bit *i.e.*, serially it is called serial transfer. Parallel shifting is much faster than serial shifting.

There are four ways possible to the shift register.

(*i*) Serial in - Serial out

(*ii*) Serial in - Parallel out

(*iii*) Parallel in - Serial out

(*iv*) Parallel in - Parallel out

(*i*) **Serial in -Serial out:** When the inputs are applied serially *i.e.*, one by one bit through a single input line, it is called serial in and when output is also taken serially then it is called serial out.

(a) Shift Left Register:

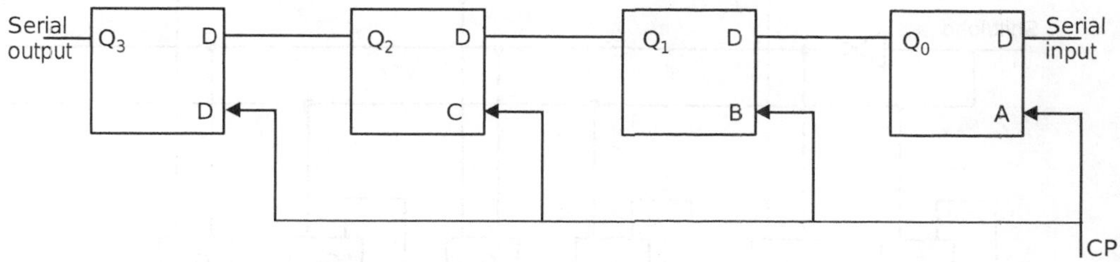

Fig. 1.31 Shift left register

In shift left register so input data whether 0 or 1 is applied to D input to flip-flop A. The clock pulse, CP is applied to all the flip-flops. Simultaneously the clock pulse occurs the input data bit at serial input reaches to Q_0 and at the same time data of stage A is shifted to stage B.

(b) Shift Right Register:

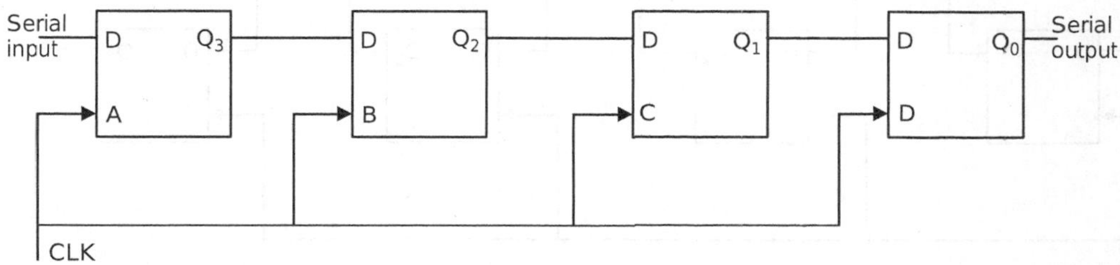

Fig. 1.32 Shift right register

It is just the inverse of shift left register. The data input is applied from the left *i.e.*, first flip-flop (A). The data input shift from MSB to LSB. When clock pulse is applied.

(ii) Serial in - Parallel out:

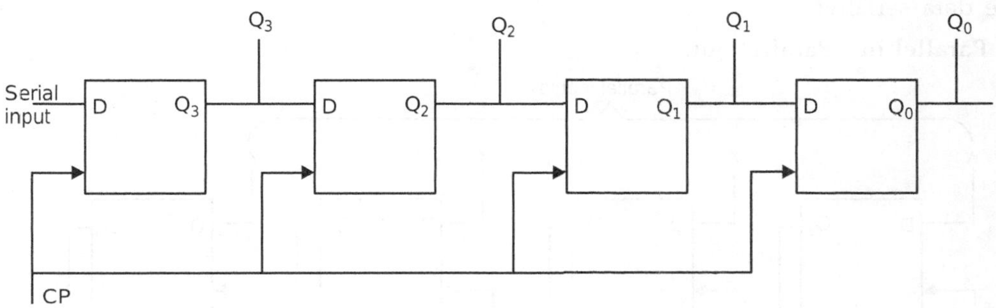

Fig. 1.33 Serial in - parallel out

Serial in-parallel out register which consists of one serial input. The output are taken from all the flip-flops. Simultaneously, it is known serial in parallel out shift register. To shift the data out in parallel data output must be available at the same time and input data is applied bit by bit.

(*iii*) Parallel in - Serial out:

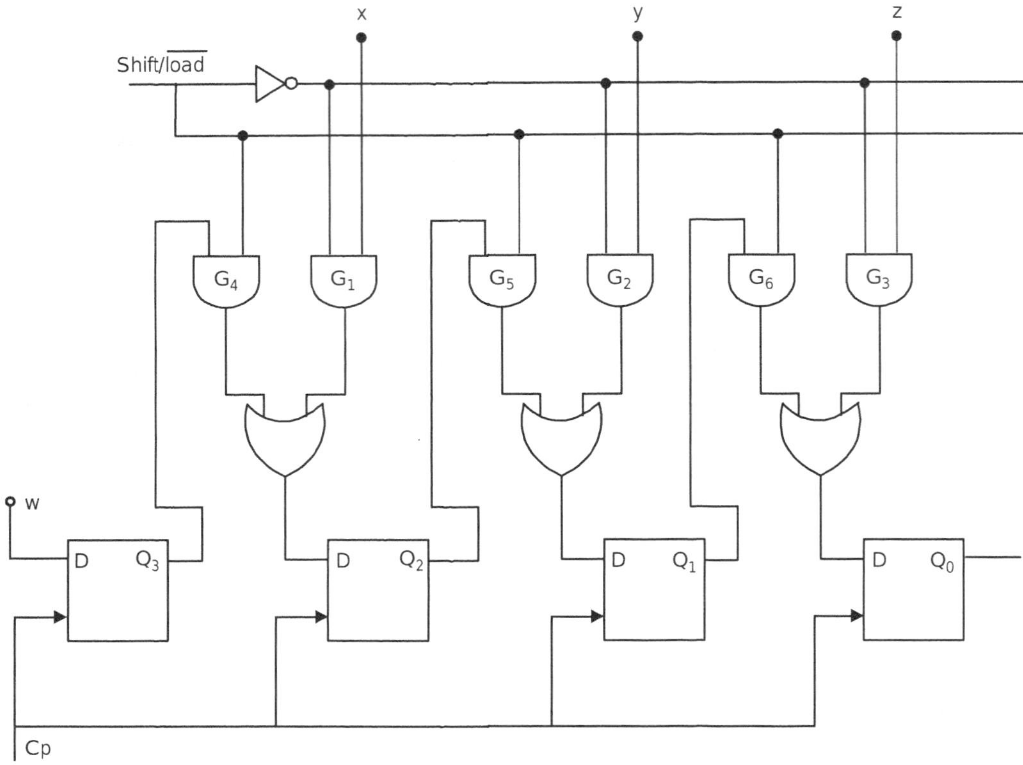

Fig. 1.34 4-Bit parallel in - serial out shift register

In this register the data inputs are applied or stored simultaneously. The output is taken bit by bit *i.e.*, serially.

It has a control input *i.e.*, SHIFT/ $\overline{\text{LOAD}}$ which controls the parallel inputs to enter and shifts the data serially.

(*iv*) Parallel in - Parallel out:

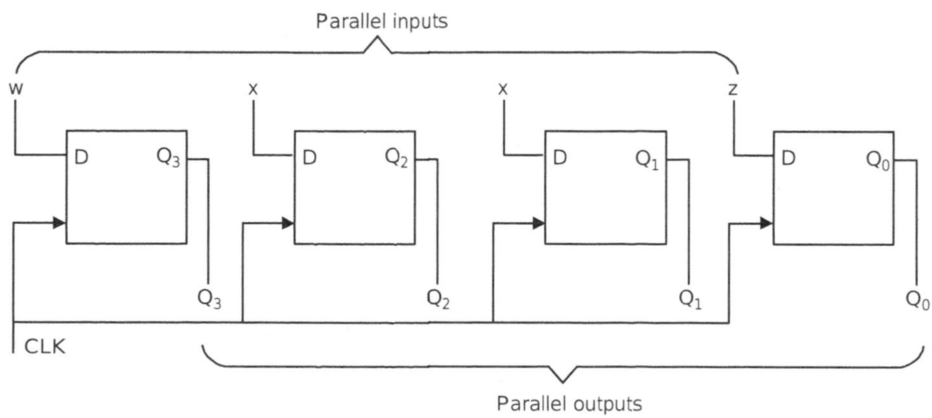

Fig. 1.35 Parallel output

In this register the data inputs are applied in parallel and outputs are taken simultaneously from each flip-flop. The parallel inputs are applied from inputs W,X,Y,Z in their respective flip-flops and parallel output are taken from Q_3, Q_2, Q_1 and Q_0 ouputs on each clock pulse.

SOLVED EXAMPLES

Example 1: *Perform the following conversions.*

(*a*) $(225)_{10} = (?)_8 = (?)_2 = (?)_{16}$

(*b*) $(1938.257)_{10} = (?)_{16}$

(*c*) $(64.AB)_{16} = (?)_8$

(*d*) $(3A9.\ BOD)_{16} = (?)_2$

Solution. Part (*a*) (*i*) $(225)_{10} = (X)_8$

Quotient	**Remainder**
$\frac{225}{8} = 28$	1
$\frac{28}{8} = 3$	4
$\frac{3}{8} = 0$	3

So the octal equivalent of 225 is $\mathbf{(341)_8}$ **Ans.**

(*ii*) $(225)_{10} = (X)_2$

Quotient	**Remainder**
$\frac{225}{2} = 112$	1
$\frac{112}{2} = 56$	0
$\frac{56}{2} = 28$	0
$\frac{28}{2} = 14$	0
$\frac{14}{2} = 7$	0
$\frac{7}{2} = 3$	1

$\frac{3}{2} = 1$ 1

$\frac{1}{2} = 0$ 1

So the binary equivalent of (225) is **$(11100001)_2$ Ans.**

(*iii*) $(225)_{10} = (X)_{16}$

Quotient	Remainder
$\frac{225}{10} = 14$	1
$\frac{14}{16} = 0$	E

So that the hexadecimal equivalent of 225 is **$(E1)_{16}$ Ans.**

Part (*b*) $(1938.257)_{10} = (2)_{16}$

Integer part = 1938

Fraction part = 27

The integer part is converted into hexadecimal by dividing it by 16. The fraction part is converted by multiplying this fraction part by 16.

Integer Part Conversion

Quotient	Remainder
$\frac{1938}{16} = 121$	2
$\frac{121}{16} = 7$	9
$\frac{7}{16} = 0$	7

$(1938)_{10} = (792)_{16}$

Fractional Part Conversion

Product	Whole Number	Fraction
0.257X16 = 4.112	4	.112
0.112X16 = 1.792	1	.792
0.792X16 = 12.679	12 = C	.679
0.679X16 = 10.864	10 = A	.864

$S_0\ (.257)_{10} = (.41CA)_{16}$

The equivalent hexadecimal number of decimal number

$(1938.257)_{10}$ = $\mathbf{(792.41CA)_{16}}$ **Ans.**

Part (*c*) $(64.AB)_{16} = (?)_8$

Step 1. Convert given number into decimal.

$$6 \rightarrow 0110$$
$$4 \rightarrow 0100$$
$$A \rightarrow 1010$$
$$B \rightarrow 1011$$

So $(64.AB)_{16} = (0110\ 0100.10101011)_2$

Step 2. Convert it into octal

001	100	100	.	101	010	110
↓	↓	↓		↓	↓	↓
1	4	4		5	2	6

= $\mathbf{(144.526)_8}$ **Ans.**

Part (*d*) $(3A9.\ BOD)_{16} = (?)_2$

Write corresponding 4 bits to each digit of the given hexadecimal number.

$$3 \rightarrow 0011$$
$$A \rightarrow 1010$$
$$9 \rightarrow 1001$$
$$B \rightarrow 1011$$
$$O \rightarrow 0000$$
$$D \rightarrow 1101$$

So $\mathbf{(1110101001.101100001101)_2}$ **Ans.**

Example 2: *Use 2's complement method to perform M-N with the given binary numbers.*

$$M = 1010100$$
$$N = 1000100$$

Solution. N = 01000100

1′s complement of N = 10111011

2′s complement = 1′s complement + 1

= 10111100

Now M – N

= M+ (2′s complement of N)

= 01010100

+ 10111100

100010000

Discard the carry

thus M – N = **00010000 Ans.**

Example 3: *Assume that X is the 2's complement of n bit binary number y. Prove that the 2's complement of x is y.*

Solution. For a positive number N_1 defined in a number system of base r, the r's complement is

$$= r^n - N \text{ if } N \neq 0$$

$$= 0 \text{ if } N = 0$$

Where n = number of digits in the integer part of N

Thus $r^n - y = x$

As X is 2's complement of y

so $2^n - y = x$

or it may be written as $2^n - x = y$

so we can say that

y is 2's complement of X.

Example 4: *Find out* $(33.57)_{10}$ *using 2's complement.* (Raj. Univ. 2002, CP)

Solution. The binary equivalent of

$$(33)_{10} = 100001$$

$$(57)_{10} = 111001$$

2's complement of 111001

= 000111

Additing it with the binary number 100001

⇒ 100001

<u>000111</u>

101000

There is no carry so taking the 2's complement 2's complement of 101000

= 011000 = $\mathbf{(-24)_{10}}$ **Ans.**

Example 5: *A number is expressed in binary 2's complement as 10011. Find its decimal equivalent value.*

Solution. 2's complement of a number = 10011

So its 1's complement will be

10011 – 1 = 10010

and the actual binary number will be 01101.

Decimal equivalent $= 2^4 \times 0 + 1 \times 2^3 + 1 \times 2^2 + 0 \times 2^1 + 1 \times 2^0$

$= 0 + 8 + 4 + 0 + 1$

$= \mathbf{(13)_{10}}$ **Ans.**

Example 6: *Prepare a truth table and logic circuit diagram for the following boolean expression.* (R.U. 2003)

(*a*) $A, B + \bar{A}, B$

(*b*) $A, \bar{B}\ C + \bar{B}\ C,$

Solution. $y = AB + \bar{A}\ B$

Truth Table

A	*B*	*y*
0	0	0
0	1	1
1	0	0
1	1	1

Logic circuit can be prepared using NOT, AND gate and OR gate.

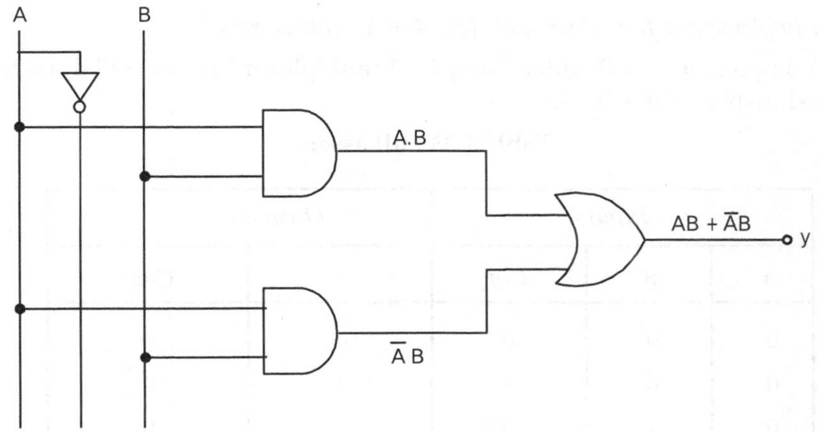

(*b*) $y = A\ \bar{B}\ C + \bar{B}\ C$

Truth Table

A	*B*	*C*	*y*
0	0	0	0
0	0	1	1
0	1	0	0
0	1	1	0
1	0	0	0
1	0	1	1
1	1	0	0
1	1	1	0

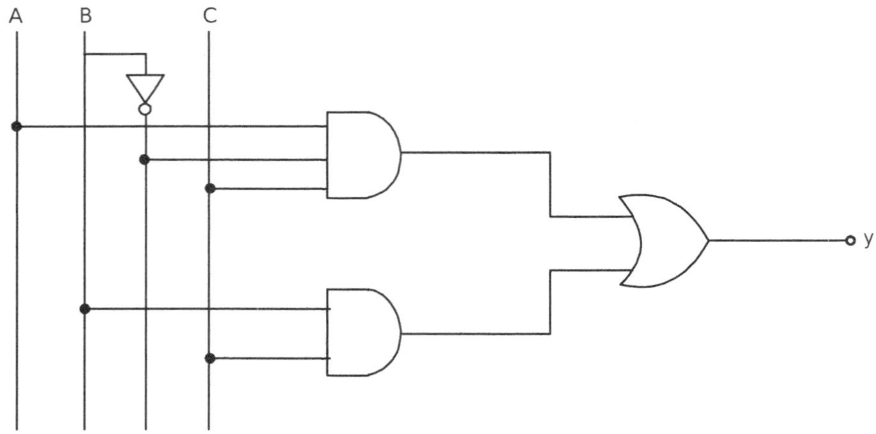

Fig. 1.36 Circuit diagram

Example 7: *Implement a full adder with two 4 × 1 multiplexers.*

Solution. To implement a full adder using 4 × 1 multiplexer first we will draw the truth table of full adder as shown in Table 1.33.

Table 1.33 Full asser

Inputs			*Outputs*	
A	*B*	*Cin*	*S*	*Cout*
0	0	0	0	0
0	0	1	1	0
0	1	0	1	0
0	1	1	0	1
1	0	0	1	0
1	0	1	0	1
1	1	0	0	1
1	1	1	1	1

We are getting two outputs sum and carry. The boolean function of S and cout Can be written as.

$$S = \Sigma n\ (1,2,4,7)$$

$$Cout = \Sigma m\ (3,5,6,7)$$

Since 4 × 1 mux is to be used, it will have only one input and two selection line. Here we use A as a input and B, C as the selection lines. For S and cout we will make the implementation table.

The two 4 × 1 mux are cascaded. The input A and A^1 are connected to lines I_0, I_1, I_2 and I_3 respectively of 4 × 1 mux for sum. The input logic 0, A^1, A^1 and logic 1 are connected to inputs of I_4, I_5, I_6 and I_7 respectively of 4 × 1 mux for Cout. So the circuit is

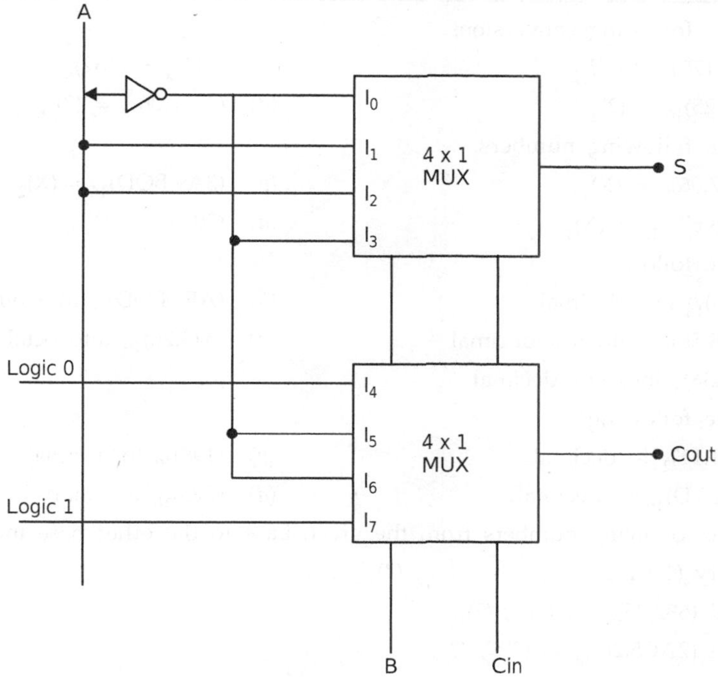

Example 8: *Implement the following function using 8 × 1 multiplexer.*

$$F(A,B,C,D) = \Sigma\ (1,2,6,7,9,11,13,15)$$

Solution. $F(A,B,C,D) = \Sigma\ (1,2,6,7,9,11,13,15)$

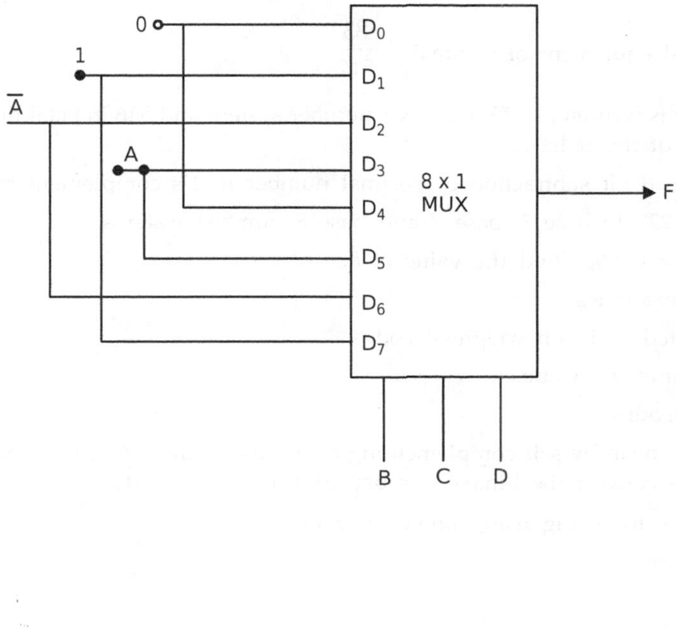

EXERCISES

1. Perform the following conversions.
   (*a*) $(175.175)_{10}$ to $(?)_2$ (*b*) $(211)_x = (152)_8$
   (*c*) $(53.625)_{10} = (?)_2$ (*d*) $(4057.06)_8 = (?)_{16}$
2. Convert the following numbers.
   (*a*) $(4057.06)_8 = (X)_{10}$ (*b*) $(3A9.BOD)_{16} = (X)_2$
   (*c*) $(2598.675)_{10} = (X)_{16}$ (*d*) $(2035)_8 = (X)_{16}$
3. Convert the following
   (*a*) $(AB6)_{16}$ into decimal (*b*) $(AF9.BOD)_{16}$ into binary
   (*c*) $(1248.56)_{10}$ into hexadecimal (*d*) $(543.26)_{10}$ into octal
   (*e*) $(247.36)_8$ into hexadecimal *[R.U. 2004]*
4. Convert the following
   (*a*) $(1001.11)_2$ to decimal (*b*) $(198)_{12}$ to decimal
   (*c*) $(2AC5.D)_{16}$ to decimal (*d*) $(725)_{10}$ to binary *[R.U. 2002]*
5. Convert the following numbers from the given base to the other base indicated.
   (*a*) Binary $(11011101)_2 \rightarrow (?)_{10}, (?)_8, (?)_{16}$
   (*b*) Octal $(632.25)_8 \rightarrow (?)_{10}, (?)_{16}$
   (*c*) Hexa $(2AC5.28)_{16} \rightarrow (?)_{10}, (?)_8$
6. Define *r*'s and (*r*-1)'s complement.
7. Use 1's and 2's complement to perform M-N with the given binary numbers.
   (*a*) M = 1010100 N = 1000100
   (*b*) M = 1000100 N = 1010100
8. What is meant by the base of the number system? Give example to illustrate the role of the base in positional number system.
9. Find the octal equivalent of decimal $1\frac{83}{512}$. *[R.U. 2003]*
10. (*a*) A number is written as 275 in radix *r* number system and 346 in octal number system. What is the value of the radix *r*.
    (*b*) Show the 8 bit subtraction of decimal number in 1's complement representation.
    (*c*) Convert 237 to base 3, base 7 and base 8 number systems. *[R.U. 2001]*
11. Given $(16)_{10} = (100)_b$. Find the value of *b*.
12. Define with examples.
    (*a*) Weighted and non weighted codes.
    (*b*) Alphanumeric Codes.
    (*c*) Gray Codes.
13. What do you mean by self complementing codes and cycle codes? Give one example for each type of code convert the binary number 100101 to gray code.
14. Implement the following using universal gate.

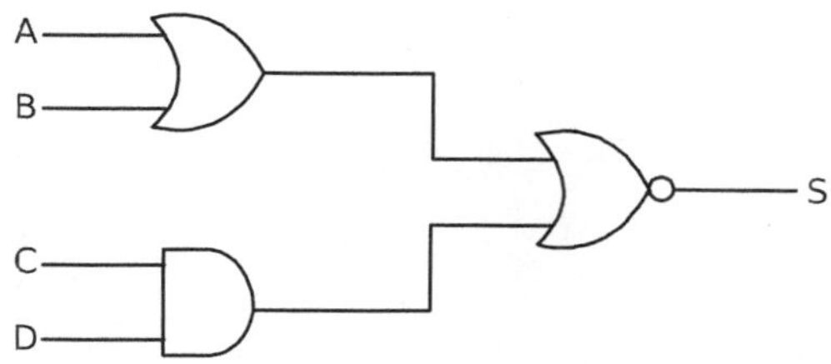

[R.U. 2004]

15. Write the difference between encoder and decoder in brief.

16. Write the difference between multiplexer and demultiplexer.

17. What is the draw back of J-K flip-flop and how it can be eliminated.

18. Write short notes on "Error detecting" and correcting codes.

19. Find the value of base/radix for a given number system.

(*a*) $(1000)_x = [(11)_2]^3$

(*b*) $(23)_x + (12)_x = (101)_x$ [R.U. 2005]

20. Define the following with one example.

(*a*) BCD Code (*b*) Excess-3 Code

21. Represent the decimal number 396 in following forms.

(*a*) Straight binary (*b*) BCD Code

(*c*) Excess– 3 code (*d*) Octal Code

(*e*) Hexadecimal Code

22. What is the main characteristics of gray code.

23. Write short notes on universal gates.

24. Write short note on design circuit using multiplexer.

25. Draw a logic diagram of full adder circuit using half adder circuit.

Chapter 2

REGISTER TRANSFER LANGUAGE

2.1 INTRODUCTION

In this chapter we are going to deal with a very special Computer Hardware language that is called Register Transfer language. In the hardware, data are stored in the registers and operations are defined on the data stored in registers. A Microoperation is a basic elementary operation defined on the data stored in registers. Microoperations are classified into 4 broad categories.

(*i*) Data Transfer Microoperation

(*ii*) Arithematic Microoperation

(*iii*) Logic Microoperations

(*iv*) Shift Microoperations.

We will discuss all these four microoperations in detail. Data can be stored in registers or in a memory location. During the execution of the program, there is a need to transfer the data from one location to the another location. Data is to be transferred from register to register, register to memory, memory to register and memory to memory. We use bus organisation to transfer the data from register to memory. A bus is defined as a common communication channel that is shared by different components. We discuss the hardware circuit that implements the basic arithmetic microoperations, like addition, subtraction etc., logic microoperations define basic four microoperations that are AND, OR, NOT and Ex-OR. Finally we discuss about shift microoperations that are used for the serial transfer of data either in the left direction or in the right direction.

2.2 REGISTER TRANSFER LANGUAGE

At the level of register transfer computer system is defined as a collection of data processing modules or blocks. These modules are made up of digital components as registers, decoders, arithematic circuits and control logic. Data are stored in the registers and operations are defined on the data stored in registers.

The operations executed on data stored in registers are known as microoperations. A microoperation is a basic elementary operation defined on the data stored in one or more registers.

The result of the operation may replace the previous results or it can be transferred to a particular memory location or another registers. Examples of microoperations are load operation, count operation, shift operation etc.

The internal hardware structure of a digital computer is best defined by specifying.

1. The set of registers-to store the data.
2. The set of microoperations-performed on the data stored in registers.
3. The set of control signals that initiate the sequence of microoperations.

The various microoperations can be defined by mnemonics or words but that is a lengthy process. So we adopt a new symbalogy to describe the transfer of data from one register to another. *"The Symbolic notation used to describe the microoperation transfers among registers is called a register transfer language.* The term register transfer implies the availability of hardware logic circuits that perform the microoperation and store the result in the same or another register. The term language is borrowed from computer programmers. A register transfer language is a system that describe the sequence of microoperations among registers in a symbolic form of a digital module. It is a convenient tool for describing the internal organisation of a digital computer in a precise manner. It helps in design process also.

Register Transfer Language is a very simple language.

2.3 MICROOPERATIONS

A microoperation is a basic elementary operation defined on the data stored in registers. The microoperations are classified into following four categories.

1. **Data transfer microoperation.**
   (*a*) *Register transfer microoperations.* These micro operations transfer the data from one register to another register.
   (*b*) *Memory transfer microoperations.* These microoperations transfer data from register to memory or memory to register.
2. **Arithmetic microoperations.** These microoperations perform arithmetic operations on data stored in registers. Addition, subtraction, multiplication, division all are arithmetic microoperations.
3. **Logic microoperations.** These microoperations perform bit manipulation operations on nonnumeric data stored in registers.
4. **Shift microoperations.** These microoperations shift the data in left or right direction stored in registers.

2.3.1 Data Transfer Microoperations

Data transfer microoperation transfer the binary information from one register to another register, from register to memory and vice versa. These microoperations does not change the information content when the information is transferred, only the data is transferred from one location to another location. The contents remain unchanged during transfer operation. Data transfer microoperations are of two types.

1. Register Transfer Microoperations
2. Memory Transfer Microoperations

2.3.1.1 Register Transfer Microoperations

These microoperations transfer the binary information from source register to destination register. A register is designated by a capital letter to denote the function of the register. Memory Address Register (MAR) holds the address for the memory unit. It is designated by MAR. Program Counter (PC) holds the next instruction in the sequence to be executed. IR is for instruction register. An *n* bit register contains bit position from 0 to (n-1), starting from the 0 in the right most position.

Fig. 2.1 depicts block diagram of register.

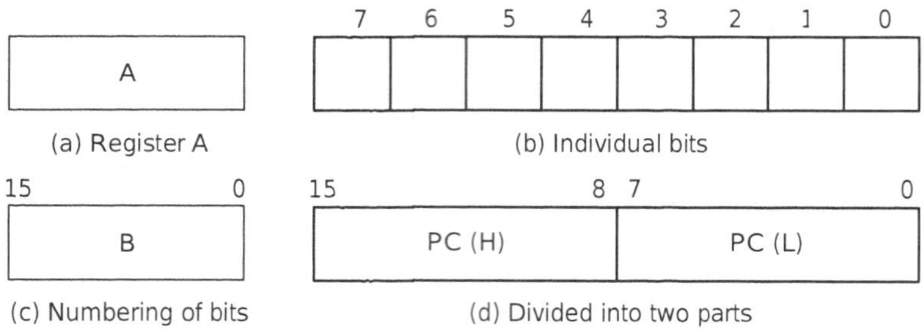

Fig. 2.1 Block diagram of register

The most common way to represent a register is by a rectangular box with the name of the register inside the box as in Fig. 2.1 (a). Registers can be represented by showing the individual bits as depicted in Fig.2.1(b). The numbering of register can be marked on the top of the box starting from 0 to (n-1) for an *n* bit register. 0 is at the right most position as in Fig. 2.1(c). Bits 0 through 7 are assigned the symbol L and bits 8 through 15 are assigned the symbol H. L is low order bytes and H is for higher order bytes as shown in Fig. 2.1 (d). PC(L) refers to the low order bytes and PC(H) to higher order bytes.

Information transferred from one register to another register can be represented in symbolic form by using a replacement operation.

$$B \leftarrow A$$

denotes a transfer of the contents of register A to contents of register B. It shows a replacement of the contents of B by contents of A. After the transfer operation the contents of source register does not change. Source register's contents remain the same.

Using a predetermined control signal data is transferred under a specific condition. The specific condition is specified by a control function. This can be shown by means of if then statement.

If (P = 1)

Then R2 ← R1

Here P is a control signal generated in the control section. A control function is a boolean variable that is equal to 1 or 0. When the value of P will be 1 then contents of register R1 will be transferred to register R2.

The control function is included as

$$P : R2 \leftarrow R1$$

The control condition is terminated by a colon (:). It indicates that transfer will take place by the hardware only when P = 1.

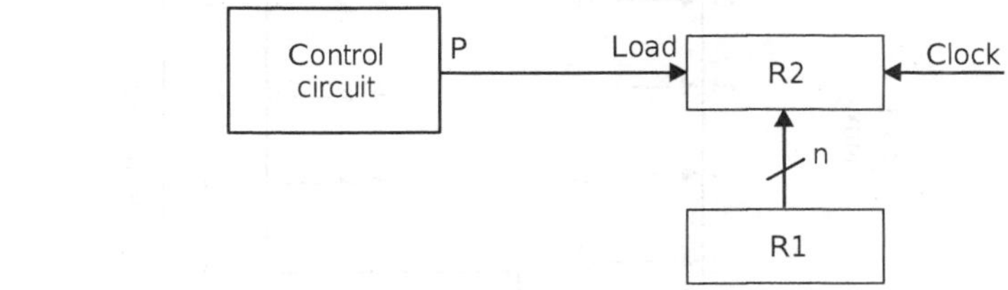

(a) Block diagram

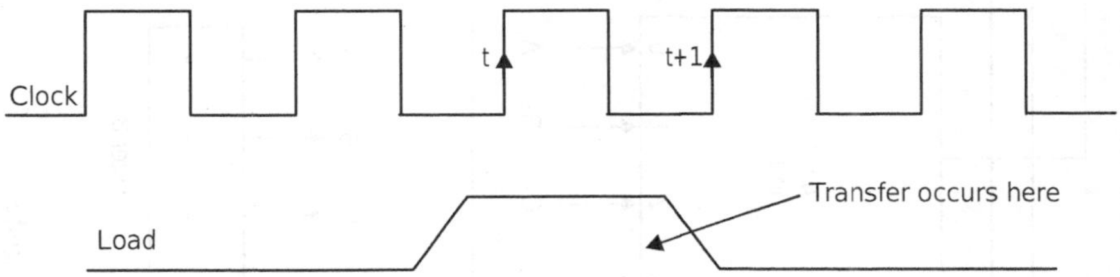

(b) Timing diagram

Fig. 2.2 Transfer from R1 to R2 when P = 1

Fig. 2.2 shows the transfer from register R1 to R2. The n outputs of register R1 are connected to the n inputs of register R2. n represents the length of the register. Transfer takes place under the control variable P. Register R2 has a load input that is activated by the control varibale P. For simplicity the control variable is synchronized with the same clock as applied to the register. As shown in the timing diagram control variable P is activated by the rising edge of a clock pulse at time t. P remains in active stage upto the next positive transition of the clok at time (t+1), find the load input active and the data inputs of R2 are then loaded into the register R1 in parallel.

Table 2.1 Basic symbols for register transfers

Symbol	*Represents*	*Examples*
1. Letters & numerals	Register with numerals	R1, PC
2. Parentheses ()	A part of register	R1(L), R2(H)
3. Arrow ←	Direction for data transfer	R2← R1
4. Comma	Separates two microoperation	R2← R1, R3← R4

Table 2.1 depicts the basic symbols used in data transfer. Registers are denoted by capital letters and numerals may follow the letters. Parenthesis are used to denote a part of a register by specifying the range of bits or by giving a symbol name to a portion of a register. The arrow denotes the direction in which transfer takes place. A comma is used to separate two or more operations that are executed at the same time.

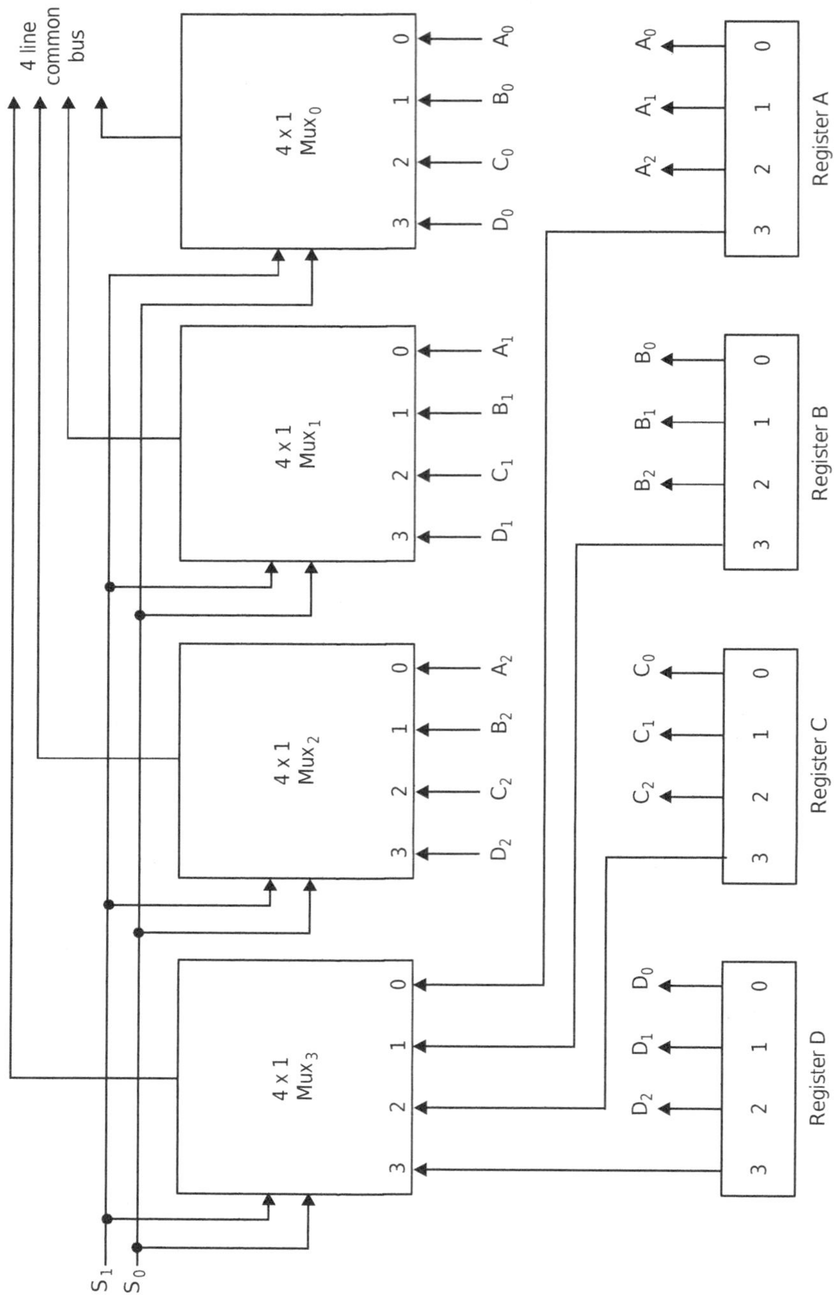

Fig. 2.3 Bus system for 4 registers

2.3.1.2 *Bus and Memory Transfer*

Bus organisation

A typical digital computer has so many registers and their data paths for transferring the information from one register to another register. If we define separate wires to link two register then number of wires will be excessive and the complexity of digital system increases. Therefore, to reduce the complexity, an efficient scheme is adopted for transfer of information in multiple register configuration, known as common bus system. A bus structure consists of a set of common lines, one for each bit of a register through which binary information is transferred one at a time. Control signals determines which register is selected for transfer.

Common bus system is constructed using multiplexers. Multiplexers are connected through a common bus system and they are allowed to select the source register whose binary information is placed on the bus. Bus system for 4 registers are shown in Fig.2.3. There are four registers A,B,C and D. Each register is containing 4 bits numbered from 0 to 3. The bus consists of four 4×1 multiplexers each having four data inputs 0 through 3 and two selection lines S_1 and S_0. In order not to complicate the diagram with 16 lines crossing each other, we use labels to show the connections from the outputs of the registers to the inputs of the multiplexers. For example output 1 of register B is connected to input 0 of MUX_2 because this input is labelled B_1.

At a time the contents of one register are transferred to the common bus. The two selection lines S_1 and S_0 are connected to the selection inputs of all four multiplexers.

Table 2.2 Function table

S_1	S_0	*Register Selected*
0	0	A
0	1	B
1	0	C
1	1	D

Table 2.2 represents the working of bus system. When $S_1S_0 = 00$. Then first inputs of the multiplexers will connect to the output lines. So from MUX_0 output is A_0 from MUX_1 output is A_1, MUX_2 output is A_2 and from MUX_3 we will get A_3 as output. So at common bus we are getting $A_3\ A_2\ A_1\ A_0$. So register A is selected for transfer. When $S_1S_0 = 01$ then second inputs of all multiplexers will be transferred on bus. This results in transferring $B_3\ B_2\ B_1\ B_0$ so register B is transferred.

Similarly when $S_1S_0 = 10$ register C is selected for transfer and when $S_1S_0 = 11$ register D is transferred on the common bus. At a time single register's contents are transferred.

In general a bus system will multiplex K registers of *n* bits each to produce an *n* line common bus.

> The number of multiplexers needed to construct the bus is equal to the number of bits in each register. The size of multiplexer must be $K \times 1$ for multiplexing K data lines.

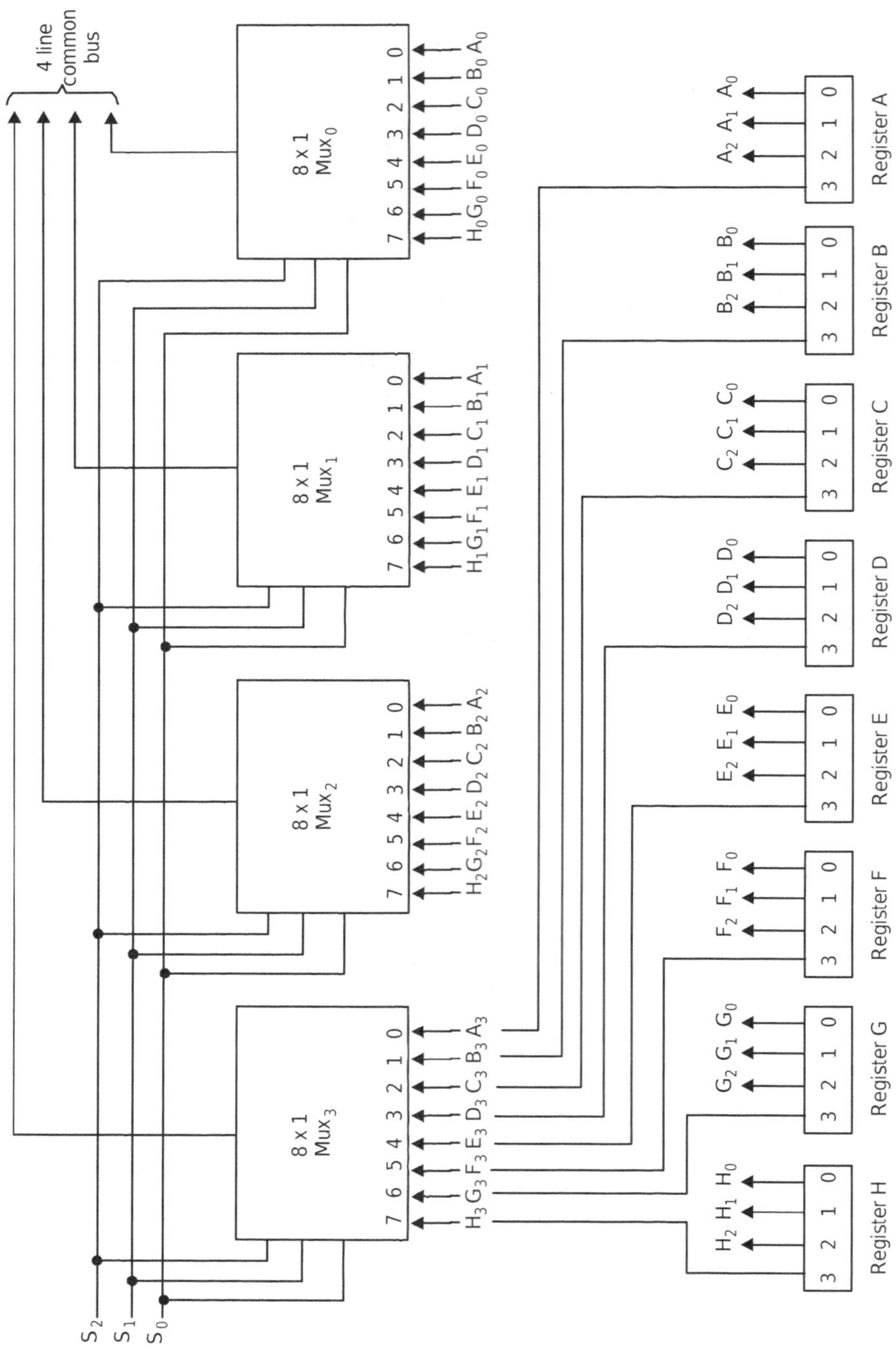

Fig. 2.4 Bus system for 8 registers

The transfer of information from a bus into one of many destination registers can be accomplished by connecting the bus lines to the inputs of all destination registers and activating the load control of the particular destination register selected. When the bus is included in the transfer, the register transfer is symbolized as follows.

$$BUS \leftarrow A, R1 \leftarrow BUS$$

The contents of register A is placed on the bus and the content of the bus is loaded into register R1 by activating its load control input.

If the bus is known to exist in the system then we can show direct transfer.

$$R1 \leftarrow A$$

Similarly we can construct bus system for 8 registers also. If registers are having 4 bits then we require 4 multiplexers of 8 × 1. Table 2.3 represents the functions table for bus system for 8 registers

Table 2.3 Function table

S_2	S_1	S_0	*Register Selected*
0	0	0	A
0	0	1	B
0	1	0	C
0	1	1	D
1	0	0	E
1	0	1	F
1	1	0	G
1	1	1	H

Fig. 2.4 depicts bus system for 8 registers when each register is containing 4 bits.

Number of Multiplexers = No. of bits in each register.

Tri state buffer transfer

A bus system can be constructed with three state gates. A three state gate is a digital circuit that exhibits three states. Two states are equivalent to conventional logic gates and third state is high impedance state. The high impedance state behaves like an open circuit, output is disconnected from all voltage sources and does not have a logic significance. Fig. 2.5 depicts graphic symbol of a three state buffer gate.

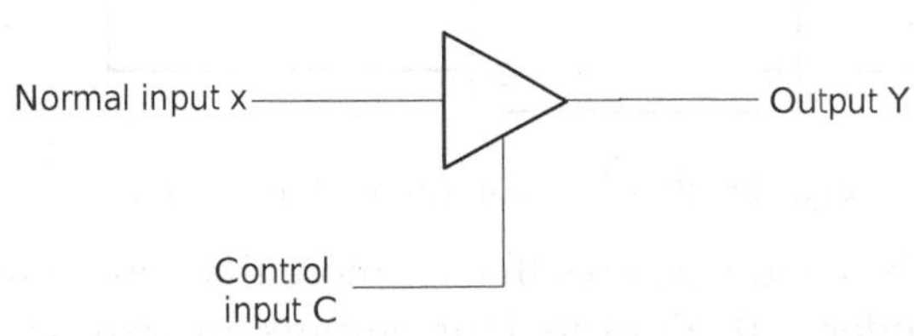

Fig. 2.5 Graphic symbol

Three state buffer is different from normal buffers. It has two input lines normal input and control input. Output state is determined by the control input. When control input is high then output line is enabled and the circuit behaves like conventional buffer, with the output is equal to the normal input. When the control input C is Zero then output line is disconnected and gate goes to a high impedance state, regardless of the value of the normal input. Because of this feature, a large number of three state gate outputs can be connected with wires to form a common bus line. Function table for three state bus is shown in Table 2.4

Table 2.4 Function table

Inputs		*Output*
X	*C*	*Y*
0	1	0
1	1	1
0	0	High impedance
1	0	High impedance

The construction of a bus system with three state buffers is demonstrated in Fig. 2.6. The outputs of four buffers are connected together to form a single bus line. The control inputs to the buffers determine which of the four normal inputs will communicate with the bus line. At a particular time only one buffer is in active state. The connected buffers must be controlled so that only one three state buffer has access to the bus line while all other buffers are maintained in a high impedance state.

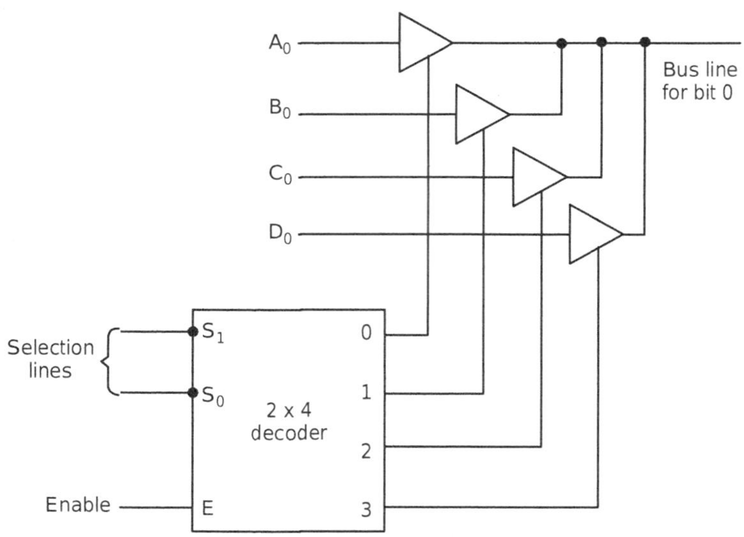

Fig. 2.6 Bus line for three state buffer

The use of decoder in the circuit ensures that no more than one control input is active when the enable input of the decoder is 0, all of its four outputs are zero and the bus line is in high impedance state because all four buffers are disabled. When the enable input is active, one of the three state buffers will be active, depending upon the values of the selection lines. This is represented in Table 2.5.

Table 2.5 Truth table

E	S_1	S_0	*Register Selected*
0	X	X	High impedance
1	0	0	A
1	0	1	B
1	1	0	C
1	1	1	D

To construct a common bus for four registers of n bits each using three state buffers, n circuits of four buffers are required. Each common output produces one of the lines for the common bus for a total of n lines. Only one decoder is necessary.

Memory transfer

There are two types of operation when data transfer takes place with reference to memory.

1. Read operation
2. Write operation

When information is transferred from memory to the outside environment it is called a read or load operation. When information is to be stored into the memory it is called a write or store operation. A memory word is symbolized by the word M. When data is transferred from registers to memory or vice-versa then read or write operations are performed. It is necessary to specify not only memory but also the address in memory to be accessed. This will be done by enclosing the address in square brackets following the letter M. As more addresses are used, this becomes unnecessary complex.

In general it is preferable to store the address value in a register and have the register supply the address to memory. This register is called Address Register (AR). The data are transferred to another register called the data register, symbalized by DR. This requires only one connection, from output of register AR to the address input of memory. Thus the memory transfer micro-operations can be summarized as

Memory read :

Read : DR ← M [AR]

This causes a transfer of information into DR from the memory word M selected by the address in AR.

Memory write :

write : M[AR] ← R2

This causes a transfer of information from register R2 into the memory word selected by the address in the register AR.

2.3.2 Arithmetic Microoperations

Arithmetic Microoperation change the information content during the transfer. The basic arithmetic microoperations are addition, subtraction, increment, decrement and shift.

The add microoperation is defined by the statement

$$R3 \leftarrow R1 + R2$$

The contents of register R1 are added with the contents of register R2 and the result of addition is transferred to the register R3.

The subtract microoperation is defined by the statement

$$R1 \leftarrow R2 - R3$$

It states that the contents of register R3 are subtracted from the contents of register R2 and the result is transferred in the register R1.

Subtraction can also be implemented using complement and addition operation.

$$R1 \leftarrow R2 + \overline{R3} + 1$$

$\overline{R3}$ indicates 1's complement of the contents of register R3. Adding 1 to the 1's complement of a number produces the 2's complement of the number.

The increment and decrement microoperations are symbolized by plus-one and minus-one operations, respectively. These microoperations are implemented with a combinational circuit or with a binary up down counter. Table 2.6 represents the arithematic microoperations.

Table 2.6 Arithmetic microoperation

Symbolic Relation	*Meaning*
$R3 \leftarrow R1 + R2$	Contents of R1 is added with R2, result transferred to R3.
$R3 \leftarrow R1 - R2$	Contents of R1 is subtracted with R2, result transferred to R3
$R1 \leftarrow \overline{R1}$	1's complement of contents of R1
$R2 \leftarrow \overline{R2} + 1$	2's complement of contents of R2
$R3 \leftarrow R_1 + \overline{R2} + 1$	Contents of R1 is added with 2's complement of contents of R2, result transferred to R3.
$R1 \leftarrow R1 + 1$	Increment the contents of R1 by one
$R1 \leftarrow R1 - 1$	Decrement the contents of R1 by one

The arithmetic microoperations of multiplication and division are not listed in the above table. These two operations are valid arithmetic microoperations but are not included in the basic set of microoperations.

The multiplication operation is implemented with a sequence of add and shift microoperations. Division is implemented with a sequence of subtract and shift microoperations.

2.3.2.1 Binary Adder

To implement the addition microoperation with hardware, we need registers to store the data and digital components that performs the arithmetic addition. The digital components that performs the addition of two bits and a previous carry is called a full adder. The digital circuit that generate the arithmetic sum of two binary numbers of any arbitrary length is called *n* bit binary adder.

The binary adder is constructed with full adder circuits connected in cascade, with the output carry from one full adder connected to the input carry of the next full adder. Let us consider a 4 bit addition. Let the binary numbers are A (A_3 A_2 A_1 A_0) as augend bits and B (B_B B_2 B_1 B_0) as addend bits. First add A_0 and B_0, then add A_1 and B_1 with previous carry generated by the addition of A_0 and B_0, now add A_2 and B_2 with the previous carry generated by the addition of A_1 and B_1. Finally A_3 and B_3 are added with the carry generated by the addition of A_2 and B_2. The carries are connected in a chain through the full adders. Fig. 2.7 depicts 4 bit binary adder.

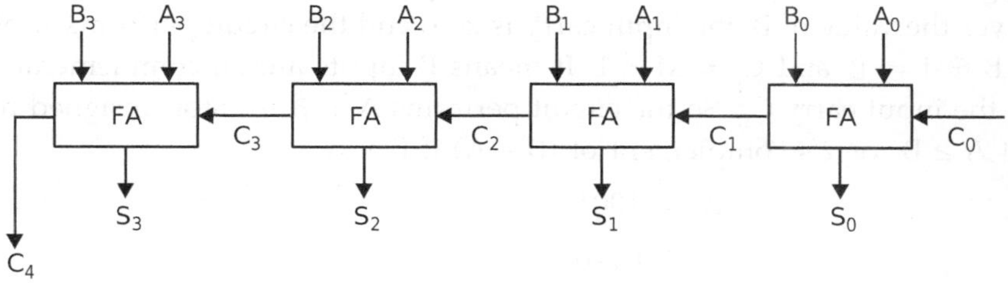

Fig. 2.7 4 bit binary adder

The input carry is C_o and the output carry is C_4. The S outputs of the full adders generate the required sum bits.

An *n* bit binary adder requires *n* full adders cascaded together where the output carry from each full adder is connected to the input carry of the next high order full adder.

2.3.2.2 Binary Adder – Subtractor

Subtraction microoperation is performed using the complement method. Subtraction A–B can be done by taking the 2's complement of B and adding it with the contents of B. The 2's complement can be obtained by adding 1 to the 1's complement of the number. The 1's complement can be done by the digital component inverter and a one can be added to the sum through the input carry.

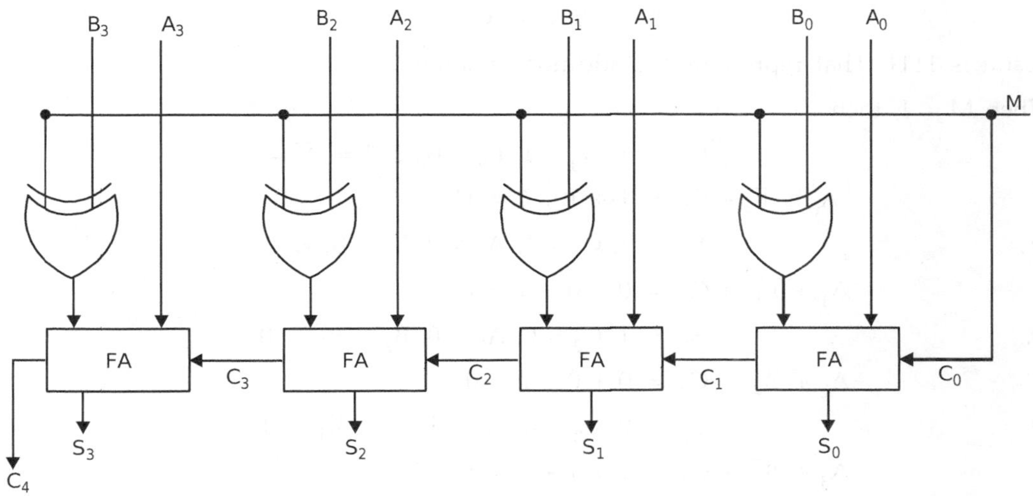

Fig. 2.8 4 bit adder - subtracter

The addition and subtraction operations can be combined into one common circuit by including an exclusive OR gate with each full adder. A 4 bit adder subtractor circuit is shown in Fig. 2.8. The mode input M controls the operation.

When $M = 0$ Circuit performs Addition operation

When $M = 1$ Circuit performs Subtraction operation

Each XOR gate receives input M and one of the input of B. When $M = 0$, we have $B \oplus 0$. The full adder receives the value of B, the input carry is zero and the circuit performs A plus B. When M=1, we have $B \oplus 1 = \overline{B}$ and $C_0 = M = 1$. It means B inputs are all complemented and a 1 is added through the input carry C_0. So the circuit performs $A + \overline{B} + 1$; for unsigned numbers this gives $(A - B)$ if $A \geq B$ or 2's complement of $(B - A)$ if $B \leq A$.

Let $A = 1001$

$B = 0110$

So $A_3\, A_2\, A_1\, A_0 = 1001$

$B_3\, B_2\, B_1\, B_0 = 0110$

When $M = 0, C_0 = 0, B_0 = B_0 \oplus 0 = 0 \oplus 0 = 0\ A_0 = 1$

$A_0 + B_0 + C_0 = 1 + 0 + 0 = 1$

i.e., $S_0 = 1, C_1 = 0, A_1 = 0, B_1 = B_1 \oplus 0 = 1$

$A_1 + B_1 + C_1 = 0 + 1 + 0 = 1$

i.e., $S_1 = 1, C_2 = 0, A_2 = 0, B_2 = B_2 \oplus 0 = 1$

$A_2 + B_2 + C_2 = 0 + 1 + 0 = 1$

i.e., $S_2 = 1, C_3 = O, A_3 = 1, B_3 = B_3 \oplus 0 = O$

$A_3 + B_3 + C_3 = 1 + 0 + 0 = 1$

i.e., $S_3 = 10, C_4 = O$

Result is 1111. That represents the addition operation.

When $M = 1$, then

$C_0 = 1, A_0 = 1, B_0 = B_0 \oplus 1 = \overline{B_0} = 1$

$A_0 + \overline{B_0} + C_0 = 1 + 1 + 1 = 11$

i.e., $S_0 = 1, C_1 = 1, A_1 = 0, B_1 = B_1 \oplus 1 = 0$

$A_1 + \overline{B_1} + C_1 = 0 + 0 + 1 = 1$

i.e., $S_1 = 1, C_2 = 0, A_2 = 0, B_2 = \overline{B_2} = 0$

$A_2 + \overline{B_2} + C_2 = 0 + 0 + 0 = 0$

i.e., $S_2 = 0, C_3 = 0, A_3 = 1, B_3 = \overline{B_3} = 1$

$A_3 + \overline{B_3} + C_3 = 1 + 1 + 0 = 10$

i.e., $S_3 = O, C_4 = 1,$

Result is 0011. That represents subtraction.

An *n* bit binary adder subtractor can be designed in the same manner. The block diagram of *n* bit binary adder subtractor is shown in Fig. 2.9

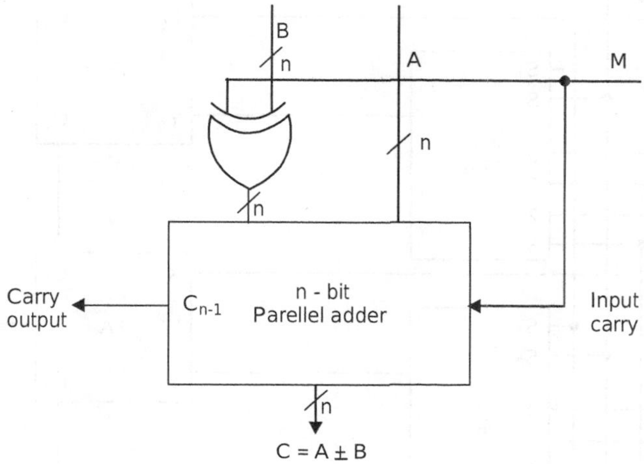

Fig. 2.9 N-bit adder subtractor

2.3.2.3 *Binary Incrementer*

The increment microoperation adds one to a number in a register. This microoperation is easily implemented with a binary counter. Every time the count enable is active. The clock pulse transition increments the contents of the register by 1 using half adder this microoperation can be implemented.

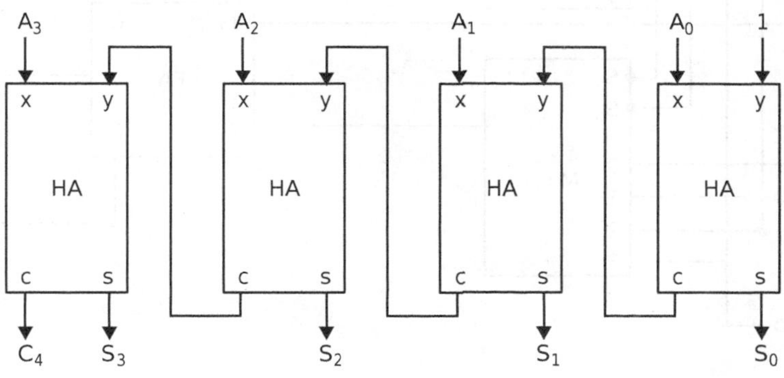

Fig. 2.10 4 bit binary incrementer

One of the inputs to the least significant half adder is connected to logic 1 and the other input is connected to the least significant bit of the number to be incremented.

The o/p carry from one half adder is connected to one of the inputs of the next higher-order half adder. The circuit receives four bits A_0 to A_3, adds 1 to it and generates the incremented output.

* *n* bit binary incrementer - requires *n* half adder.

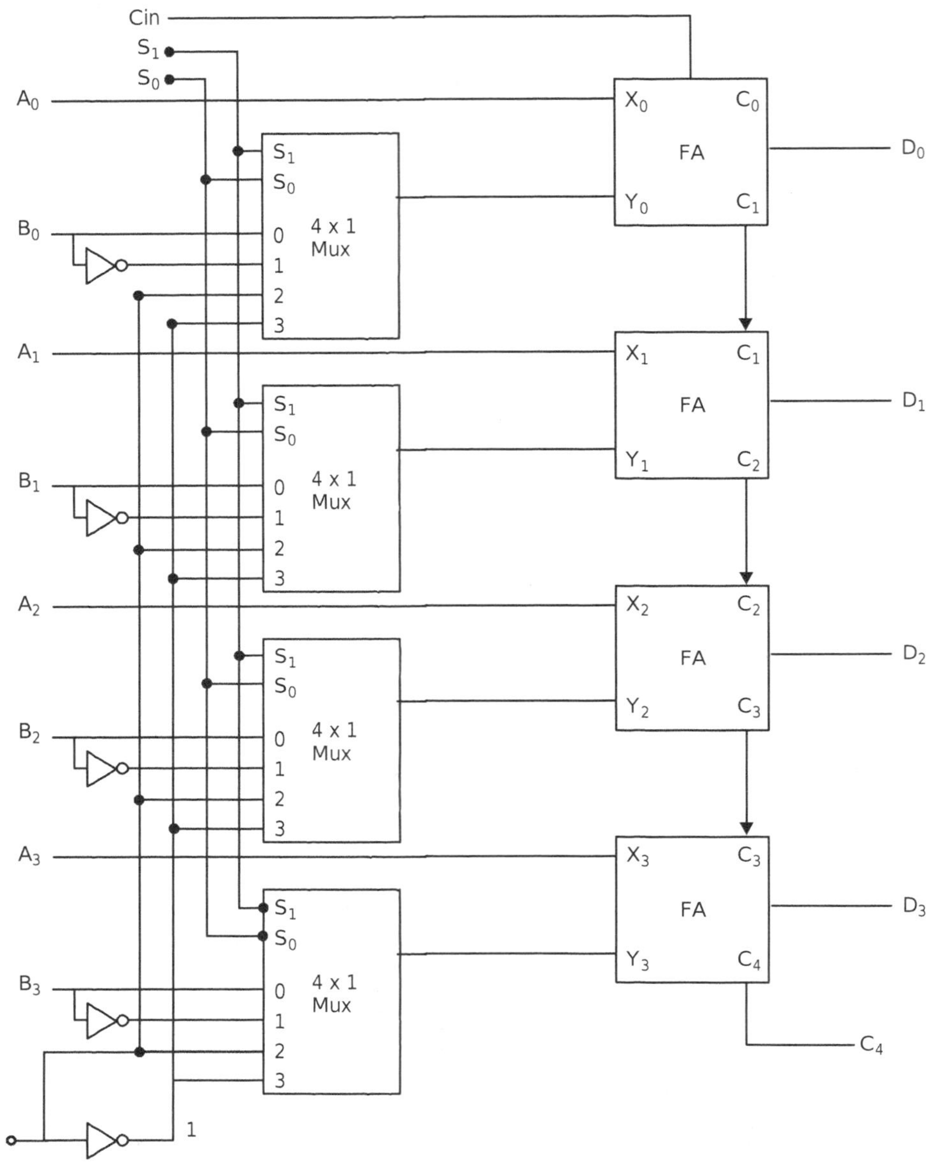

Fig. 2.11 4 bit arithmetic circuit

2.3.2.4 Arithmetic Circuits

The various arithmetic microoperations can be implemented in one composite arithmetic circuit. The basic component of an arithmetic circuit is the parallel adder. The diagram is shown in Fig. 2.11. It has four full adder circuits that constitute the 4 bit adder and four multiplexers for choosing different operations. There are two 4 bit inputs A and B and 4 bit output D. The four inputs from A go directly to the X inputs of the binary adder. Each of the four inputs from B are connected to the data inputs of the multiplexers. The four multiplexers are controlled by two selection inputs S_1 and S_0. The input carry *Cin* goes to the carry input of the FA in the least significant position.

The output of the binary adder is defined as

$$D = A + Y + Cin$$

Where

A = 4 bit binary number at the X inputs

y = 4 bit binary number at the Y inputs

It is possible to generate eight arithmetic microoperations listed in Table 2.7.

Table 2.7 Arithmetic circuit function

S1	*Cin*	*So*	*Input Y*	*Output D = A + Y + Cin*	*Microoperations*
0	0	0	B	A + B	Add microoperation
0	1	0	B	A + B + 1	Add with carry
0	0	1	$\overline{B}$	$A + \overline{B}$	Subtract with borrow
0	1	1	$\overline{B}$	$A + \overline{B} + 1$	Subtract
1	0	0	0	A	Transfer A
1	1	0	0	A + 1	Increment A
1	0	1	1	A –1	Decrement A
1	1	1	1	A	Transfer A

Case 1 : When $S_1 S_0 = 0$.

Cin = 0 then output D = A + B

If *Cin* = 1 then output D = A + B + 1

Both cases perform the add microoperation with or without adding the input carry.

Case 2: When $S_1S_0 = 01$ the complement of B is applied to the *y* inputs of the adder.

If *Cin* = 1 then $D = A + \overline{B} + 1 \Rightarrow A - B$

If *Cin* = 0 then $D = A + \overline{B} \Rightarrow A - B - 1$

Case 3 : When $S_1 S_0 = 10$, all 0's are inserted into the *y* inputs.

If *Cin* = 0 then output D = A + 0+0 = A

If *Cin* = 1 then output D = A + 1

In the first case we have a direct transfer from input A to output D. In the second case, the value of A is incremented by 1.

Case 4 : When $S_1 S_o = 11$, all 1's are inserted into the *y* inputs.

If *Cin* = 0 then output D = A + all 1's

$$D = A + (2\text{'s complement of } 1)$$
$$= A - 1$$

If $Cin = 1$ then output $D = A - 1 + 1 = A$

Which causes a direct transfer from input A to output D.

∴ The microoperation D = A is generated twice so there are only seven distinct microoperations in the arithmetic circuit.

2.3.3 Logic Microoperations

Logic microoperations specify binary operations for string of bits stored in register. Each bit of the register is considered separately and treat them as binary variables. Some of the basic logic microoperations that can be performed on boolean or binary data are NOT, AND, OR and XOR operation.

These logic microoperations can be applied bitwise to n bit logical data units. For example the exclusive OR microoperation with the contents of two registers R1 and R2 is symbolised by the statement.

$$P : R1 \leftarrow R1 \oplus R2$$

Here P is a control variable. As a numerical example assume that each register has four bits. Let the content of R1 be 1001 and the content of R2 be 1100. The exclusive OR microoperation stated above symbolizes the following logic computation.

1001 Contents of R1
1100 Contents of R2
0101 Contents of R1 after P = 1

Logic microoperations are very useful for bit manipulation of binary data and for making logical decisions. Special symbols will be adopted for logic microoperations OR, AND and complement to distinguish them from the corresponding symbols used to express boolean functions.

$\vee$ denotes OR microoperation

$\wedge$ denotes AND microoperation

In all there are 16 different logic operations that can be performed with two binary variables. These can be derived from all possible truth tables obtained with two binary variables as shown in Table 2.8. In this table each of the 16 columns from F_0 to F_{15} represents a truth table of one possible Boolean function for the two variables x and y. The functions are determined from the 16 binary combinations that can be assigned to F.

Table 2.8 Truth table for 16 functions of two variables

x	y	F_0	F_1	F_2	F_3	F_4	F_5	F_6	F_7	F_8	F_9	F_{10}	F_{11}	F_{12}	F_{13}	F_{14}	F_{15}
0	0	0	0	0	0	0	0	0	0	1	1	1	1	1	1	1	1
0	1	0	0	0	0	1	1	1	1	0	0	0	0	1	1	1	1
1	0	0	0	1	1	0	0	1	1	0	0	1	1	0	0	1	1
1	1	0	1	0	1	0	1	0	1	0	1	0	1	0	1	0	1

The 16 Boolean functions of two variables x and y are expressed in the first column of Table 2.9. The 16 logic microoperations are derived from these functions by replacing variable X by the binary content of register A and variable y by the binary content of register B. Table 2.9 represents these 16 different logic microoperations.

Table 2.9 Logic microoperations

Boolean-function	*Microoperation*	*Name*
$F_o = o$	$F \leftarrow 0$	Clear
$F_1 = xy$	$F \leftarrow A \wedge B$	AND
$F_2 = XY^1$	$F \leftarrow A \wedge \overline{B}$	
$F_3 = X$	$F \leftarrow A$	Transfer A
$F_4 = X^1Y$	$F \leftarrow \overline{A} \wedge B$	
$F_5 = Y$	$F \leftarrow B$	Transfer B
$F_6 = X \oplus Y$	$F \leftarrow A \oplus B$	Exclusive OR
$F_7 = X+Y$	$F \leftarrow A \vee B$	OR
$F_8 = (X+Y)^1$	$F \leftarrow \overline{A \vee B}$	NOR
$F_9 = (X \oplus Y)^1$	$F \leftarrow \overline{A \oplus B}$	Exlusive NOR
$F_{10} = \overline{Y}$	$F \leftarrow \overline{B}$	Complement B
$F_{11} = X+Y^1$	$F \leftarrow A \vee \overline{B}$	
$F_{12} = X^1$	$F \leftarrow \overline{A}$	Complement A
$F_{13} = X^1+Y$	$F \leftarrow \overline{A} \vee B$	
$F_{14} = (XY)^1$	$F \leftarrow \overline{A \wedge B}$	NAND
$F_{15} = 1$	$F \leftarrow$ all 1's	Det to all 1's

2.3.3.1 *Hardware Implementation*

Four basic logic Microoperation are

$\rightarrow$ AND, OR, XOR, COMPLEMENT

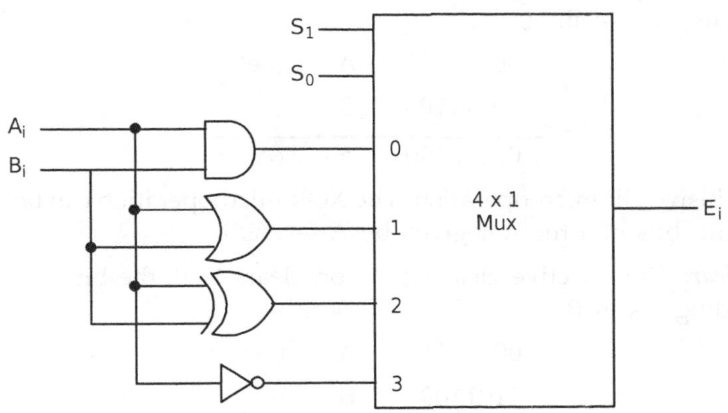

Fig. 2.12 Hardware implementation

Table 2.10 Function table

S_1	S_0	*O/P*	*Operation*
0	0	$E = A \wedge B$	AND
0	1	$E = A \vee B$	OR
1	0	$E = A \oplus B$	EX – OR
1	1	$E = \bar{A}$	NOT

The hardware implementation of logic microoperations requires that logic gates be inserted for each bit or pairs of bits in the registers to perform the logic function required. Circuits consists of four gates and a multiplexer. Each of the four basic logic microoperations is generated through a gate that performs the required logic. The outputs of the gates are applied to the data inputs of the multiplexer. The selection variables will go to all *n* stages. Table 2.10 represents the function table.

2.3.3.2 Applications

The logic microoperations are used for manipulation of individual bits or a portion of a word stored in a register. They can be used to change the bit values, delete group of bits or inserting new bit values.

(*a*) *Selective Set:* The Selective set operation sets to 1, the bits in register A where there are corresponding 1's in register B. It does not affect the bit positions where there are corresponding 0's in register B.

e.g.,

0011011	A	(Before)
1101100	B	
1111111	A	(After)

The OR logic microoperation can be used to selectively set bits of a register A. The boolean expression $A \leftarrow AVB$ can be used to implement selective set operation.

(*b*) *Selective Complement:* The selective complement operation complements bits in A where there are corresponding 1's in B. It does not affect bit positions in A that have corresponding 0's in B.

e.g.,

00111000	A	(Before)
10011100	B	
00100100	A	(After)

It is the exclusive OR microoperation. The XOR microoperation can be used to selectively complement bits of a register given by $A \leftarrow A \oplus B$.

(*c*) *Selective Clear:* The selective clear operation clears to 0, the bits in A where there are corresponding 1's in B.

e.g.,

0011011	A	(Before)
1101100	B	
0010011	A	(After)

The boolean operation performed on the individual bits in AB[1]. The corresponding logic operation is $A \leftarrow A \wedge \overline{B}$.

(*d*) *Clear Operation:* Clear operation compares the corresponding bits in A and B and produces an all 0's results if all the bits of A and B are equal. This operation is achieved by exclusive OR microoperation.

e.g.,

10010011	A	(Before)
10010011	B	
00000000	A	(After)

$A \leftarrow A \oplus B$

(*e*) *Mask Operation*: The mask operation is similar to the selective clear operation except that the bits of A are cleared only where there are corresponding 0's in B. The mask operation is an AND microoperation.

e.g.,

11001101	A	(Before)
10011001	B	
10001001	A	(After)

The boolean operation is $A \leftarrow A \wedge B$.

2.2.4 Shift Microoperation

Shift Microoperations are used to transfer the data serially. These are used in combination with arithmetic logic and other data processing operations. This operation shift the contents of register in left or right direction. At the same time when the bits are shifted the last or first flip-flop receives the binary information from the serial input. During shift left operation the serial input transfers a bit into the last flip-flop at the right most position.

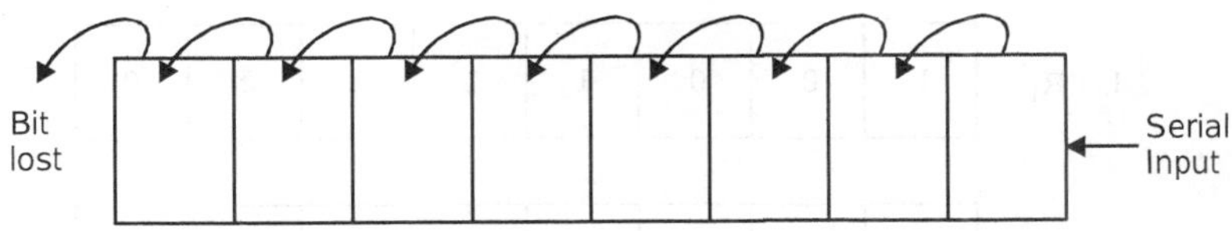

The rest of the bits are shifted towards left by one bit position.

Similarly during a shift right operation the serial input transfer a bit into the first flip-flop at the left most position

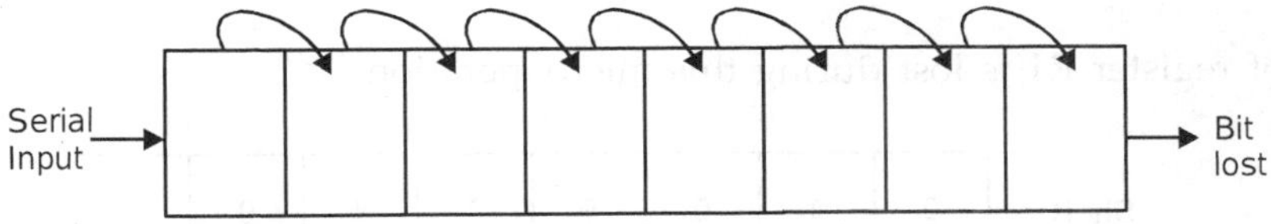

The rest of the bits are shifted towards right by one bit position.

There are three types of shift microoperation. Each microoperation can be done in left or in right direction.

(*i*) Logical Shift

(*ii*) Circular Shift

(*iii*) Arithmetic Shift.

These are shown in Table 2.11.

Table 2.11 Shift microoperations

Symbolic Designation	*Description*
1. R ← Shl R	Shift left register R
2. R ← Shr R	Shift right register R
3. R ← Cil R	Circular Shift left register R
4. R ← Cir R	Circular Shift right register R
5. R ← ashl R	Arithmetic Shift left R
6. R ← ashr R	Arithmetic Shift right R.

(*i*) *Logical Shift:* A logical shift transfers *0* through the serial input. Shl denotes logical shift left operation while Shr denotes logical shift right operation.

For example: R1 ← Shl R1

R2 ← Shr R2

are two microoperations that specify a 1 bit shift to the left of the content of register R1 and a 1 bit shift to the right of the content of register R2. The bit transferred to the end position through the serial input is assumed to be 0 during a logical shift.

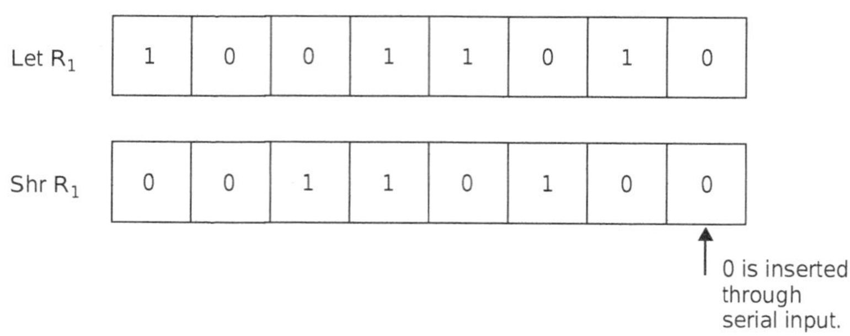

MSB of register R1 is lost during this microoperation.

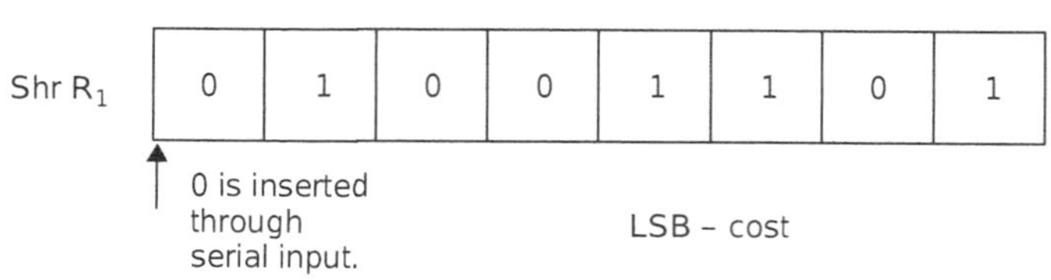

(*ii*) *Circular Shift:* It is also known as rotate microoperation. It circulates the bits of the register around both the ends without any loss of information. This is done by connecting the serial output of the shift register to the serial input. We use the notation Cil and Cir for circular shift left microoperation and circular shift right microoperation.

For example:

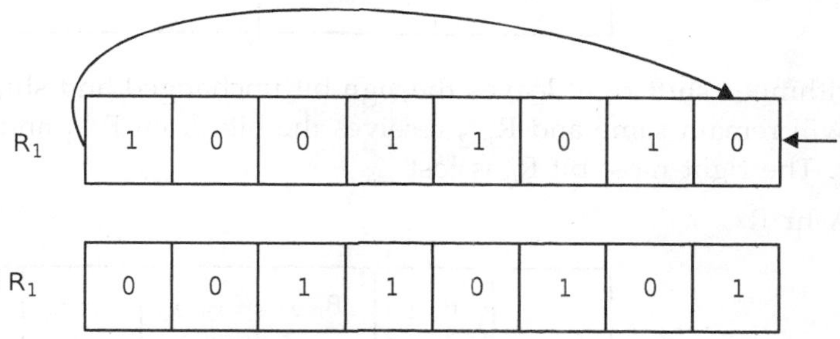

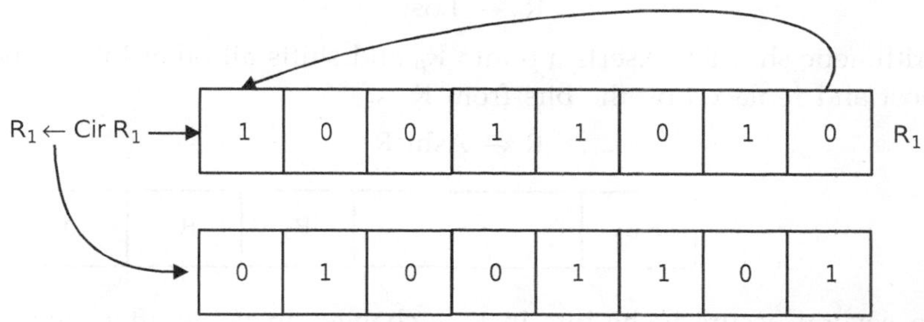

There is no loss of information in case of circular left and right microoperation.

(*iii*) *Arithmetic Shift:* An arithmetic shift microoperation shifts a signed binary number to the left or right direction. An arithmetic shift left multiplies a signed binary number by 2 and arithmetic shift right divides a signed binary number by 2.

For example:

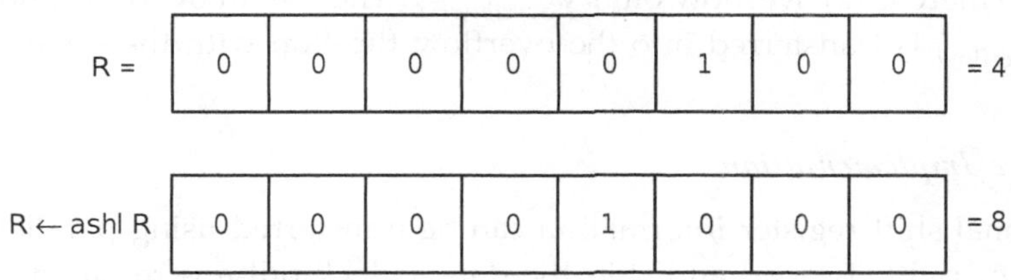

So, ashl R multiplies the number by 2.

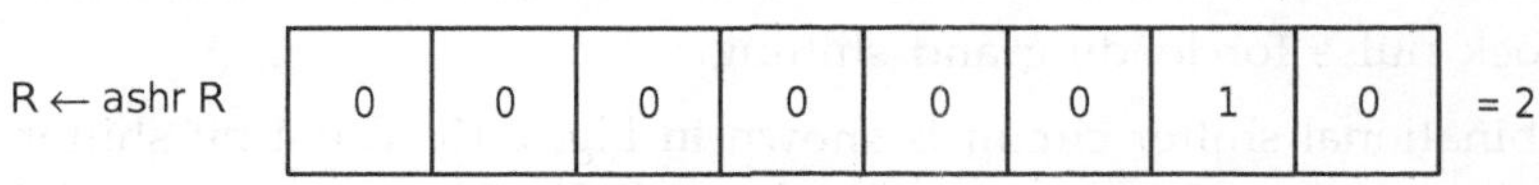

So, ashr R divides the number by 2.

Arithmetic shifts must leave the sign bit unchanged because while dividing or multiplying the number by 2 sign of the number remains same.

The left most bit of the number holds the sign and the remaining bits represent the actual number. The sign bit is 0 for positive numbers and 1 for negative numbers in all representations.

R_{n-1}	R_{n-2}	- -	R_1	R_0

The arithmetic shift right leaves the sign bit unchanged and shifts the number to the right. Thus R_{n-1} will remain same and R_{n-2} receives the bits from R_{n-1} and so on for the other bits in the register. The right most bit R_0 is lost.

$R \leftarrow \text{Ashr } R$

R_{n-1}	R_{n-1}	R_{n-2}	R_{n-3}	- - -	R_1

$$R_0 \leftarrow \text{Lost}$$

The arithmetic shift left inserts a 0 into R_0 and shifts all other bits to the left. The initial bit of R_{n-1} is lost and replaced by the bits from R_{n-2}.

$$R \leftarrow \text{Ashl } R$$

R_{n-2}	- - -	R_1	R_0	0

A sign several occurs if the bits in R_{n-1} changes in value after shift. This happens if the multiplication by 2 causes an overflow.

Overflow: An overflow occurs after an arithmetic shift left if initially before the shift micro-operation R_{n-1} is not equals to R_{n-2}. An overflow flip-flop can be used to detect an arithmetic overflow.

$$V_{\text{overflow}} = R_{n-1} \oplus R_{n-2}$$

If $V_{\text{overflow}} = 0$ there is no overflow bit if $V_{\text{overflow}}=1$. There is an overflow and a sign reversal after the shift. V_{overflow} is transferred into the overflow flip-flop with the same clock pulse that shifts the register.

2.3.4.1 Hardware Implementation

In a bidirectional shift register information can be transferred using parallel load and then shifting either left or right. To load and shift the data a clock pulse is required. The contents of a register that has to be shifted is first placed onto a common bus whose output is connected to the combinational shifter and then shift number is then loaded back into the register. This requires only one clock pulse for loading and shifting.

A combinational shifter circuit is shown in Fig. 2.13. The 4 bit shifter has four data inputs A_0 through A_3 and four data outputs H_0 through H_3. There are two serial inputs one for serial left (I_L) and other for shift right (I_R).

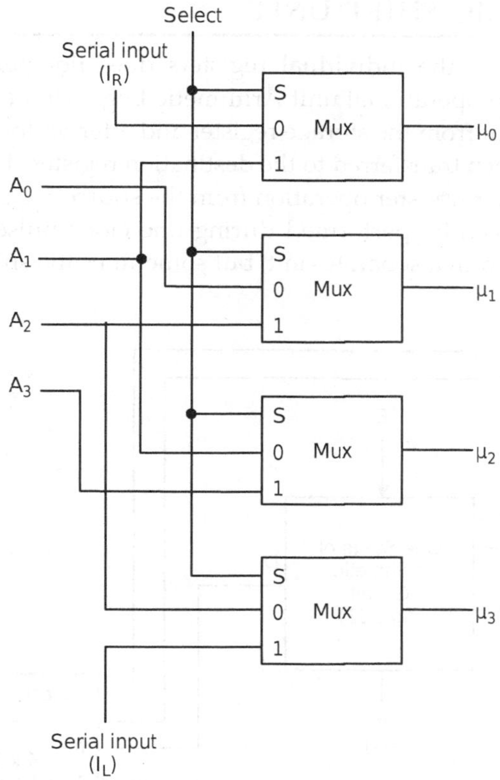

Fig. 2.13 4 bit combinational circuit shifter

When the selection input

S = 0 then output H_0 H_1 H_2 H_3 is I_R A_0 A_1 A_2

Input data are shifted right.

When S = 1 then output H_0 H_1 H_2 H_3 is A_1 A_2 A_3 I_L

Input data are shifted left.

Function table is depicted in Table 2.12.

Table 2.12 Function table

Select	*Outputs*			
S	H_0	H_1	H_2	H_3
0	I_R	A_0	A_1	A_2
1	A_1	A_2	A_3	I_L

∴ *n* data inputs = *n* multiplexers

The two serial inputs can be controlled by another multiplexer to provide the three possible types of shifts.

2.4 ARITHMETIC LOGIC SHIFT UNIT

In actual implementations the individual registers does not perform the various micro-operations directly, instead an operational unit Arithmetic Logic Unit (ALU) performs the micro-operations. The ALU gets input from the storage register and after performing the microoperations, the result of the operation is then transferred to the destination register. The ALU is a combinational circuit so that the entire register transfer operation from the source registers through the ALU and into the destination register can be performed during one clock pulse period. The shift micro-operations are often performed in a separate unit, but sometimes the shift unit is made part of the overall ALU.

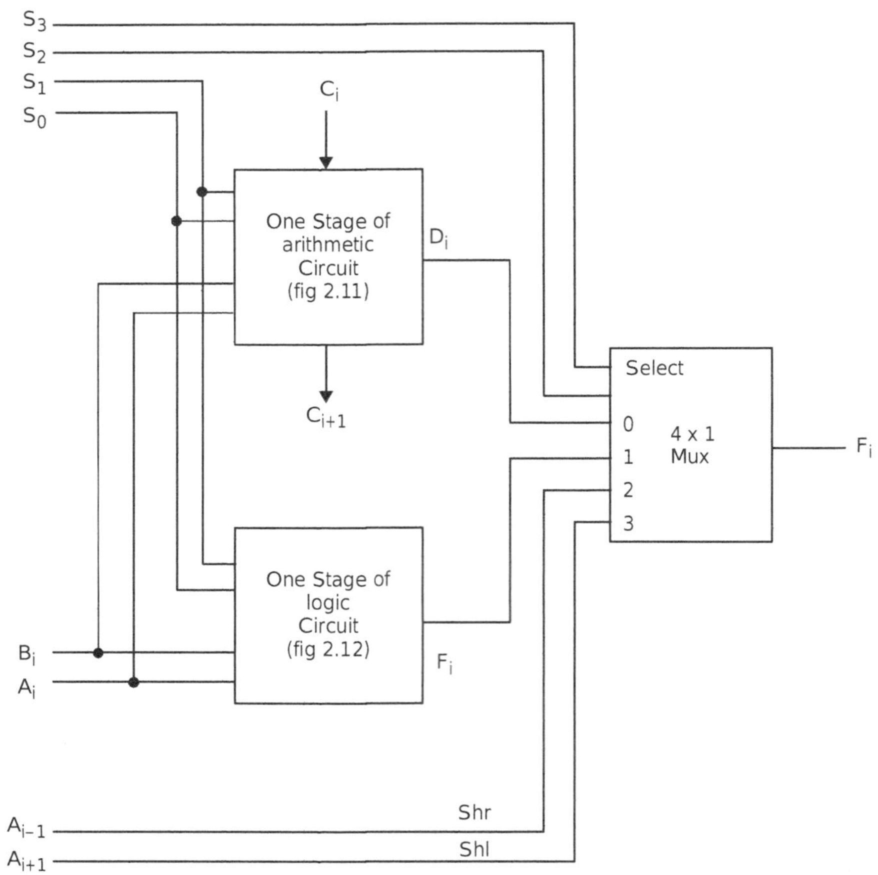

Fig. 2.14 One stage of arithmetic logic shift unit

Inputs A_i and B_i are applied to both the arithematic and logic units S_1 and S_0 selects the particular microoperation A 4 × 1 multiplexer is used to choose between an arithmetic output, logic output or a shift operation. The multiplexer receives input A_{i-1} for the shift left operation and A_{i+1} for shift right operation.

This circuit provides eight arithmetic operation, four logic operations and two shift operations. Each operation is specified with the combination of 5 variables S_3, S_2, S_1, S_0 and *Cin*. Input carry *Cin* is used in case of arithmetic operations only.

Table 2.13 lists all 14 operations.

When S_3 S_2 = 00

– Eight arithmetic microoperations are selected.

When S_3 S_2 = 01

– Four logic microoperations are selected.

When S_3 S_2 = 10

– Shift left operation is selected

When S_3 S_2 = 11

– Shift right operation is selected.

Table 2.13 Truth table for arithmetic logic shift unit

Operation Select					*Operation*	*Function*
S_3	S_2	S_1	S_0	*Cin*		
0	0	0	0	0	F = A	Transfer A
0	0	0	0	0	F = A + 1	Increment A
0	0	0	1	0	F = A + B	Addition
0	0	0	1	1	F = A + B + 1	Add with carry
0	0	1	0	0	$F = A + \overline{B}$	Subtract with borrow
0	0	1	0	1	$F = A + \overline{B} + 1$	Subtraction
0	0	1	1	0	F = A - 1	Decrement A
0	0	1	1	1	F = A	Transfer A
0	1	0	0	X	$F = A \wedge B$	AND
0	1	0	1	X	$F = A \vee B$	OR
0	1	1	0	X	$F = A \oplus B$	XOR
0	1	1	1	X	$F = \overline{A}$	Complement A
1	0	X	X	X	F = Shl A	Shift left
1	1	X	X	X	F = Shr A	Shift right

SOLVED EXAMPLES

Example 1: *A digital computer has a common bus system for 16 registers of 32 bits each. The bus is constructed with multiplexers (ref. to Fig. 2.3)*

(i) How many selection variables are needed in each multiplexer.

(ii) What is the size of each multiplexer.

(iii) How many multiplexers are required.

Solution: (*i*) There are total 16 registers that we have to select. So we need 4 control variables or selection variables because using 4 variables we can select 2^4 registers. So $2^4 = 8^{16}$

(*ii*) No. of registers = size of multiplexer.

The size of multiplexer will be 16 × 1 since we have to select one of the 16 registers for data transfer.

(*iii*) No. of bits in each register is equal to the total number of multiplexers so we require total 32 multiplexer.

Example 2: *Design a 2 bit incrementer circuit using half adder.*

Solution. Let we are having 2 bit data in register A and bits are marked as A_1A_0.

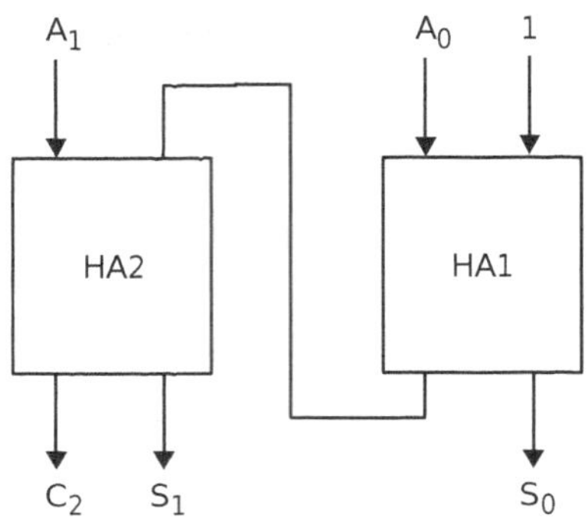

At half adder 1 we are having $A_0 + 1$. Output is S_0 and the generated carry is transferred to the second half adder.

Example 3: *Design an arithmetic circuit with one selection variable S and two n bit data inputs A and B. The circuit generates the following four arithmetic operations in conjunction with carry input Cin draw the logic diagram for first 2 bits.*

Solution.

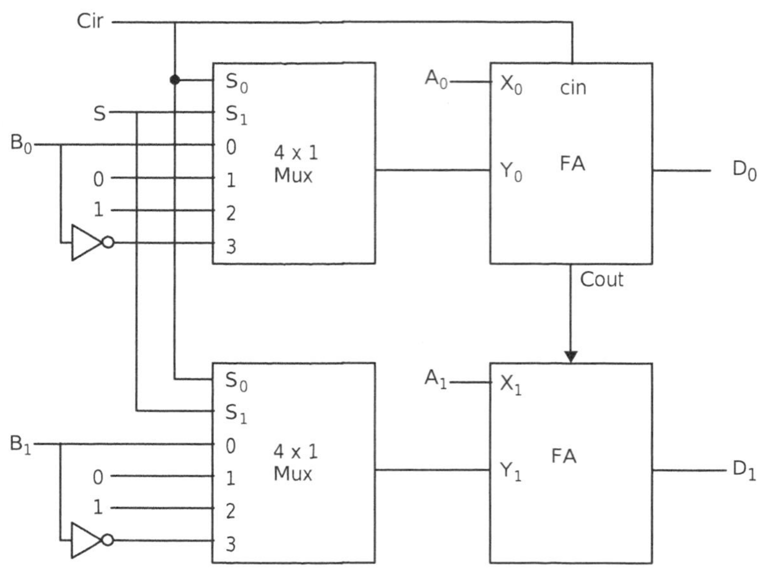

S	*Cin*	*Operation*
0	0	D = A + B
0	1	D = A + 1
1	0	D = A – 1
1	1	$D = A + \overline{B} + 1$

When $S = 0$ and $Cin = 0$

$Y_0 = B_0,\ Y_1 = B_1$

Output $D_0 = X_0 + Y_0 + Cin$

$D_1 = X_1 + Y_1 + Cout$

$= \mathbf{A + B}$

When $S = 0\ Cin = 1$

Output $D_0 = X_0 + Y_0 + Cin = A_0 + 1$

$D_1 = X_1 + Y_1 + Cout = A_1 + Cout$

$= A + 1$

Similarly $S = 1$, and $Cin = 0$

then output $D = A - 1$

and for $S = 1$ and $Cin = 1$

output $D = A - B$

Example 4: *If a register R is containing binary value 10011100. What will be the value of register R arithmetic right operation, starting from the initial value 10011100 determine the value of the register after arithmetic shift left microoperation comment about overflow situation.*

Solution. Let

R = 1 0 0 1 1 1 0 0

R ← Ashr A

1	1	0	0	1	1	1	0

L & B of R is lost.

R =	1	0	0	1	1	1	0	0

R =	0	0	1	1	1	0	0	0

Sign several occurs after the shift microoperation so overflow will occurs.

$$V_s = R_{n-1} \oplus R_{n-2}$$

$$= 1$$

Example 5: *The output of 4 registers R_0, R_1, R_2 and R_3 are connected through 4 to 1 MUX to the input of fifth register R_5. Each register is 8 bit long. The required transfers are dictated by four timing variables T_0 through T_3 as follows:*

$$T_0 \leftarrow R_5 \leftarrow R_0$$
$$T_1 \leftarrow R_5 \leftarrow R_1$$
$$T_2 \leftarrow R_5 \leftarrow R_2$$
$$T_3 \leftarrow R_5 \leftarrow R_3$$

The timing variables are mutually exclusive which means that only one variable is equal to 1 at any given time. While the other three are equal to 0 (zero). Draw the block diagram showing the hardware implementation of the register transfer include the connections necessary from timing variable to the selection input of the MUX and to the load of R_5.

Solution. Given four registers R_0, R_1, R_2, R_3. Given that three registers are connected to 4 through 1 MUX to inputs of R_5. Capacity of each register is 8 bit.

$$T_0 \leftarrow R_5 \leftarrow R_0$$
$$T_1 \leftarrow R_5 \leftarrow R_1$$
$$T_2 \leftarrow R_5 \leftarrow R_2$$
$$T_3 \leftarrow R_5 \leftarrow R_3$$

That means when timing variable is active, data transfer occurs from R_0 to R_5 and when T_1 is active, the transfer occurs from R_1 to R_5 and S_0 on. Given that only one out of four timing variable can be active at a time others remains 0 (zero). This is shown by the following table.

Result	T_0	T_1	T_2	T_3	S_1	S_0	R_s *Load*
No transfer occurs	0	0	0	0	X	X	0
$R_5 \leftarrow R_0$	1	0	0	0	0	0	1
$R_5 \leftarrow R_1$	0	1	0	0	0	1	1
$R_5 \leftarrow R_2$	0	0	1	0	1	0	1
$R_5 \leftarrow R_3$	0	0	0	1	1	1	1

When

$$S_1\,S_0 = 00 \qquad R_5 \leftarrow R_0$$
$$S_1\,S_0 = 01 \qquad R_5 \leftarrow R_1$$
$$S_1\,S_0 = 10 \qquad R_5 \leftarrow R_2$$
$$S_1\,S_0 = 11 \qquad R_5 \leftarrow R_3$$
$$S_1 = T_2 + T_3$$
$$S_0 = T_1 + T_3$$
$$\text{Load} = T_0 + T_1 + T_2 + T_3$$

Block diagram consists of 5 register R_0, R_1, R_2, R_3, R_5, two selection time, S_1 S_0, one load time, one MUX.

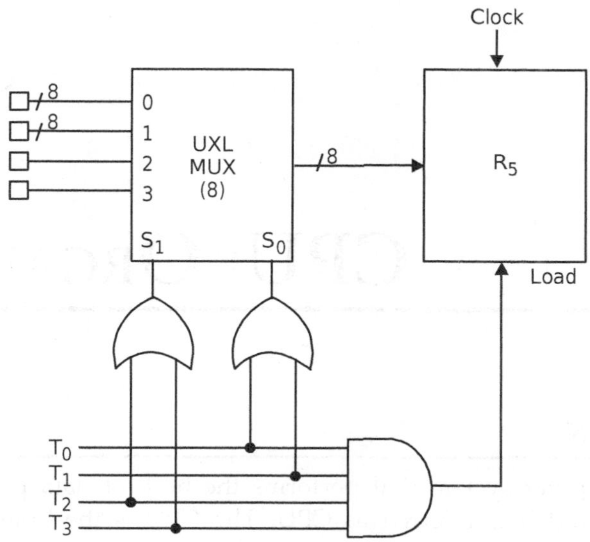

EXERCISES

1. The outputs of two registers R_0 and R_1 are connected through a 2 × 1 multiplexers to the inputs of third register R_2. Each register is 4 bit wide the required transfers are controlled by the two timing variables To and T_1 as follows.

   $T_0 : R_2 \leftarrow R_0$ $\qquad$ $T_1 : R_2 \leftarrow R_1$

   The timing variables are mutually exclusive. Draw the block diagram showing the hardware implementation of the register transfers. Include the connections necessary from the two timing variables to the selection inputs of the multiplexers and to the load input of register R_2.
2. Explain bus system for 4 registers using tri state buffers and a decoder. Each register is containing 4 bits.
3. A digital computer has a common bus system for 8 registers of 32 bits each. The bus is constructed with multiplexers.
   (*i*) How many selection variables will be there in each multiplexer.
   (*ii*) What is the size of each multiplexer.
   (*iii*) How many multiplexers are there in the bus.
4. Show the block diagram of the hardware that implements the following register transfer statement.

   $Y \ T_2 : \ R_2 \leftarrow R_1, R_1 \leftarrow R_2$
5. Design a 4 bit combinational circuit decrementer using four full adder circuits.
6. The following transfer statements specify a memory explain the memory operations in each case.

   (*i*) $R_1 \leftarrow M\ [AR]$ $\qquad$ (*ii*) $M\ [AR] \leftarrow R_2$

   (*iii*) $R_1 \leftarrow M\ [R_1]$
7. Starting from an initial value of R = 01101010, determine the sequence of binary values in R after a logical shift left, followed by a circular shift right, followed by a logical shift right and a circular shift left.

Chapter 3

CPU ORGANISATION

3.1 INTRODUCTION

The part of the computer system that performs the bulk of data processing is known as Central Processing Unit and it is referred as CPU. The CPU is the brain of a computer. The program which is to be executed is stored in the main memory. A program is a sequence of instructions to perform a specified task. The CPU fetches instruction codes from the memory and decodes them. The CPU also reads data from the memory, which are required for instruction execution. When the required data for the execution of an instruction is at hand, the CPU executes the instruction.

The CPU is made up of three major parts as depicted in Fig 3.1.

(*i*) Arithmetic and logic unit (ALU)

(*ii*) Control unit

(*iii*) Register set.

CPU contains a number of registers to store data temporarily during the execution of a program. The number of registers differ from processor to processor. The function of an ALU is to perform arithmetic and logic microoperations for executing the instructions. The control unit supervises the transfer of information among various registers and instructs the ALU as to which operation to perform. It also controls all other devices such as memory, input and output devices connected to the CPU.

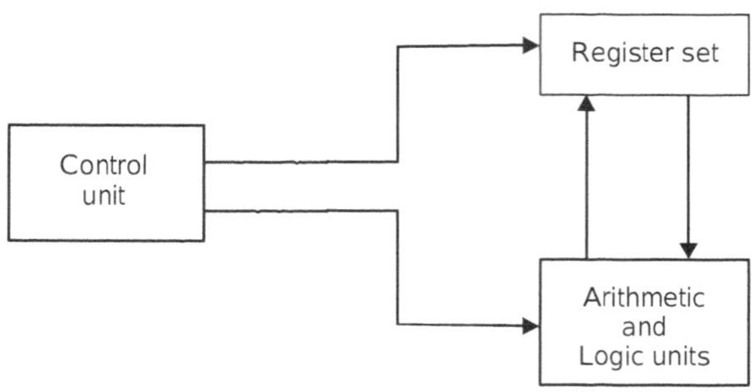

Fig. 3.1 Components of CPU

Besides executing programs the CPU also controls input devices, output devices and other components of the computer. It controls input and output devices to receive and send data. Under its control programs and data are stored in the memory and displayed on the CRT screen.

3.2 CPU ORGANISATION

The primary function of CPU is to execute sequence of instructions, execute the programs that are stored in an external main memory. A program residing in the memory unit of the computer consists of a sequence of instructions. The program is executed in the computer by going through a cycle for each instruction. Each instruction cycle in turn is subdivided into a sequence of phases. In the basic computer each instruction cycle consists of the following phases:

1. Fetch the instruction from memory
2. Decode the instruction
3. Fetch the operand
4. Execute the instruction.

Upon completion of step 4 the control goes back to step 1 to fetch the next instruction from memory. This process continues indefinitely unless a HALT instruction is encountered. The overview of CPU behaviour during execution of the instruction can be explained using the following flow chart.

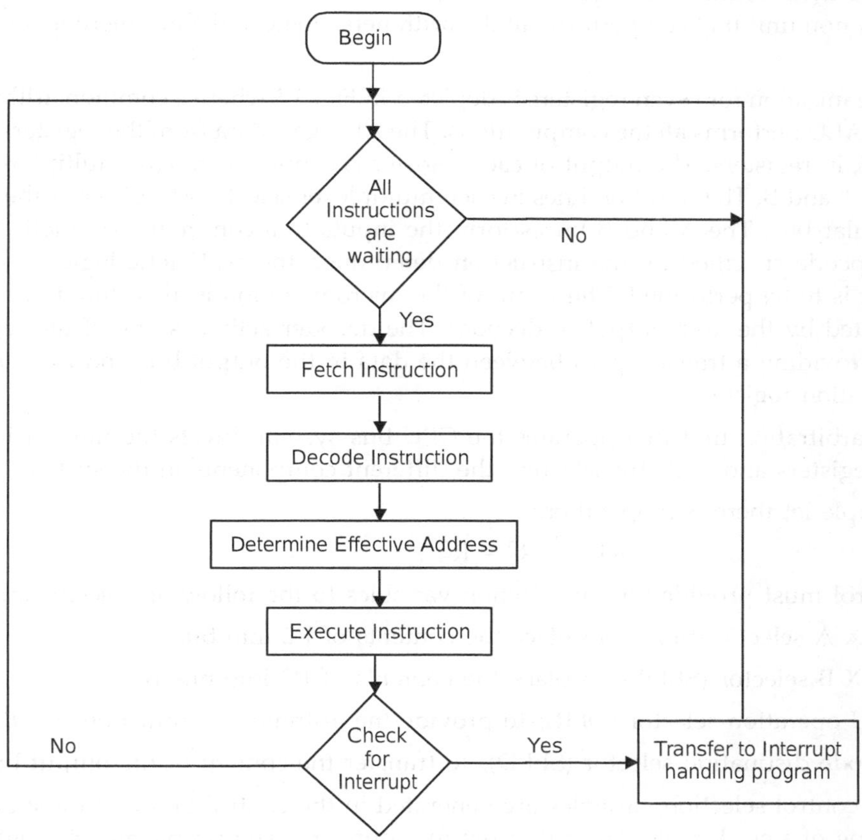

Fig. 3.2 Instruction cycle

Once we have determined the tasks a CPU will perform we must design an instruction set architecture capable of handling these tasks. We select the instructions a program could use to write the application programs and the registers used by these instructions. If instructions have to execute using Fetch phase instructions are fetched from the memory. We decode the instruction, determine the effective address and execute the instruction. Now we check for interrupt. If there is no interrupt we repeat the process for the next instruction and if there is any interrupt control is transferred to interrupt handling program after executing this interrupt handling program we begin our process again.

3.2.1 Register Set Organisation

Memory locations are used to store the data values, temporary results, return addresses and partial results during the execution of instructions. Having to refer to memory locations for such applications is time consuming because memory access is the most time consuming operation in a computer. The CPU can access registers more quickly than it can access main memory. Register to register operations generally execute faster than do register to memory or memory to memory instructions. It is more convenient and more efficient to store these intermediate values in processor registers. Each instruction specifies how the registers will be used and the computers are called general purpose register set machines. When there are large number of registers in the CPU, it is most efficient way to connect the registers through common bus system. Hence it is necessary to provide a common unit that can perform all the arithmetic, logic and shift microoperations in the processor.

A bus organisation for seven registers is depicted in Fig. 3.3 where a common arithmetic logic and shift unit ALU performs all the computations. The ALU gets data from the registers and stores the result back in registers. The output of each register is connected to two multiplexers to form the two buses A and B. The selection lines in each multiplexer select one register or the input data for the particular bus. The A and B buses form the inputs to a common Arithmetic Logic Unit (ALU). The opcode specified by the instruction determined the arithmetic logic or shift micro-operation that is to be performed. The result of the microoperation is also stored back in one of registers selected by the load output of decoder. The decoder activates one of the register load inputs, thus providing a transfer path between the data in the output bus and the inputs of the selected desination register.

The bus arbitration unit that operates the CPU bus system directs the flow of information through the registers and ALU by selecting the different components in the system.

For example let there is a operation:

$$R1 \leftarrow R2 - R3$$

The control must provide binary selection variables to the following selector inputs:

1. MUX A selector (SELA)–to place the contents of R2 into bus A.
2. MUX B selector (SELB)– to place the contents of R3 into bus B.
3. ALU operation selector (OPR);–to provide the arithmetic subtraction A – B.
4. Decode distination selector (SELD);–to transfer the content of the output bus into R1.

The four control selection variables are generated in the control unit and must be available at the beginning of a clock cycle. The data from the source register propagates through the gates in the multiplexers and the ALU, to the output bus and onto the inputs of the destination register.

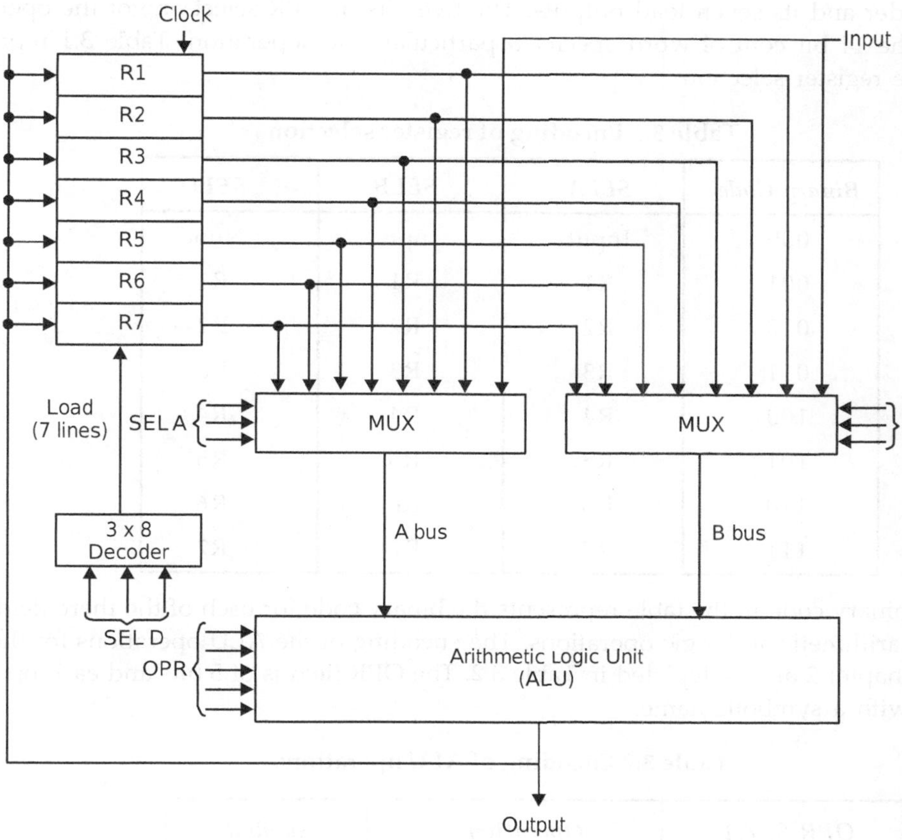

(a) Block diagram

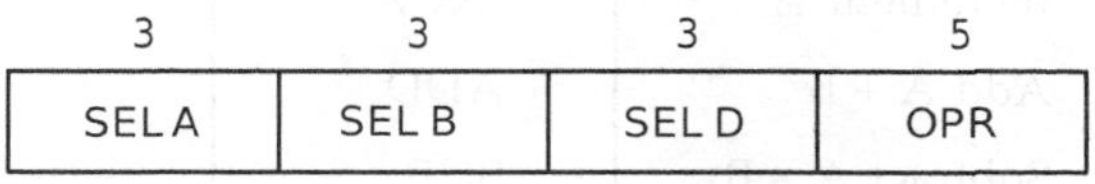

(b) Control word

Fig. 3.3 Register set with common ALU

3.2.1.1 Control Word

There are 14 binary selection inputs in the unit and their combined values specified a control word. Control word is represented in Fig 3.3 (b), There are four fields in the control word. These are:

- SELA
- SELB
- SELD
- OPR.

The three bits of SELA select a source register for the A inputs of the ALU. The three bits of SELB select a register for the B input of the ALU. The three bits of SELD select a destination register using the decoder and its seven load outputs. The five bits of OPR select one of the operations in the ALU. The 14 bit control word specify a particular microoperation. Table 3.1 represents encoding of the register selections.

Table 3.1 Encoding of register selection

Binary Code	*SELA*	*SELB*	*SELD*
000	Input	Input	None
001	R1	R1	R1
010	R2	R2	R2
011	R3	R3	R3
100	R4	R4	R4
101	R5	R5	R5
110	R6	R6	R6
111	R7	R7	R7

The 3 bit binary code in the table represents the binary code for each of the there fields. The ALU provides arithmetic and logic operations. The encoding of the ALU operations for the CPU is taken from chapter 2 and is depicted in Table 3.2. The OPR field is of 5 bits and each operation is designated with a symbolic name.

Table 3.2 Encoding of ALU operations

OPR Select	*Operation*	*Symbol*
00000	Transfer A	TSFA
00001	Increment A	INCA
00010	Add A + B	ADD
00101	Subtract A – B	SUB
00110	Decrement A	DECA
01000	AND A and B	AND
01010	OR A and B	OR
01100	XOR A and B	XOR
01110	Complement A	COMA
10000	Shift right A	SHRA
11000	Shift left A	SHLA

A 14 bit control word specify a microoperation in the CPU. The control word can be derived from the selection variables.

For example there is an operation

R1 ←R2 – R3

R2 ←A input of the ALU

R3 ←B input of the ALU.

R1 ←Destination register and ALU operation to subtract A–B.

The control word is specified using four fields. Binary value of each field can be obtained from Table 3.1 and 3.2.

Field:	SELA	SELB	SELD	OPR
Symbol:	R2	R3	R1	SUB
Control word:	010	011	001	00101

So the control word is 01001100100101.

The increment and decrement transfer microoperations do not use the B inputs of the ALU. The most common efficient way to generate control words with a large number of bits is to store them in a memory unit. A memory unit that stores control words is referred to as a control memory. By reading consecutive control words from memory, it is possible to initiate the desired sequence of microoperations for the CPU. This type of control is referred to as microprogrammed control.

3.2.2 Stack Organisation

A useful feature that is included in the CPU of most computers is a stack. A stack is a last in first out list in which items that are inserted last are deleted first. A stack is a storage device that stores the information. The stack in digital computers is essentially a memory unit with an address register. The register that holds the address for the stack is called Stack Pointer (SP) because its value always points to the top item of the stack. Basically two operations are defined on stack.

(*i*) Insertion

(*ii*) Deletion.

The operation of inserting an item on the stack is called push operation and the operation of deleting an item from the stack is known as pop operation. Both these operations are implemented by incrementing or decrementing the stack pointer register.

3.2.2.1 Register Stack

A stack can be placed in a portion of large memory or it can be organized as a collection of finite number of memory words or registers. Fig. 3.4 shows the organisation of a 32 word stack. The stack pointer register SP contains a binary value that is equal to the address of the word that is present on the top of the stack.

There are four items in the stack A, B, C and D. D is at the top of the stack. Stack pointer register (SP) containing the address where item D is present. To delete an item from the stack, the stack is popped by reading the memory word at address 4 and decrementing the content of SP. Item C is now on the top of the stack and SP holds the address 3. To insert a new item, the stack is pushed by incrementing SP and writing a word in the next higher location in the stack.

In a 32 word stack, the stack pointer contains 5 bits because $2^5 = 32$. There are two 1 bit registers FULL and EMTY. These two registers describe underflow and overflow conditions. The one bit register FULL is set to 1 when the stack is full and the one bit register EMTY is set to 1 when the stack is empty of items. DR is the data register that holds the binary data to be written into or read out of the stack.

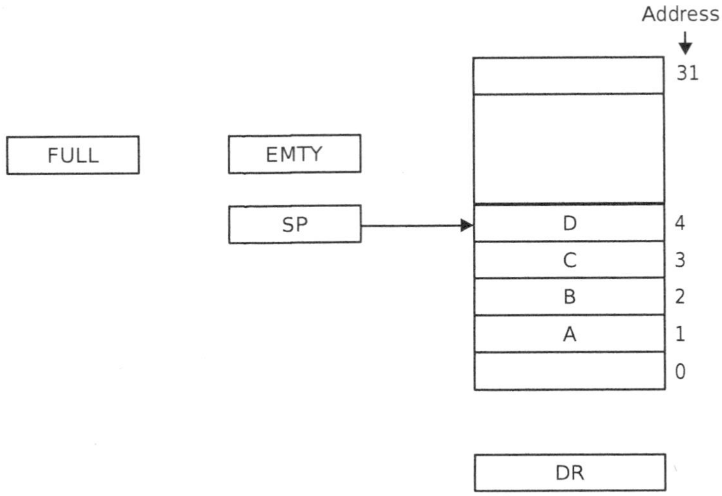

Fig. 3.4 Block diagram of 32 word stack

Initially SP is cleared to 0. EMTY is set to 1 and FULL is cleared to 0. It means SP points to the address 0 and the stack is marked empty and not full. A new item is inserted with a push operation if the stack is not full (if FULL = 0). The push operation is implemented with the following sequence of microoperations.

SP ← SP + 1 //incrementing SP//

M [SP] ← DR //writing item on top of stack//

If (SP = 0) then (FULL ← 1) //Check overflow condition//

EMTY ← 0 //Mark the stack is not empty//

The stack pointer is incremented so that is points to the address of the next higher word. During memory write operation, the word is placed on top of the stack from DR register. The first item stored in the stack is at address 1. The last item is stored at address 0. If SP reaches 0, the stack is full of items and FULL is set to 1. Once an item is stored in location 0 there are no more empty registers in the stack. If an item is written in the stack, obviously the stack cannot be empty. So EMTY is cleared to 0.

A new item is read from stack if the stack is not empty means EMTY = 0. This can be achieved by a POP operation which consists of the following sequence of microoperations.

DR ← M [SP] // Read item from top of the stack//

SP ← SP–1 //Decrement stack pointer//

If (SP = 0) then (EMTY ←1)//Check underflow condition//

FULL ← 0 //Mark the stack not full//

The top item is read from the stack into DR. The SP is then decremented.

If its value reaches zero, the stack is empty. So EMTY is set to 1. This condition is reached if the item read was in location 1. Once this item is read out. SP is decremented and reaches the value 0, which is initial value of SP. The advantage of a register stack is that the instructions do not explicitly reference their operands, the opcodes are very short. Also because the stack is within the CPU, the operands are close to the ALU. Hence execution of these instructions is very fast.

3.2.2.2 Memory Stack

A stack can be implemented in random access memory attached to a CPU. The implementation of a stack in the CPU is done by assigning a part of memory for stack operation and using a processor register as a stack pointer.

Fig 3.5 depicts that a computer's memory is partitioned into three segments.

(*i*) Program

(*ii*) Data

(*iii*) Stack.

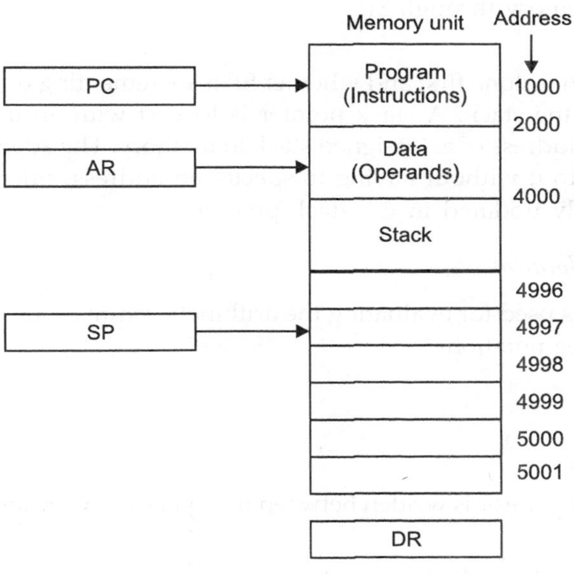

Fig. 3.5 Computer memory with three segments

A program is a set of instructions Program Counter (PC) is used to manage this segment. PC points to the next instruction that is to be executed. The handle data segment Address Register (AR) is used. AR points to an array of data. Stack segment is managed using Stack Pointer (SP). SP points at the top of the stack. The three registers are connected to a common address bus and either one can provide an address for memory. Program Counter (PC) is used during the fetch phase to read the instruction. AR is used during the execution phase to read an operand. SP is used to push or pop items into or from the stack.

As represented in the figure the initial value of SP is 5000 and the stack grows with decreasing addresses. Thus the first item stored in the list is at address 5000, the second item is stored at address 4999. No provisions are available for stack limit checks.

Items in the stack communicate with a data register DR. A new item it inserted with the push operation as follows:

$$SP \leftarrow SP - 1$$
$$M [SP] \leftarrow DR$$

A memory write operation inserts the word from DR into the top of the stack. A memory write operation inserts the word from DR into the top of the stack. A new item is deleted with a pop operation as follows:

$$DR \leftarrow M [SP]$$
$$SP \leftarrow SP + 1.$$

Most computers do not provide hardware to check for stack overflow or underflow condition. The limits of a stack can be checked using two registers. One register holds the upper limit of the stack and the other register holds the lower limit of the stack. After a push operation, SP is compared with the upper limit register and after a pop operation, SP is compared with the lower limit register.

The two microoperations needed for push or pop operation.

(*i*) An access to memory through SP.

(*ii*) Updating SP.

Which microoperation is done first and whether SP is incrementing or decrementing depends upon the organisation of the stack. A stack pointer is loaded with an initial value. This initial value must be the bottom address of an assigned stack in memory. The advantage of memory stack is that the CPU can refer to it without having to specify an address, since the address is always available and automatically updated in the stack pointer.

3.2.2.3 Reverse Polish Notation

A stack organisation is used for evaluating the arithmetic expressions. Arithmetic expressions can be represented in three notations.

(*i*) Infix Notation

(*ii*) Prefix Notation

(*iii*) Postfix Notation.

In infix notation each operator is written between the operands. Consider the simple arithmetic expression:

$$(A + B) \ * \ (C + D)$$

Addition operator is between the operands A and B or C and D. The star is between two addition results. To evaluate this expression first we compute A + B and store this result. Then (C + D) is done and then multiply both the partial results. From this example we see that to evaluate arithmetic expressions in infix notation it is necessary to scan back and then determine the next operation to be performed.

The polish mathematician Lukasiewicz showed that arithmetic expressions can be represented in prefix notation. This representation places the operator before the operands. Like +AB. This representation is also known as polish notation.

The postfix notation referred to as Reverse Polish Notation (RPN) places the operator after the operands like AB+.

The reverse polish notation is in a form suitable for stack manipulation.

The conversion from infix notation to reverse polish notation must take into consideration the operational hierarchy adopted for infix notation. This hierarchy dictates that we first perform all arithmetic inside inner parenthesis, then inside outer parenthesis and do multiplication and division operations before addition and subtraction operations. Consider the expression.

(A – B) * [C * (D + E) * F]

To convert this expression into postfix notation we first evaluate inner parenthesis. Next we evaluate square brackets. Multiplication is performed with higher precedence over addition and subtraction. Converted expression is

AB – DE + C * F * *.

3.2.2.4 Evaluation of Arithmetic Expressions

Reverse polish notation combined with a stack arrangement of registers is the most efficient way known for evaluating arithmetic expressions.

The stack is particulary useful for handling long complex problems including chain calculations. It is based on the fact that any arithmetic expression can be expressed in parentheses free polish notation. The procedure consists of first converting the arithmetic expression into its equivalent reverse polish notation.

Consider the following arithmetic expression P written in postfix notation:

P: 5 6 2 + * 1 2 4 /–

First we add right parenthesis at the end of P to obtain

5 6 2 + * 12 4 /–)

The elements of P have been labelled from left to right. Expression is scanned from left to right when an operand is encountered then it is added to the stack, when an operator is encountered then two top elements are popped. Operation is performed on these two elements and the result is again placed on the top of the stack.

Evaluation of expression is represented by the following table.

Table 3.3 Evaluation of arithmetic expression

Symbol Scanned	*Stack*
5	5
6	5,6
2	5, 6, 2
+	5, 8
*	40
12	40, 12
4	40, 12, 4
/	40, 3
–	37
)	

3.2.3 Single Accumulator Organisation

An accumulator machine uses a single operational register, called an accumulator to hold the result of arithmetic, logical or shift operation. All operations are performed with an implied accumulator register. The instruction format in this type of computer uses on address field. For example, the instruction that specifies an arithmetic addition is defined by an assembly language instruction as

ADD X

where X is the address of the operand. The ADD instruction in this case results in the operation AC $\leftarrow$ AC + M [X]. AC is the accumulator register and M [X] symbolizes the memory word located at address X.

The instruction do not explicitly reference the accumulator. The accumulator is an amplicit operand of each instruction and hence accumulator machine instructions are mostly 1 address instructions. For accumulator machines, LOAD instruction copy a value from memory to an accumulator and a STORE instruction copy the value from the accumulator to memory. Like

STORE T

$\Rightarrow$ M [T] $\leftarrow$ AC.

Transfer the contents of accumulator register to a memory location designated by T.

LOAD A

$\Rightarrow$ AC $\leftarrow$ M [A].

Transfer the contents of memory location designated by A to the accumulator register.

Accumulator organisation of a computer supports one address or zero address instructions. Zero address example.

Complement Accumulator one address example:

STORE T

LOAD A.

3.3 INSTRUCTION FORMATS

The basic computer has three types of instructions:

1. Memory reference instructions
2. Register reference instructions
3. Input-output instructions.

Each format contains three bits and the remaining 13 bits depends upon the operand code encountered. These formats are represented in Fig. 3.6.

A memory reference instruction uses 12 bits to specify an address and one bit to specify the addressing mode I. I is equal to 0 for direct address and to 1 for indirect address. Instruction format is the function of the control unit within the CPU to interpret each instruction code and provide the necessary control functions needed to process the instruction. The most common fields found in instruction format are:

(*i*) An operation code field that specifies the operation that is to be performed.

(*ii*) An address field that designates a memory address or a processor register.

(*iii*) A mode field that specifies the way the operand or the effective address is determined.

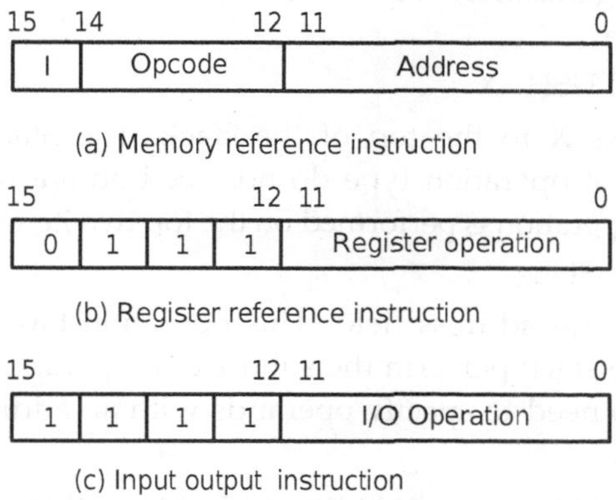

Fig. 3.6 Basic computer instruction formats

The operation code field of an instruction is a group of bits that define various processor operations such as addition, subtraction, complement and shift. The mode field of an instruction code specify a variety of alternatives for choosing the operands from the given address. Operations specified as part of computer instructions are executed on some data stored either in memory or in processor register. The operand that is present in memory is specified by a memory address and the operand that is present in a register is specify by a register address. A register address is a binary number of K bits that defines one of 2^K registers in the CPU. Thus a CPU with 32 processor registers R0 through R15 will have a register address field of 5 bits. Computers may have instructions of several different lengths containing varying number of addresses. The number of address fields in the instruction format of a computer depends upon the internal organisation of its registers. There are three types of CPU organisation that we have discussed in section 3.1.

In accumulator type organisation all operations are performed with an implied accumulator register. The instruction format of computer uses one address field. For example the instruction that specifies an arithmetic subtraction is defined by an assembly language instruction is

SUB X

X is the address of the operand.

In general register type of organisation instruction format needs three register address fields. Thus the instruction for an arithmetic addition may be written in assembly language as

ADD R1, R2, R3

It denotes the operation R1 ← R2 + R3. The number of address fields in the instruction can be reduced from three to two if the destination register is the same as one of the source registers. Thus the instruction

ADD R1 , R2

This implies R1 ← R1 + R2, general register type computers employ two or three address fields in their instruction format. Each address field may specify a memory location or a processor register.

Computers with stack organisation requires one address field in case of PUSH and POP instructions. So the instruction

PUSH X

will push the word at address X to the top of the stack. The Stack Pointer (SP) is updated automatically. The instruction of operation type do not need an address field in stack organised computers. This is because the operation is performed on the top two items of the stack. The instruction

SUB.

This instruction is having no address field. This operation has the effect that the top two elements are popped from the stack perform the subtraction operation on them and pushing the result on the stack. There is no need to specify operands with an address field since all operands are implied to be in the stack.

Most computers fall into one of the three types of organisations.

To illustrate the influence of the number of addresses on computer program, we consider the following arithmetic expression

T = (P – Q) * (R + S).

Using zero, one, two or three address instructions. We use the following symbols:

ADD – Addition
MUL – Multiplication
SUB – Subtraction
MOV – Transfer type instruction
LOAD – Data transfer to Accumulator
STORE – Data transfer from Accumulator.

3.3.1 Three Address Instructions

Computers with three address instruction formats use three address field in each instruction. Each address field can specify either a processor register or a memory operand. The program in assembly language that evaluates T = (P – Q) * (R + S) is explained below:

SUB R1, P, Q	R1 ←M [P] – M [Q]
ADD R2, R, S	R2 ←M [R] + M [S]
MUL T, R1, R2	M [X] ←R1 * R2

It is assumed that the computer has two processor registers R1 and R2. The symbol M [P] denotes at memory address symbolized by P.

Advantage

It results in short programs when evaluating arithmetic expressions.

Disadvantage

The binary coded instructions require too many bits to specify three addresses.

Example

Cyber 170. The instruction formats use either three register address fields or two register address fields and one memory address field.

3.3.2 Two Address Instructions

Two address instructions are the most common in commercial computers. Again each address field can specify either a processor register or a memory word. The program to evaluate T = (P – Q) * (R + S) is as follows:

MOV	R1, P	R1 ← M [P]
SUB	R1, Q	R1 ← R1 – M [Q]
MOV	R2, R	R2 ← M [R]
ADD	R2, S	R2 ← R2 + M [S]
MUL	R1, R2	R1 ← R1 * R2
MOV	T, R1	M [T] ← R1

The MOV instruction is used to moves or transfers the operands to and from memory and processor registers. Destination register is assumed to be a source register.

3.3.3 One Address Instructions

One address instructions use an implied accumulator (AC) register for all data manipulation. The program to evaluate T = (P – Q) * (R + S) is as follows:

LOAD	P	AC ← M [P]
SUB	Q	AC ← AC – M [Q]
STORE	A	M [A] ← AC
LOAD	R	AC ← M [R]
ADD	S	AC ← AC + M [S]
MUL	A	AC ← AC * M [A]
STORE	T	M [T] ← AC

Firstly P is loaded into the accumulator. Then contents of accumulator is subtracted from M [Q]. A is the address of the temporary memory location required for storing the intermediate result. Each instruction is of one address only. The advantage of this type of instruction is that less number of memory locations are required. For all type of data manipulation implied accumulator is used.

3.3.4 Zero Address Instructions

In case of stack organisation the instructions that represents insertion or deletion of an item require one address. While instructions that represent basic arithmetic operations like addition, subtraction etc., requires zero address field. The program T = (P – Q) * (R + S) is represents by the following instructions in stack organised computer.

PUSH	P	TOS ← P
PUSH	Q	TOS ← Q
SUB		TOS ← (P – Q)
PUSH	R	TOS ← R

PUSH	S	TOS ← S
ADD		TOS ← (R + S)
MUL		TOS ← (P – Q) * (R + S)
POP	T	M [T] ← TOS

Here TOS represents the top of stack. To evaluate arithmetic expressions in stack computers, it is necessary to convert the expressions into reverse polish notation. The name "zero address" is given to this type of computer because of the absence of an address field in the computational instructions.

3.4 ADDRESSING MODES

There are three fields in an instruction:

(*i*) Opcode

(*ii*) Address field

(*iii*) Mode field.

The Opcode field in the instruction represents the operation which is to be performed. The operation is performed on some data that is to be stored in computer registers or memory words. There are several ways to specify an operand. These are called addressing modes. The way the operands are chosen during the execution of a program is depend on the addressing mode of the instruction. Addressing modes define a rule or a way by which the value of the operand is referenced or we reach where the value of operand is present. The operand can be present in processor register, memory, I/O port and in the instruction itself. Addressing modes define a technique to reach where the operand that is required in our instruction is present.

Computers use addressing techniques for the purpose of accommodating one or both of the following provisions:

(*i*) To give programming versatility to the user by providing facilities such as pointer to memory. Counters for loop control, indexing of data and program relocation.

(*ii*) To reduce the number of bits in the addressing field of the instruction.

To understand the various addressing modes, it is imperative that we understand the basic operation cycle of the computer. An instruction cycle is divided into three major phases.

(*i*) Fetch the instruction from memory

(*ii*) Decode the instruction

(*iii*) Execute the instruction.

There is one register PC (Program Counter) that keeps track of the instructions in the program stored in memory. PC holds the address of the next instruction that is to be executed. Whenever an instruction is fetched from memory. PC is incremented by 1. The second phase of the machine cycle determines the operation that we have to performed the addressing mode of the instruction and the location where the operand is present. Then we execute the instruction and returned to step 1 to fetch the next instruction from memory. The availability of the addressing modes gives the experienced assembly language programmer flexibility for writing program that are more efficient with respect to the number of instructions and execution time.

Now discussing the addressing modes following standard terms are used:

(i) Address (A)

Contents of an address field in the instruction that refers to a memory location.

(ii) Register (R)

Contents of an address field that refers to a register in the instruction.

(iii) Program Counter (PC)

The Program Counter (PC) keeps tracks of the instructions in the program stored in memory. It holds the address of the instruction that is to be executed and incremented every time when an instruction is fetched from memory.

(iv) Effective Address (EA)

The effective address is the address of the operand when the operand is actually stored. It is defined to be the memory address obtained from the computation dictated by the given addressing mode.

3.4.1 Implied Addressing

In this type of addressing mode operands are defined implicitly as a part of definition of the instruction itself.

For example, Increment accumulator instruction.

Complement accumulator instruction are implied mode instructions because the operand in the accumulator register is implied in the definition of the instruction. All register reference instructions that use accumulator are implied mode instruction. Zero address instructions in stack organised computers are implied mode instructions since it is implied that operands are present on the top of the stack.

3.4.2 Immediate Addressing

This is the simplest form of addressing modes. The operand itself is a part of instruction. In other words we can say that an immediate mode instruction contains an operand field rather than an address field.

OPERAND = A

OP	A

For example, MOV R, O

This instruction is of type immediate mode instruction. Value of the operand can be in processor register or it can be present in memory word. This mode can be used constants and set initial values of variables.

The advantage of immediate addressing is that no memory reference other than the instruction fetch is required to obtain the value of the operand. So it saves one memory cycle in the instruction cycle. The disadvantage is that the size of the number is restricted to the size of address field.

3.4.3 Direct Addressing

In this type of addressing effective address of the operand is present in the instruction. This is very simple form of addressing. The operand is present in memory. When we access the Effective Address (EA), then we get the value of the operand that is required during the execution of the instruction.

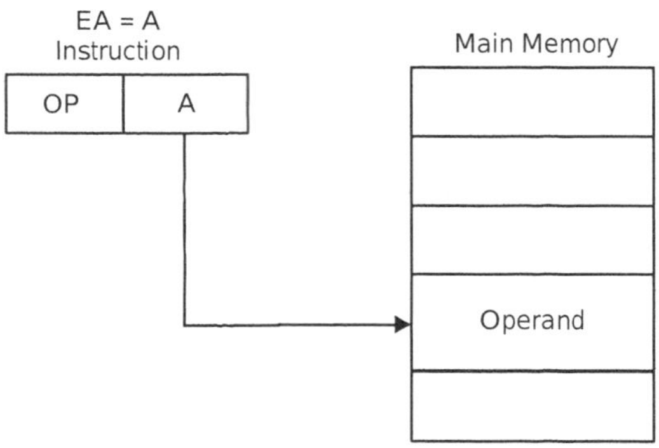

Fig. 3.7

This addressing technique was common in earlier generation of computers but it is not common in current architectures. It requires only one memory reference.

3.4.3.1 Limitation

It provides only a limited address space. When there are K bits in the address field then we can access 2^k units of storage area.

3.4.4 Indirect Addressing

With direct addressing, the length of the address field is less than the word length thus limiting the address range. One solution of this problem is indirect addressing technique. In this technique address field of the instruction represents the another address field rather than the actual value of the operand. So in this mode the address field of the instruction gives the address where the effective address is stored in memory. Control fetches the instruction from memory ands uses its address part to access the memory again to read the effective address.

$$EA = (A)$$

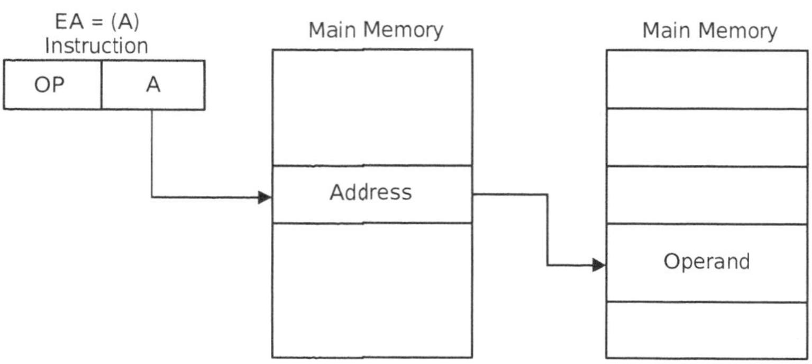

Fig. 3.8

The parenthesis are interpreted as meaning "Contents of". The advantage of this approach is that for a word length of n, an address space of 2^n is now available. The disadvantage is that it requires two memory references to fetch the operand, one to get its address and a second to get its value.

3.4.5 Register Addressing

It this mode the operands are in registers that reside within the CPU. It is similar to direct addressing. The only difference is that the address field refers to a register rather than a main memory address.

$$EA = R$$

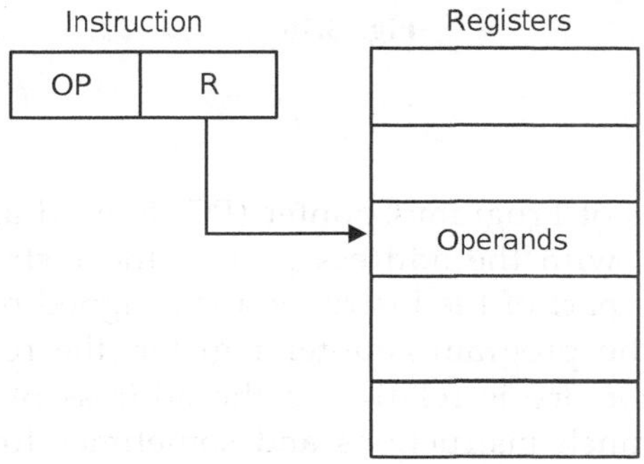

Fig. 3.9

Advantages

(*a*) Only a small address field is needed.

(*b*) No memory reference is required. The memory access time for a register is much less than that for a main memory address because registers are internal to CPU.

Disadvantage

Address space is very limited. Since number of registers are limited.

3.4.6 Register Indirect Addressing

Register indirect addressing is similar to indirect addressing. In this case address field refers to a register and in indirect addressing address fields refer to a memory location. The instruction specifies a register in the CPU whose contents give the address of the operand in memory. When there is indirect register addressing, the program generates the address of the operand and places it in operational register for later use. A reference to the register is then equivalent specifying a memory address.

The advantage of a register indirect mode instruction is that the address field of the instruction uses fewer bits to select a register than would have been required to specify a memory address directly.

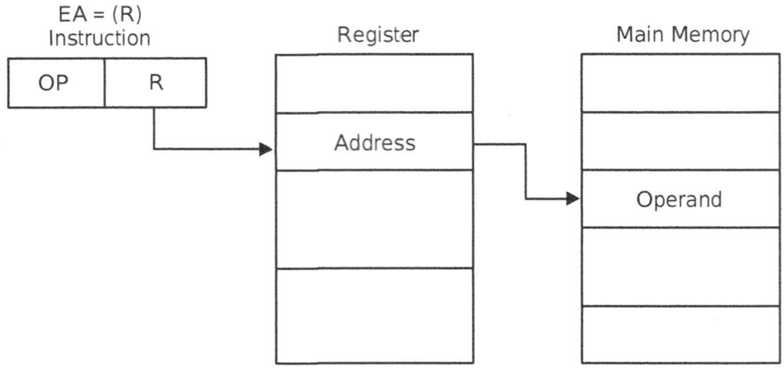

Fig. 3.10

3.4.7 Relative Addressing

In this technique contents of Program Counter (PC) is used as a base address. Contents of program counter is added with the address part of the instruction in order to get the effective address. The address part of the instruction is a signed number. When this number is added to the contents of the program counter register, the result produces an effective address whose position in memory is relative to the address of the next instruction. This addressing is common for branch instructions and sometimes for immediate data but this technique is considered absolute for data addressing. We have to be take care that when we are adding the contents of the program counter then we have to see that value in the decode phase of the instruction cycle. Because when an instruction is fetched from memory, the value of program counter is updated.

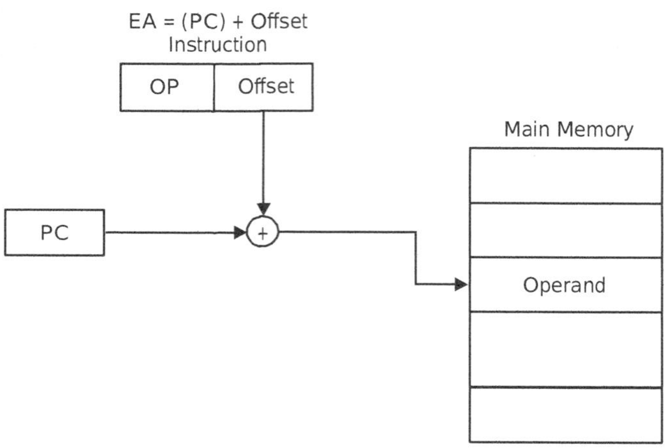

Fig. 3.11

3.4.8 Indexed Addressing

In this addressing mode the contents of an index register is added with the address part of the instruction to obtain the effective address. An index register is a special CPU register that contains an index value. The distance between the beginning address and the address of the operand is the index value stored in the index register.

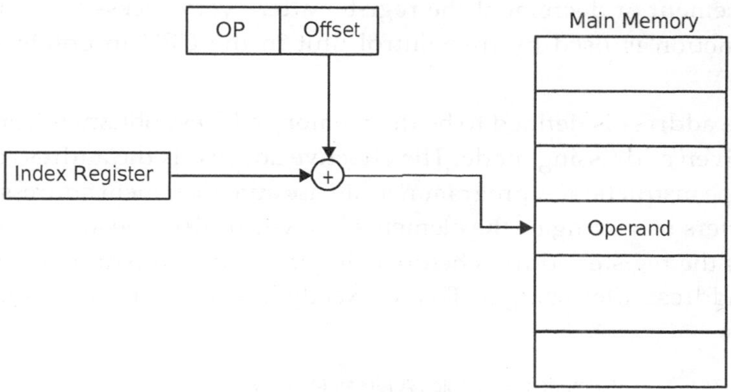

Fig. 3.12

3.4.9 Base Register Addressing

In this mode the contents of the base register is added with the address part of the instruction in order to obtain the effective address. It is same as index addressing except now the register is a base register. An index register in assumed to hold an index number that is relative to the address part of the instruction. The base register may be a general purpose register or a general purpose register set machine.

The Effective Address (EA) of the operand is then sum of the displacement and the content of the base register.

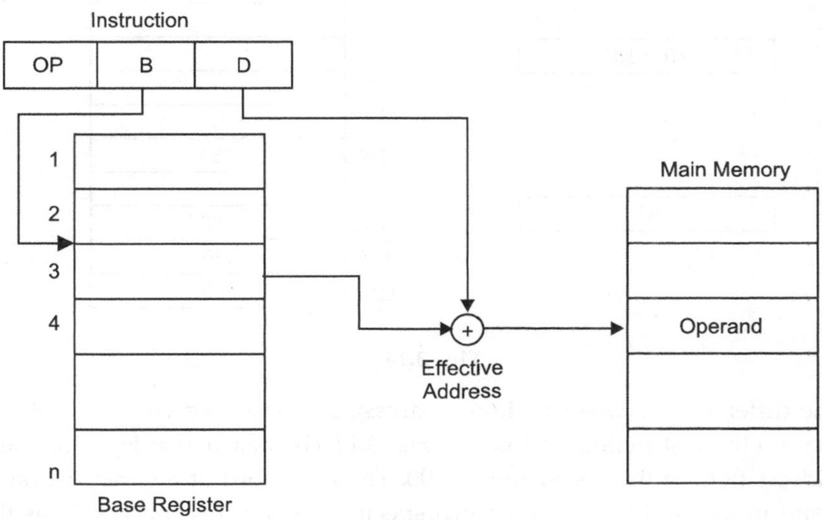

Fig. 3.13

$$EA = (B) + D$$

Each base register can point to any location in memory.

3.4.10 Auto Increment and Auto Decrement Addressing

It is special addressing mode that automatically increment or decrement the index register. When the address stored in the register refers to a table of data in memory. It is necessary to increment or decrement the register after every access to the table. The address field of an instruction is used by the control unit in the CPU to obtain the operand from memory.

The effective address is defined to be the memory address obtained from the computation dictated by the given addressing mode. The effective address is the address of the operand in a computational type instruction. A programmer can use auto increment addressing to sequentially access the characters in a string or the elements in a vector list. The auto increment addressing mode increments the register address before using it and the auto decrement addressing mode decrements the address after using it. That is exactly how typical computers manipulate stack registers.

Numerical Example : Address Memory

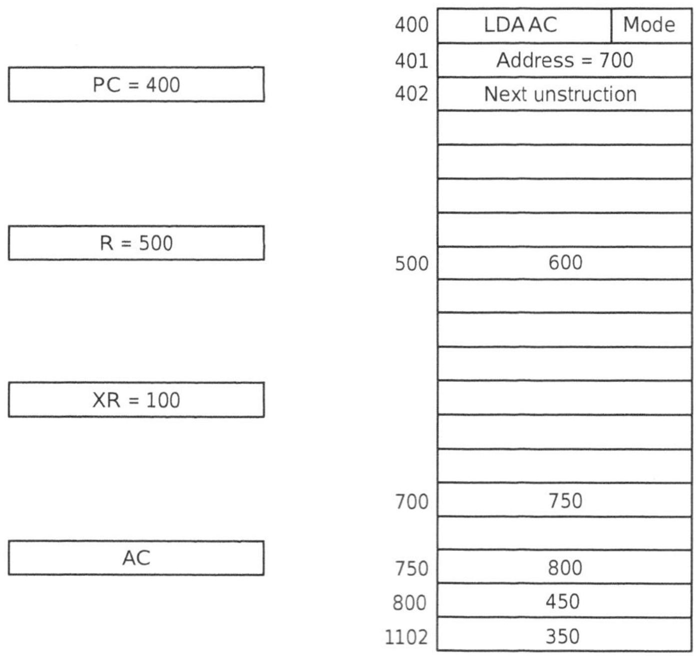

Fig. 3.14

To show the difference between various addressing modes, we will show the effect of the addressing modes on the instructions defined in Fig. 3.14 The instruction is written at the address 400 and 401. Address field of the instruction is 700. The first word of the instruction specifies the operation code and mode, and the second word specifies the address part. PC has the value 400 for fetching the instruction. After the execution of the instruction accumulator register will receive the value.

Now for each addressing mode technique we will calculate the Effective Address (EA).

(*i*) **Direct addressing mode.** Address that is mentioned in the instruction will contain the value of the operand.

So Effective Address = 700

Contents of AC = 750

(*ii*) **Immediate addressing mode.** Value of the operand is a part of instruction itself.

So Contents of AC = 700

Effective Address = 401.

(*iii*) **Indirect addressing mode.** Two memory references are required. So when we access 700 location, we will get again an address that is 750. When we access 750 then we will get the value of the operand.

So Effective Address = 750

Contents of AC = 800.

(*iv*) **Register direct addressing mode.** Contents of register provides the value of the operand.

So Contents of AC = 500.

(*v*) **Register Indirect addressing mode.** Contents of register provides the effective address of the operand.

So Effective address = 500

Contents of AC = 600.

(*vi*) **Relative addressing mode.**

Effective address = Contents of program counter (PC) + Address that is part of the instruction

EA = 402 + 700 = 1102

Here we are taking the value of program counter as 402. Because addressing mode is determined in the decode phase of the instruction cycle. Value of program counter is updated when an instruction is fetched from memory, so PC is updated as 402. Since 400 and 401 are the location when the instruction is written and next instruction is at address 402.

So Effective address = 1102

Contents of AC = 350.

(*vii*) **Indexed addressing mode.** In the index mode the effective address is XR + 700 = 100 + 700 = 800 and the operand is 450.

So Effective address = 800

Contents of AC = 450

Table 3.4 lists the values of the effective address and the operand loaded into the AC for seven addressing modes.

Table 3.4 Tabular list of example

Addressing Mode	*Effective Address*	*Contents of AC*
1. Direct Addressing	700	750
2. Immediate	401	700
3. Indirect Addressing	750	800
4. Register Direct	–	500
5. Register Indirect	500	600
6. Relative	1102	350
7. Indexed	800	450

3.5 DATA TRANSFER AND MANIPULATION

Instruction set of a computer determines the machine's computational capabilities. Instruction set architecture provides flexibility to the programmer. Computers provide an extensive set of instructions to give the user the flexibility to carry out various computational tasks. The instruction set of different computers differ from each other mostly in the way the operands are determined from the address and mode fields. Operations are represented by binary codes and binary code for one computer can be different from another computer. It may also happen that the symbolic name given to instructions in assembly language notation is different in different computers, even for the same instruction. An instruction contains three fields:

1. Opcode
2. Address Field
3. Mode Field.

According to the address field an instruction can be classified as three address instruction, two address, one address and zero address instructions. Instructions can be classified according to the opcode field. Opcodes are of different types and according to the type of opcode instructions can be classified into three categories:

1. Data Transfer Instructions
2. Data Manipulation Instructions
3. Program Control Instructions.

Data transfer instructions transfer data from one location to another without changing the contents. Data manipulation instructions are those that perform arithmetic, logic and shift operations. Program control instructions provide decision making capabilities and are responsible for changing the execution sequence. The instruction set of a particular computer determines the register transfer operations and control decisions that are available to the user.

3.5.1 Data Transfer Instructions

Data transfer instructions move the data from one location to another location in computer without changing the contents. The most common data transfer takes place between memory and processor registers, between processor registers and input or output devices and between the processor registers themselves. Each instruction is represented by mnemonic symbol. Typically there are eight data transfer instructions. These are represented in Table 3.5.

Table 3.5 Data transfer instructions

Name	*Mnemonic Symbol*
Load	LD
Store	ST
Move	MOV
Exchange	XCH
Input	IN
Output	OUT
Push	PUSH
Pop	POP

The load instruction has been used mostly to designate a transfer from memory to a processor register usually an accumulator.

The store instruction designates a transfer from processor register to memory. The move instruction transfer data from one processor register to another, from processor register the memory, from memory to processor register or between two memory words. The exchange instruction swap information between two register or a register and a memory word. The input and output instructions transfer data among processor registers and input or output terminals. The push and pop instructions transfer data between processor registers and a memory stack. The instructions listed in the table is associated with a variety of addressing modes. As an example consider the load to accumulator instruction when used with eight different addressing modes. To be able to write assembly language programs for a computer, it is necessary to know the type of instructions available and also to be familiar with the addressing modes used in the particular computer.

3.5.2 Data Manipulation Instructions

Data manipulation instructions perform operations on data and provide the computational capabilities for the computer. These instructions change the contents of registers on which the instructions operates. The data manipulation instructions in a typical computer are usually divided into three basic types:

1. Arithmetic Instructions
2. Logical and Bit Manipulation Instructions
3. Shift Instructions.

Each instruction when executed in the computer must go through the fetch phase that reads the binary code of the instruction from memory. The operands are brought in processor registers according to the rules of the instruction addressing mode. The last step is to execute the instruction in the processor.

1. Arithmetic Instructions

The four basic arithmetic operations are addition, subtraction, multiplication and division. Some computers provide instructions for all four operations and some computers provides only addition and subtraction directly. Multiplication and division is generated from these two operations. Typical arithmetic instructions are listed in Table 3.6.

Table 3.6 Typical arithmetic instructions

Name	*Mnemonics*
Increment	INC
Decrement	DEC
Add	ADD
Subtract	SUB
Multiply	MUL
Divide	DIV
Add with Carry	ADDC
Subtract with Borrow	SUBB
Negation	NEG

Increment operation adds 1 to the value that is stored in registers or memory word. The decrement instruction subtracts 1 from a value stored in a register or in a memory word. A number with all 0's, produces a number with all 1's, when decremented. The addition, subtraction, multiplication and divide instructions may be available for different types of data. An arithmetic instruction may specify fixed print or floating point data, binary or decimal data, single precision or double precision data.

Execution of arithmetic instructions generally set the processor status flags or the condition codes to indicate the outcome of the operation. Examples of such outcomes are the conditions generated as a carry or a borrow, an overflow or an underflow, the result is 0 or the result is negative. Thus the condition code register is an implicit operand for most of these instructions. A special carry flip-flop is used to store the carry from an operation. The instruction add with carry performs the addition of two numbers plus the value of the carry from the previous computation. In the same way the "subtract with borrow" instruction subtracts two words and a borrow which may have resulted from a previous subtract operation. The negative operation represents the 2's complement of a number.

2. Logical and Bit Manipulation Instructions

Logical instructions perform binary operations on bits stored in registers. These instructions manipulate individual bits or a group of bits that represent binary coded information. These logical instructions consider each bit of the operand separately and treat it as a boolean variable. These instructions can be used to set, clear and export specific groups of bits and perform many other operations. Typical logical and bit manipulation instructions are listed in Table 3.7.

The clear instruction sets all the bits to 0. The complement instruction produces 1's complement of the number by changing the 1 bit into 0 or 0 into 1 bit.

Table 3.7 Typical logical and bit manipulation instructions

Name	*Mnemonics*
Clear	CLR
Complement	COM
AND	AND
OR	OR
Exclusive OR	XOR
Clear Carry	CLRC
Set Carry	SETC
Complement Carry	COMC
Enable Interrupt	EI
Disable Interrupt	DI

The AND, OR and XOR operation produce the corresponding logical operations on individual bits of the operands. There are three bit manipulation operations possible

CLRC—Set the carry bit to 0

SETC—Set the carry bit to 1

COMC—Complement the carry bit.

The three logical instructions are usually applied to do just that. A flip-flop that controls the interrupt facility and is either enabled or disabled by means of bit manipulation instructions.

3. *Shift Instructions*

Shift instructions are used to shift the contents of an operand. These instructions move the bits of a word either in the left direction or in the right direction. The bits shifted in at the end of the word determines the type of shift used. There are three types of shift operations:

(*i*) Logical Shift

(*ii*) Circular Shift

(*iii*) Arithmetic Shift.

In either case the shift may be to the right or to the left. Table 3.8 represents the typical shift instructions.

The logical shift inserts a 0 to the end bit position. The end position is the left most bit for shift right and the right most bit position for the shift left.

Table 3.8 Typical shift instructions

Name	*Mnemonics*
Logical Shift Left	SHL
Logical Shift Right	SHR
Arithmetic Shift Left	SHLA
Arithmetic Shift Right	SHRA
Rolate Left	ROL
Rotate Right	ROR
Rotate Left Through Carry	ROLC
Rotate Right Through Carry	RORC

The arithmetic shift considers the sign bit of the number. Arithmetic shift left operation multiply a number by 2 while arithmetic shift right operation divides a number by two. The arithmetic shift right instruction must preserve the sign bit in the left most position. The sign bit is shifted to the right together with the rest of the number, but the sign bit itself remains unchanged.

The rotate instructions produces a circular shift. Bits shifted out at one end of the word are not lost as in a logical shift but are circulated back into the other end. The rotate through carry instruction treats a carry bit as an extension of the register whose word is being rotated. So a rotate left through carry instruction transfers the carry bit into the right most bit position of the register, transfer the left most bit position into the carry and at the same time shifts the entire register to the left.

Instruction set architects provide the various shift instructions for a number of different reasons. For example for extracting fields from the words and for extending the precision of integers. In chapter-2 we have already discussed shift instructions in detail.

3.5.3 Program Control Instructions

Instructions are always stored in consecutive memory locations or executed in serial manner. An instruction is fetched from the memory and executed. When instruction is fetched from memory every time the value of the program counter is incremented. After executing the instructions control again returns to the fetch cycle with the program counter containing the address of the next instruction that have to fetch from the memory. This process continues until an HALT instruction is encountered.

A program control type instruction change the default execution sequence of the program. These instructions change the address value in the program counter and cause the flow of control to be altered. Program control instructions specify conditions for altering the content of the program counter, while data transfer and manipulation instructions specify conditions for data processing operations. Change in the value of the program counter causes a break in the sequence of instruction execution. Some typical program control instructions are listed in Table 3.9.

Table 3.9 Typical program control instructions

Name	*Mnemonics*
Branch	BR
Jump	JMP
Skip	SKP
Call	CALL
Return	RET
Compare	CMP
Test	TST

Branch and Jump instructions when executed causes a transfer of the value of an address in the program counter. Since the program counter contains the value of the next instruction's address that is to be executed, the next instruction come from the address specified by the branch instruction. Branch or Jump instruction's may by conditionally or unconditionally. An unconditional branch change the value of program counter without specifying any condition.

If it is conditional, when the given condition is met, the program counter is loaded with the branch address and the next instruction is taken from this address. If the condition is false, the program counter is not changed and the next instruction is taken from the next location in sequence. The branch and jump instructions are used inter changeably to mean the same thing, but sometimes they are used to denote different addressing modes.

SKIP does not need an address field. It skips the next instruction in sequence. This is done by incrementing the program counter during the execute phase in addition to its being incremented during the fetch phase. It can be conditional or unconditional.

The call and return instruction's are used in conjunction with subroutines. It is discussed in later sections. The compare instruction performs a subtraction between two operands. Certain status bit condition's are set as a result of the operation. Now we discuss these status bits.

3.6 STATUS BIT CONDITIONS

It is convenient to supplement the ALU circuit in the CPU with a status register where status bit condition can be stored for further analysis. Status bits are also called condition-code bits or flag bits. Fig. 3.5 shows the block diagram of an 8-bit ALU with a 4-bit status register. The four status bits are symbolized by C, S, Z and V. The bits are set or cleared as a result of an operation performed in the ALU.

1. Bit C (Carry) is set to 1 if the end carry C_8 is 1. It is cleared to 0 if the carry is 0.
2. Bit S (Sign) is set 1 if the highest order bit F_7 is 1. It is set to 0 if the bit is 0.
3. Bit Z (Zero) is set to 1 if the output of the ALU contains all 0's. It is cleared to 0 otherwise. In other words, Z = 1 if the output is zero and Z = 0 if the output is not zero.

4. Bit V (overflow) is set to 1 if the exclusive–OR of the last two carries is equal to 1, and cleared to 0 otherwise. This is the condition for an overflow when negative numbers are in 2's complement. For the 8-bit ALU, V = 1 if the output is greater than +127 or less than –128.

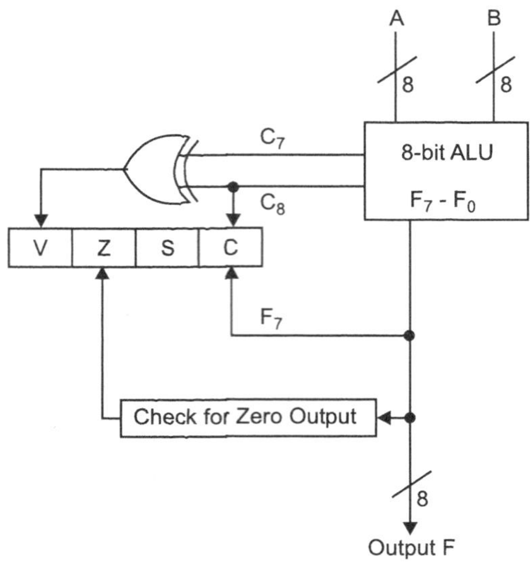

Fig. 3.15 Status register bits

The status bits can be checked after an ALU operation to determine certain relationships that exist between the values of A and B.

If bit V is set after the addition of two signed numbers, it indicates an overflow condition. If Z is set after an exclusive – OR operation, it indicates that A = B. This is so because $x \oplus x = 0$, and the exclusive – OR of two equal operands gives an all 0's result which set the Z-bit.

A single bit in A can be checked to determine if it is 0 or 1 by masking all bits except the bit in question and then check the Z status bit.

For example.

Let A = 101 x 11 00.

where x is the bit to be checked. The AND operation of A with B = 00010000 produces a result 000 x 0000.

If $x = 0$, the Z-status bit is set.

If $x = 1$, the Z-bit is cleared since the result is not zero.

The AND operation can be generated with the TEST instruction listed in Table 3.5 if the original content of A must be preserved.

3.7 SUBROUTINE CALL AND RETURN

A subroutine is a self-contained sequence of instructions that performs a given computational task.

In another way "A subroutine is a group of instructions written separately from the main program to perform a function that occurs repeatedly in the main program." For example, if a time delay is required between three successive events, three delays can be written in the main program. To avoid the repetition of the same delay instruction, the subroutine technique is used. Delay instructions are written once, separately from the main program, and are called by the main program when needed.

During the execution of a program, a subroutine may be called to perform its function many times at various points in the main program. Each time a subroutine is called, a branch is executed to the beginning of the subroutine to start executing its set of instructions. After the subroutine has been executed, a branch is made back to the main program.

The instruction that transfers program control to a subroutine is known by different names. The most common names used are call subroutine, jump to subroutine, branch to subroutine, or branch and save address. A call subroutine instruction consists of an operation code together with an address that specifies the beginning of the subroutine. The instruction is executed by performing two operations:

1. The address of the next instruction available in the program counter is stored in a temporary location so the subroutine knows where to return.
2. Control is transferred to the beginning of the subroutine.

The last instruction of every subroutine, commonly called return from subroutine, transfer the return address from the temporary location into the program counter. Transfer of program control to the instruction whose address was originally stored in the temporary location.

Different computers use a different temporary location for storing the return address. Some store the return address in the first memory location of the subroutine, some store it in a fixed location in memory some store it in a processor register and some store it in a memory stack. The advantage of a stack for the return address is that when a succession of subroutines is called, the sequential return addresses can be pushed into the stack. The return from subroutine instruction causes the stack to pop and the contents of the top of the stack are transferred to the program counter. A subroutine call is implemented with the following microoperations:

SP ← SP – 1	Decrement stack pointer.
M [SP] ← PC	Push content of PC onto the stack.
PC ← effective address	Transfer control to the subroutine.

The instruction that returns from the last subroutine is implemented by the following micro-operations:

PR ← M [SP]	Pop stack and transfer to PC.
SP ← SP + 1	Increment stack pointer.

By using a subroutine stack, all return addresses are automatically stored by the hardware in one unit.

A recursive subroutine is a subroutine that calls itself. If only one register or memory location is used to store the return address, and the recursive subroutine calls itself, it destroys the previous return address. When a stack is used, each return address can be pushed into the stack without destroying any previous values. This solves the problem of recursive subroutines because the next subroutine to exit is always the last subroutine that was called.

3.8 PROGRAM INTERRUPT

The program interrupt is used to handle a variety of problems that arise out of normal program sequence. Program interrupt refers to the transfer of program control from a currently running program to another service program as a result of an external or internal generated request. The transfer control from the current program to another program is called an interrupt routine.

The interrupt routine actually performs tasks such as initiating an input-output operation or responding to an error encountered by the I/O device. Control returns to the original program after a service program is executed.

The interrupt procedure is similar to subroutine call except:

1. The interrupt is usually initiated by an internal or external signal rather than from an execution of an instruction.
2. The address of the interrupt service program is determined by the hardware rather than from the address field of an instruction.
3. An interrupt procedure stores all the information necessary to define the state of the CPU rather than storing only the PC.

After a program has been interrupted and interrupt routine been executed, the CPU must return to exactly the same state that it was when the interrupt occur. The state of the CPU at the end of the execute cycle is determine from:

(*a*) The content of the PC.

(*b*) The content of all processor register.

(*c*) The content of contain status condition.

3.8.1 Program Status Word (PSW)

The collection of all status bit conditions in the CPU is sometimes called a program status word or PSW.

It includes the status bits from the last ALU operation and it specifies the interrupts that are allowed to occur and whether the CPU is operating in that supervisor or user mode. Many computers have a resident operating system that controls and supervises all other programs in the computer. When the CPU is executing a program that is part of the operating system, it is said to be in supervisor or system mode.

The CPU is normally in the user mode when executing user programs. The mode that the CPU is operating at any given time is determined from special status bit in the PSW.

The hardware procedure for processing an interrupt is very similar to the execution of a subroutine call instruction. The state of the CPU is pushed into a memory stack and the beginning address of the service routine is transferred to the program counter. The beginning address of the service routine is transferred to the program counter. The beginning address of the service routine is determined by the hardware rather than the address field of an instruction.

The CPU does not respond to an interrupt until the end of an instruction execution. Just before going to the next fetch phase, control checks for any interrupt signals. If an interrupt is pending, control goes to a hardware interrupt cycle. During this cycle, the contents of PC and PSW are pushed onto the stack. The branch address for the particular interrupt is then transferred to PC and a new PSW is loaded into the status register. The service program can now be executed starting from the batch address and having a CPU mode as specified in the new PSW.

3.8.2 Types of Interrupts

There are three major types of interrupts:

1. External Interrupts
2. Internal Interrupts
3. Software Interrupts.

External Interrupts comes from I/O devices, from a circuit monitoring the power supply, or from any other external source. *e.g.*, that cause external interrupts are I/O device requesting transfer of data, I/O device finished transfer of data, elapsed time of an event or power failure. Power failure interrupt may have as its service routine a program that transfers the complete state of the CPU into a nondestructive memory in the few millisec. before power ceases.

Internal Interrupts arise from illegal or erroneous use of an instruction or data. Examples of interrupts caused by internal error conditions are register overflow, attempt to divide by zero, an invalid operation code, stack overflow and protection violation.

The difference between internal and external interrupts is that the internal interrupts is initiated by some exceptional condition caused by the program itself rather than by an external event.

External and Internal Interrupts are initiated from signals that occur in the hardware of the CPU. A software interrupt is initiated by executing an instruction. Software interrupt is a special call instruction that behaves like an interrupt rather than a subroutine cell. In can be used by the programmer to initiate an interrupt procedure at any desired point in the program.

The most common use of software interrupt is associated with a supervisor call instruction. This instruction provides means for switching from a CPU user mode to the supervisor mode.

SOLVED EXAMPLES

Example 1: *A two word instruction is stored in memory at an address designated by C. The address field is stored at address C + 1 and is designated by the symbol A. The operand that is used during the execution of the instruction is stored at the address B. Value of index register is X. Explain how B is calculated from the other addresses if the addressing mode of the instruction is:*

(*i*) *Direct*

(*ii*) *Indirect*

(*iii*) *Relative*

(*iv*) *Indexed.*

Solution. Instruction is of two words, that are designated by the address C and C + 1. The operand is present at the address B. It means B is the effective address.

$$EA = (B)$$

Index register is containing value X.

$$IR = X.$$

$$\boxed{PC = C} \quad \text{Program Counter}$$

Instruction format can be represented as

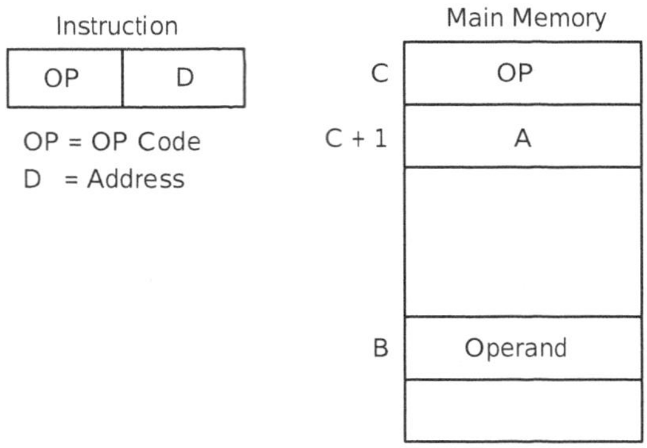

(i) Direct addressing mode

The address that is part of the instruction is the effective address.

So EA = A

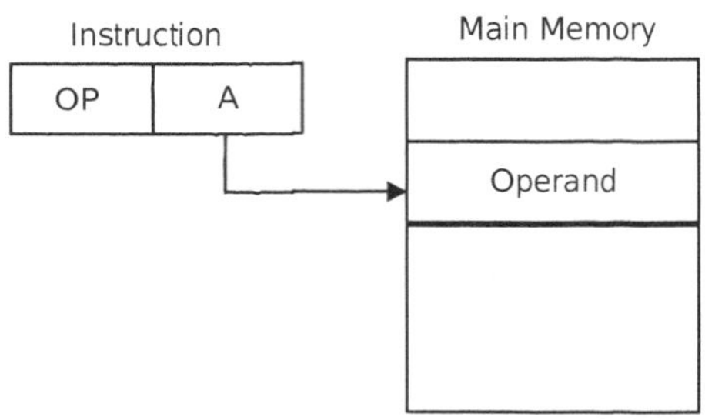

(ii) Indirect addressing mode

Address field of the instruction refers to the address of a word in memory which contains the address of the operand.

So EA = M (A)

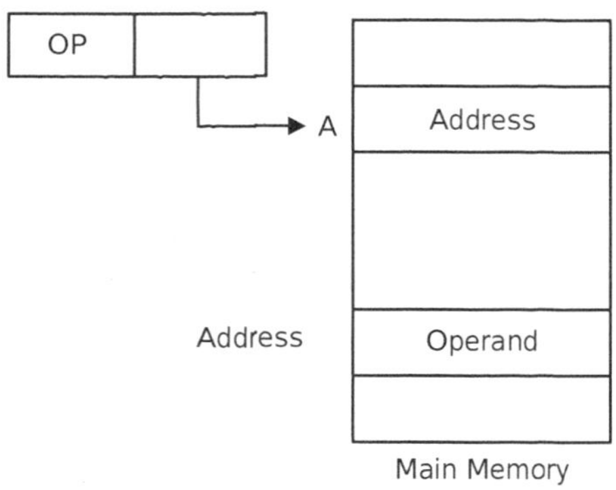

(iii) Relative addressing mode

Effective address = Address field of the instruction + Contents of program counter register

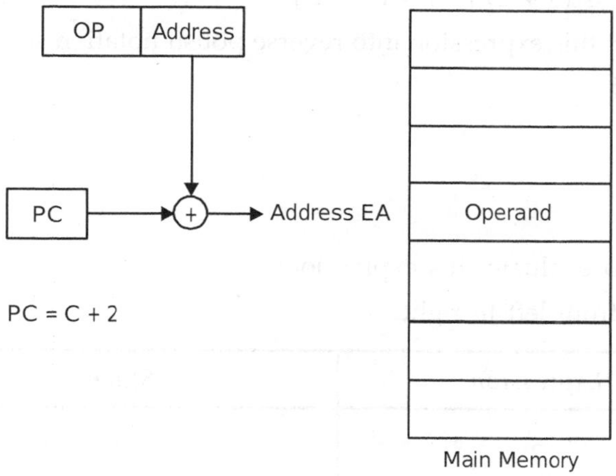

So EA = C + 2 + A

Value of program counter is incremented in decode phase. So value of PC is C + 2.

(iv) Indexed addressing modes

Effective address Address field of the instruction

+

Contents of indexed register

IR = X

So EA = X + A

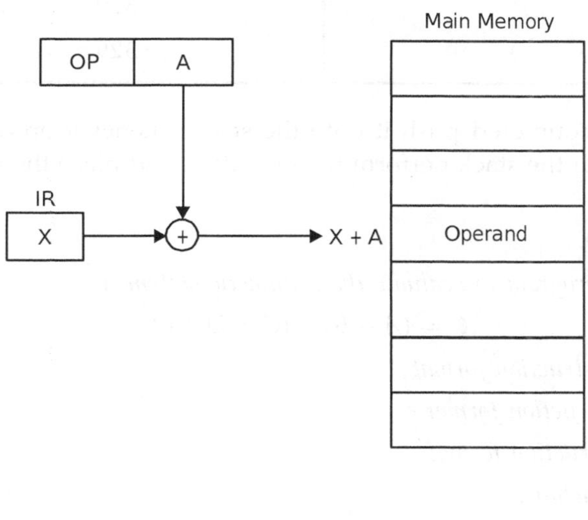

Example 2: *Convert the following numerical arithmetic expression into reverse polish notation and show the stack operations for evaluating the numerical result of:*

(5 + 2) [3 + 4 (9 + 2)].

Solution. Expression is (5 + 2) [3 + 4 (9 + 2)]

First of all we convert this expression into reverse polish notation scanning from left to right

52 + [3 + 4 * (92 +)]

52 + [3 + 92 + 4 *]

52 + [92 + 4 * 3 +]

52 + [92 + 4 * 3 + *].

Now stack is used to evaluate this expression:

Scan the expression from left to right.

Expression	*Stack*
5	5
2	5, 2
†	7
9	7, 9
2	7, 9, 2
+	7, 11
4	7, 11, 4
*	7, 44
3	7, 44, 3
+	7, 47
*	329
)	329

When operand is encountered push it onto the stack whenever an operator is incountered pop the two elements from the stack perform the operation and place the result on the top of the stack.

So final result is 329.

Example 3: *Write a program to evaluate the arithmetic statement:*

$$X = (A - B) \div (C + D * E)$$

(*i*) *Three address instruction format*

(*ii*) *Two address instruction format*

(*iii*) *One address instruction format*

(*iv*) *Using a stack machine.*

Solution. (*i*) Three address instruction format:

SUB	X, A, B	M [X] ← M [A] – M [B]
MUL	Y, D, E	M [Y] ← M [CD] * M [E]
ADD	T, C, Y	M [T] ← M [C] + M [Y]
DIV	X, X, T	M [X] ← M [X] / M [T]

(*ii*) Two address instruction format:

It reduces the space requirement.

MOV	X, A
SUB	Y, B
MOV	T, D
MUL	T, E
ADD	T, C
DIV	X, T

(*iii*) One address instruction format:

LOAD	D	AC ← M [D]
MUL	E	AC ← AC * M [E]
ADD	C	AC ← AC + M [C]
STORE	Y	M [Y] ← AC
LOAD	A	AC ← M [A]
SUB	B	AC ← AC – M [B]
DIV	Y	AC ← AC/M [Y]
STORE	X	M [X] ← AC

(*iv*) Using a stack machine: In stack computers insertion and deletion operation use one address instruction format. And arithmetic operations use zero address instruction formats.

PUSH	A	TOS ← M [A]
PUSH	B	TOS ← M [B]
SUB		TOS ← M [A] – M [B]
PUSH	D	TOS ← M [D]
PUSH	E	TOS ← M [E]
MUL		TOS ← M [D] * M [E]
DUSH	C	TOS ← M [C]
ADD		TOS ← M [D] * M [E] + M [C]
DIV		$TOS \leftarrow \frac{M[A] - M[B]}{M[D] * M[E] + M[C]}$
POP	X	M (x) ← TOS

Example 4: *How many memory reference are required in each case.*

(*i*) *Indirect addressing mode*

(*ii*) *Direct addressing mode*

(*iii*) *A branch type.*

Solution. (*i*) In indirect addressing mode we have to perform the followings:

(*a*) Fetch the instruction from memory – 1 memory reference.

(*b*) Fetch the effective address – 1 Memory reference.

(*c*) Fetch the operand – 1 memory reference.

So total we need three memory reference.

(*ii*) Direct addressing mode:

(*a*) Fetch the instruction from memory –1 memory reference.

(*b*) Fetch the operand using the address that is present in the instruction –1 memory reference.

So total we need two memory reference.

(*iii*) In a branch type:

(*a*) First fetch the instruction – 1 memory reference.

(*b*) Then fetch the effective address and transfer to PC – 1 memory reference.

So we need two memory references.

Example 5: *Convert the following arithmetic expression into reverse polish notation:*

$$A + (B * C - (D/E \uparrow F) * G) * H.$$

Solution. Index notation $A + (B * C - (D/E \uparrow F) * G) * H$.

$$\Rightarrow A + (B * C - (D \,/\, E\, F \uparrow) * G) * H$$

$$\Rightarrow A + ((B * C) - (\, D\, E\, F \uparrow \,/\, *\, G)) * H$$

$$\Rightarrow A + ((B * C) - (\, D\, E\, F \uparrow \,/\, G\, *\,)) * H$$

$$\Rightarrow A + ((BC\, *) - (D\, E\, F \uparrow \,/\, G\, *)) * H$$

$$\Rightarrow A + (BC\, *\, D\, E\, F \uparrow \,/\, G\, *\, -\,) * H$$

$$\Rightarrow A + (BC\, *\, D\, E\, F \uparrow \,/\, G\, *\, -\, H\, *)$$

$$\Rightarrow A\, B\, C\, *\, D\, E\, F \uparrow \,/\, G\, *\, -\, H\, *\, +$$

So the equivalent postfix notation is

$$\boxed{A\, B\, C\, *\, D\, E\, F \uparrow / G\, *\, -\, H\, *\, +}$$ **Ans.**

Example 6: *A computer has 32 bits instructions and 12 bits addresses if there are 250 two address instructions, how many one address instructions can be there?*

Solution. A two address instruction format can be represented as

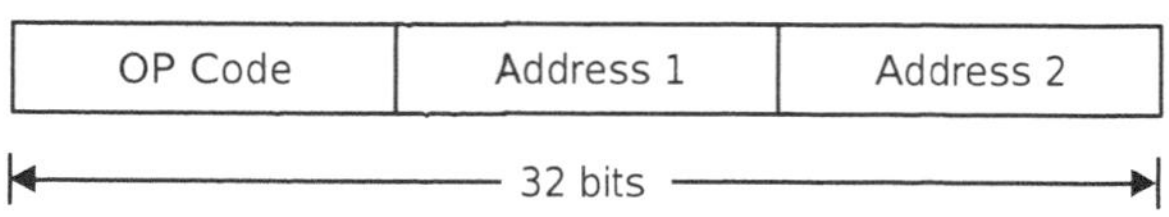

Address field is of 12 bits so the instruction format can be represented as

← 8 bits →	← 12 bits →	← 12 bits →	
OP Code	Address 2	Address 1	= 32 bits

with 12 bits address field total combinations of instructions is $2^{12} = 4096$.

So Total possible instructions = 4096.

Two address instructions = 250.

So possible combinations for one address instructions is 4096 – 250 = 3846

← 8×2^{12} →	← 12 →	
OP Code	Address 1	one address instruction

Therefore maximum number of one address instruction

8×2^{12} Ans.

EXERCISES

1. What are the different instruction types? Is there any impact of addressing modes in instruction set design of a machine?
2. Explain different types of addressing modes in detail. What must be the address field of an indexed addressing mode instruction to make it the same as a register indirect mode instruction?
3. What is interrupt and interrupt controller? Explain different types of interrupt.
4. How stack data structure is used to implement subroutine call and return?
5. Give examples of external interrupts and five examples of internal interrupts. What is the difference between a software interrupt and a subroutine call?
6. An instruction is stored at location 400 with its address field at location 401. The address field has the value 500. A processor register R_1 contains the value 200. Evaluate the effective address if the addressing mode of the instruction is

   (*a*) Direct

   (*b*) Immediate

   (*c*) Relative

   (*d*) Register indirect

   (*e*) Indexed.

   Value in index register is 200.
7. A computer has 16 bits instructions and 6 bit addresses if there are 60 two address instructions, how many one address instructions can be there.
8. If the memory unit of a computer has 256 K words of 32 bits each the computer has an instruction format with four fields an operation code (opcode). A field to specify one of 8 addressing modes, a register field to specify one of 64 registers and a memory address field. Specify the instruction format and the number of bits in each field if the instruction is one memory word.

9. Convert the following infix expressions into equivalent reverse polish notation:

(*a*) (A – B) / (D + E) * F)

(*b*) ((A + B) / D) ↑ ((E – F) * G)

(*c*) $\dfrac{A * [B + C * (D + E)]}{F * (G + H)}$.

10. Convert the following arithmetic expressions from reverse polish notation to infix notation:

(*a*) A B D + * E / F G H K / + * –

(*b*) A B – D E / *

(*c*) A B D ↑ + E F – / G +

11. Convert the following numerical arithmetic expression into reverse polish notation and show the stack operations for evaluating the numerical result:

$$(12 / (7 - 3) + 2 * (1 + 5).$$

12. Perform the logic AND, OR and XOR with the two binary strings 10011001 and 10101010.

Chapter 4

PIPELINING AND PARALLEL PROCESSING

4.1 INTRODUCTION

Early computer systems were single user system. At a time only one program was executed by the ALU of the central processing unit. All the resources were assigned to that program only. There was a large difference between the speed of the CPU and the speed of the I/O devices & memory. In this single program environment CPU became idle for a long time that degrades the performance of CPU. The utilisation for CPU was very less and through put was not upto the expectation. This gives the concept of parallel processing and multiprogramming. When one process is busy with the I/O devices, CPU can be assigned to the another process. This increases the utilisation of CPU and performance of the computer system.

In this chapter we discuss the trends towards parallel processing. Flynn's gave the classification of computers on the concept of parallel processing. Pipelining is a technique based on parallel processing that decompose a sequential process into subprocesses. We will discuss the concept of pipelining and types of pipelining in detail. In the last section we will discuss about RISC and CISC architecture.

4.2 PARALLEL PROCESSING

Parallel processing implies simultaneous processing of information. It is used to provide simultaneous data processing tasks for the purpose of increasing the computational speed of a computer system. In case of sequential processing each instruction is processed in a sequential manner. At a time only one task is performed. A parallel processing system is able to perform concurrent data processing to achieve faster execution time. In parallel processing when an instruction is executed by the CPU, the next instruction can be read from memory. The system may have two or more ALUs and be able to execute two or more instructions at the same time. The system may have two or more processors that can operate concurrently. The purpose of parallel processing is to speed up the computer processing capability and increase its throughput, that is, the amount of processing that can be accomplished during a given interval of time. The amount of hardware increases with parallel processing thus the cost of the system increases.

Parallel processing can be viewed from various levels of complexity. At the lowest level, we distinguish between serial and parallel operations by the type of registers. Register with serial load (shift registers) operate in serial fashion one bit at a time while registers with parallel load operate with all the bits of the word simultaneously. Parallel processing can be achieved by:

(*i*) Multiplicity of functional units.

(*ii*) Parallelism and pipelining within the CPU.

(*iii*) Overlapped CPU and I/O operations.

(*iv*) Use of hierarchical memory system.

(*v*) Balancing of subsystem bandwidths.

(*vi*) Multiprogramming and time sharing.

The early computers hand only one arithmetic and logic units in its CPU. Furthermore the ALU could only perform one function at a time. In practice many of the functions of the ALU can be distributed to multiple and specialized functional units which can operate in parallel. For example CDC-6600 computer has 10 functional units built into the CPU that is shown in Fig. 4.1.

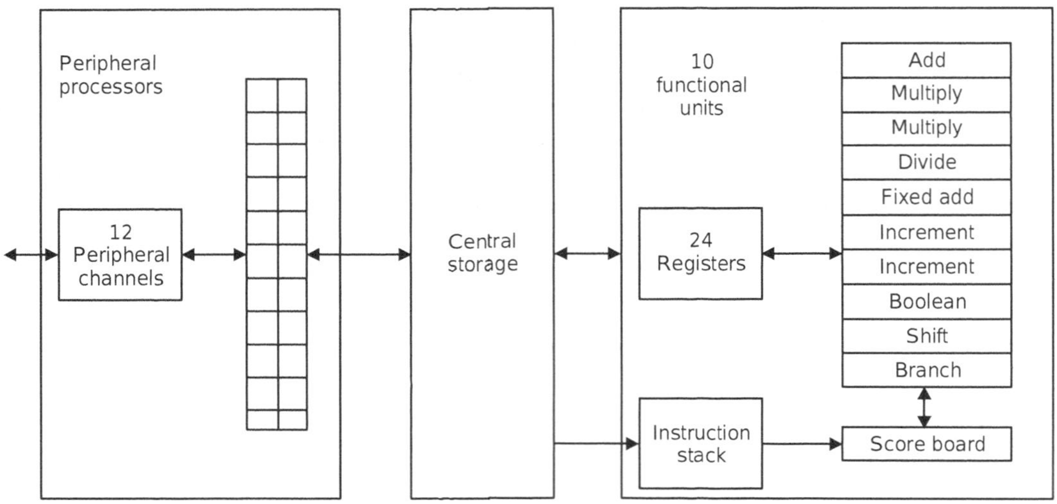

Fig. 4.1. System architecture of CDC-6600 computer

I/O operations can be performed simultaneously with the CPU computations by using separate I/O controllers, channels and I/O processors. The direct memory access (DMA) channel can be used to provide direct information transfer between the I/O devices and the main memory. Various phases of instruction executions are now pipelined, including instruction fetch, decode, operand fetch, arithmetic logic execution and store result. The speed gap between the CPU and the main memory can be closed up by using fast cache memory between them. The cache should have an access time that is equals to the access time of processor. Input-output channels with different speeds can be used between the slow I/O devices and the main memory. These I/O channels perform buffering and multiplexing functions to transfer the data from multiple disks into main memory. Multiprogramming and time sharing are software approaches to achieve concurrency in a uniprocessor system. We can mix the execution of various types of programs in the computer to balance bandwidths among the various functional units. Multiprogramming on a uniprocessor is centered around the sharing of the CPU by many programs. Parallel computers are those systems that emphasize parallel processing. We divide parallel computers into three architectural configuration.

(*a*) Pipeline computers

(*b*) Array processors

(*c*) Multiprocessor system.

4.3. FLYNN'S CLASSIFICATION

There are a variety of ways that the parallel processing can be classified . It can be considered from the internal organisation of the processors, from the interconnection structure between processors or the flow of information through the system. One of the most classification is the Flynn's classification. M.J. Flynn classifies architectures into four categories based on the presence of single or multiple streams of instructions and data, where an instruction stream is a set of sequential instructions to be executed by a single processor and the data stream is the sequential flow of data required by the instruction stream. Parallel processing may occur in the instruction stream, in the data stream or in both the streams. Flynn's classification divides computers into four major groups.

- Single Instruction Single Data Stream (SISD)
- Single Instruction Multiple Data Stream (SIMD)
- Multiple Instruction Single Data Stream (MISD)
- Multiple Instruction Multiple Data Stream (MIMD).

(*i*) *SISD (Single Instruction Single Data Stream):* This is the Von-Neumann concept of serial computer in which only one instruction is executed at any time. SISD represents the organisation of a single computer that is containing a control unit, a processor unit and a memory unit. Instructions are executed in the serial processing and the system may or may not have internal parallel processing capabilities. SISD is referred as serial scalar computer.

CU: Control Unit
EU: Execution Unit
MU: Memory Unit

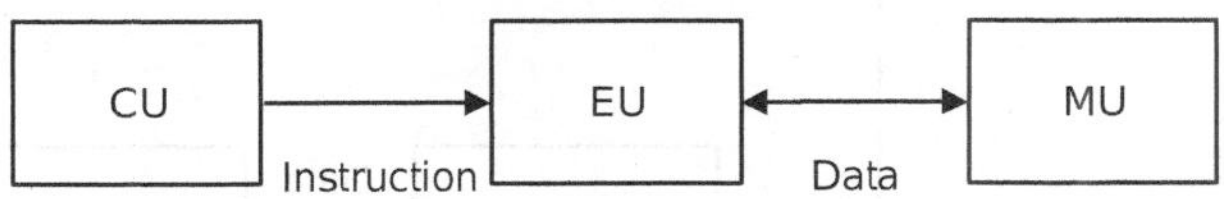

Fig. 4.2 SISD architecture

All SISD machines has a single register called Program Counter (PC). This register enforces serial execution of instructions. When an instruction is fetched from memory, the program counter is updated to contain the address of the next instruction to be fetched and executed in the serial order.

Parallel processing may be achieved by means of multiple functional units or by pipeline processing.

(*ii*) *MISD (Multiple Instruction Single Data Stream):* This implies that multiple instructions are operated in the single data stream. This class of machines has been challenged by many computer architects as impractical or impossible, at present there is no working examples of this type.

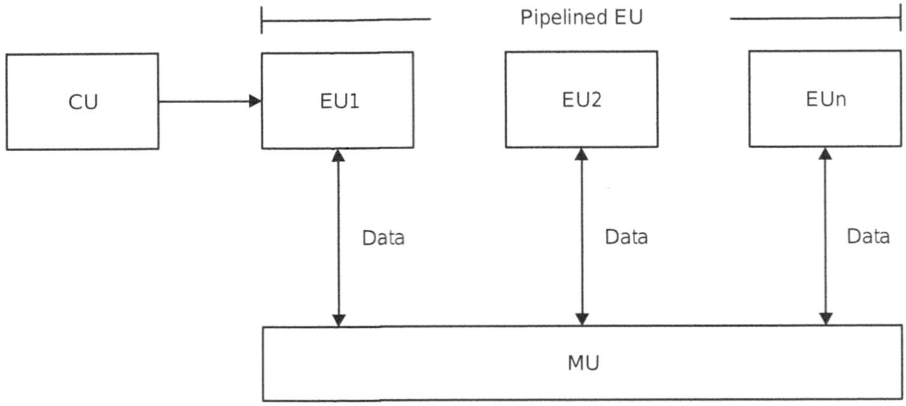

Fig. 4.3 MISD architecture

Under a single control unit, there are many execution units. All the execution units are operated simultaneously on the same data stream. Highly pipelined architectures, such as systolic arrays and vector processors are often classified under this type of machine. Pipeline architectures perform vector processing through a series of stages, each of which performs a particular function and produces an intermediate result.

(iii) SIMD (Single Instruction Multiple Data Stream): This implies that a single instruction is applied to a set of data stream. Instructions are applied on the different data simultaneously.

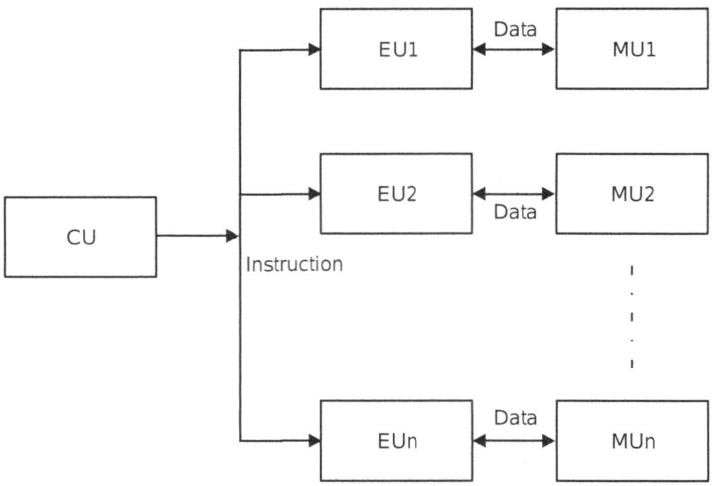

Fig. 4.4 SIMD architecture

There is a single control unit that invoked many separate processing units. SIMD machines support vector processing. All the execution units are operated under the supervision of a single control unit. All execution units receive the same instruction from the control unit but operate on different items of data. Shared memory unit is divided into modules so that it can communicate with all the processors simultaneously.

(iv) MIMD (Multiple Instruction Multiple Data Stream): This includes machine with several processing units in which multiple instructions can be applied to different data simultaneously.

MIMD machines are most complex but they hold the greatest promise for efficiency accomplished through concurrent processing. Here concurrency implies that not only multiple processors are being operated simultaneously but multiple programs are being executed in the same time frame, concurrent to each other.

MIMD can be worked with shared memory or with distributed memory. Fig. 4.5 depicts this.

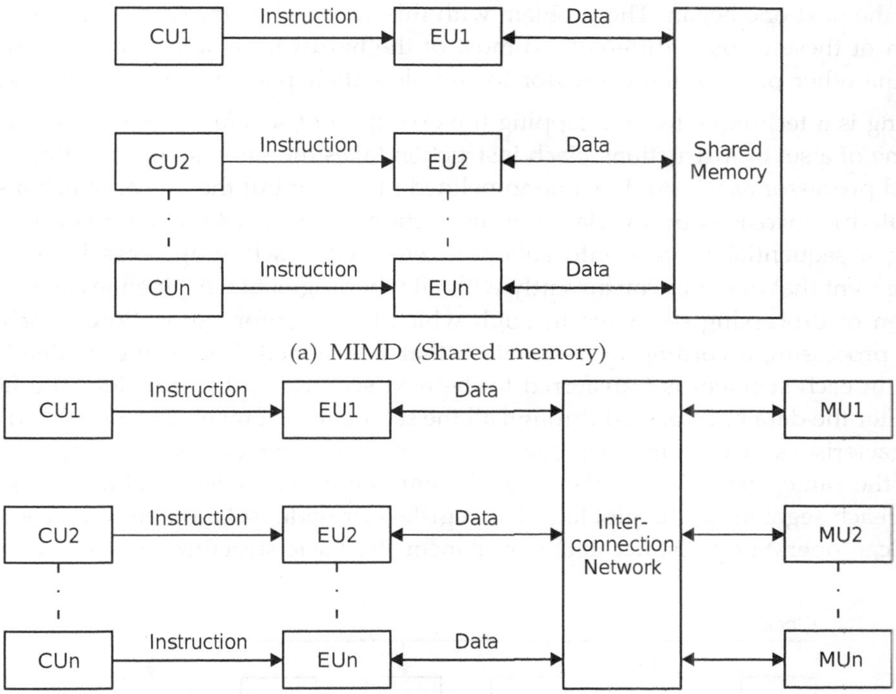

(*b*) MIMD (Distributed memory)

Fig. 4.5 MIMD architecture

Flynn's classification has proved to be a good method for the classification of computer architectures for almost three decades. Fig.4.6 shows a classification that represents some of the features of proposed architectures.

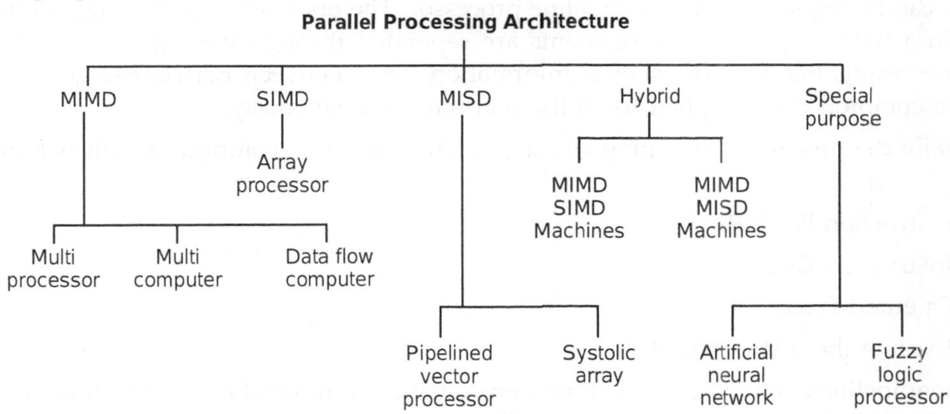

Fig. 4.6 Parallel processing architecture

4.4 PIPELINING

Early computers executed instructions in a very straight forward fashion. The processor fetched an instruction from memory, decoded it to determine what operation is performed, read the instruction's inputs from the register file, performed the computation required by the instruction and wrote the result back into the register file. Each instruction was completely finished before execution of the next one began. The problem with this approach is that the hardware needed to perform each of these steps is different. So most of the hardware is idle at any given moment, waiting for the other parts of the processor to complete their part of executing an instruction.

Pipelining is a technique for overlapping the execution of several instructions to reduce the execution time of a set of instructions. Each instruction takes the same amount of time to execute in a pipelined processor as it would in a nonpipelined processor but the rate at which instructions can be executed is increased by overlapping instruction execution. Pipelining is a technique of decomposing a sequential process into suboperations, with each subprocess is assigned to a dedicated segment that operates concurrently with all other segments. A pipeline can be described as a collection of processing segments through which binary information flows. Each segment performs its processing according to the subtask that is assigned. The result obtained from the computation in each segment is transferred to the next segment in the pipeline. The final result is obtained after the data have passed through all the segments. Segments are also called as stages. It is the characteristics of the pipelines that several computations can be in progress in distinct segments at the same time. The overlapping of computation is made possible by associating a register with each segment in the pipeline. The registers provide isolation between each segment so that each can operate on distinct data simultaneously. Basic structure of pipeline is depicted in Fig. 4.7.

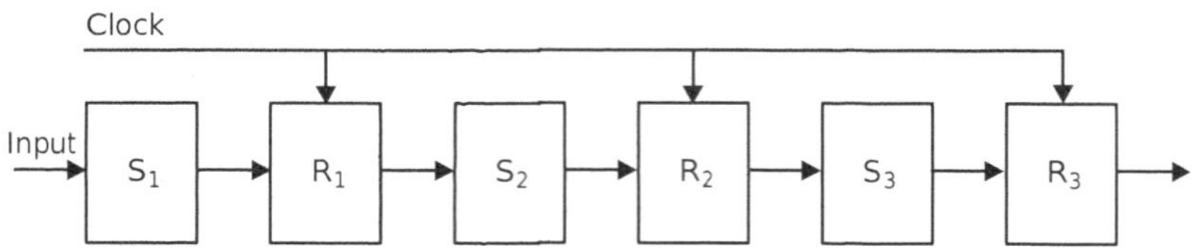

Fig. 4.7. Three segment pipeline

Any operation that can be decomposed into a sequence of suboperations of about the same complexity can be implemented by a pipeline processor. The operands pass through all the three segments in a fixed sequence. The segments are separated through the registers that hold the intermediate results between the stages. Information flows between adjacent stages under the control of a common clock applied to all the registers simultaneously.

Normally the process of executing an instruction in a digital computer involves four major steps.

(*i*) Instruction Fetch (IF)

(*ii*) Instruction Decoding (ID)

(*iii*) Operand Fetch (OF)

(*iv*) Execute the instruction (EX).

In a nonpipelined computer, these four steps must be completed before the next instruction can be issued. Fig. 4.8 shows the space time diagram for a nonpipelined processor.

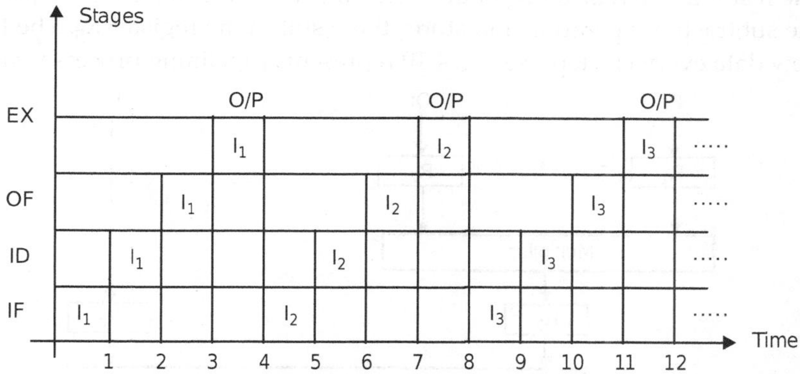

Fig. 4.8. Space time diagram for nonpipeline system

For the nonpipelined computer, it takes four pipeline cycles to complete one instruction. Space-time diagram for a pipelined computer is depicted in Fig. 4.9. It is clear that once a pipeline is filled up, an output result is produced from the pipeline on each cycle. The instruction cycle has been effectively reduced to one fourth of the original cycle time by such overlapped instructions.

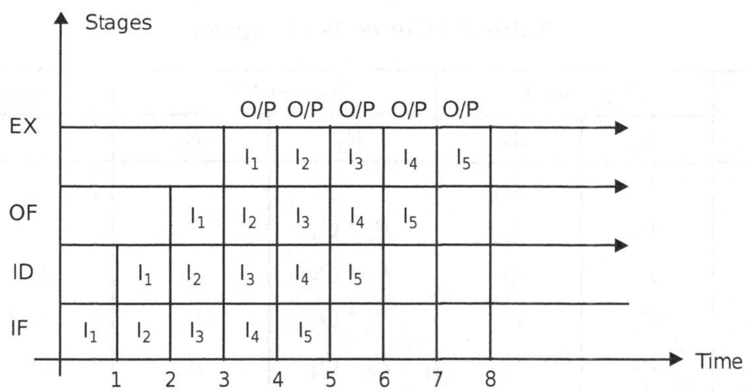

Fig. 4.9. Space time diagram for pipelined computer

Due to the overlapped instruction and arithmetic execution, it is obvious that pipeline machines are better turned to perform the same operations repeatedly through the pipeline.

The pipeline organization will be demonstrated by means of a simple example. Suppose we want to perform the combined multiply and substraction operations with a stream of numbers.

$$Pi * Qi - Ri$$

$$\text{for } l = 1, 2, 3... 6$$

Each suboperation is to be implemented in a segment within a pipeline. Each segment has some registers to store the data and a combinational circuit to perform the operations on the data present in the registers. The suboperations performed in each segment of the pipeline are as follows:

$$Pi \leftarrow R_1, Qi \leftarrow R_2$$

$$R_3 \leftarrow R_1 * R_2, R_4 \leftarrow Ri$$

$$R_5 \leftarrow R_3 - R_4$$

First *Pi* and *Qi* are transferred in registers R_1 and R_2. In the second cycle we multiply *Pi* and *Qi* and store the result in the register R_3 at the same time *Ri* is transferred to register R_4 and finally we perform the subtraction operation and stores the result in the register R_5. The five registers are loaded with new data every clock pulse Fig. 4.10 represents pipelining processing for this example.

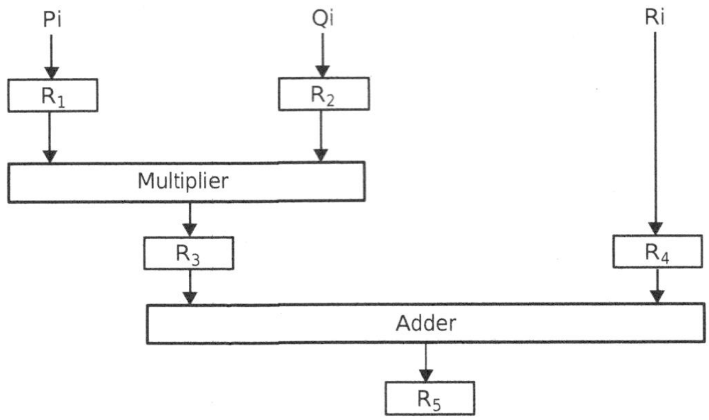

Fig. 4.10. Pipeline processing

The effect of each clock pulse is shown in Table 4.1.

Table 4.1 Contents of registers

Clock	*Segment 1*		*Segment 2*		*Segment 3*
Cycle	R_1	R_2	R_3	R_4	R_5
1.	P_1	Q_1			
2.	P_2	Q_2	$P_1 * Q_1$	R_1	
3.	P_3	Q_3	$P_2 * Q_2$	R_2	$P_1 * Q_1 - R_1$
4.	P_4	Q_4	$P_3 * Q_3$	R_3	$P_2 * Q_2 - R_2$
5.	P_5	Q_5	$P_4 * Q_4$	R_4	$P_3 * Q_3 - R_3$
6.	P_6	Q_6	$P_2 * Q_5$	R_5	$P_4 * Q_4 - R_4$
7.	–	–	$P_6 * Q_6$	R_6	$P_5 * Q_5 - R_5$
8.	–	–	–	–	$P_6 * Q_6 - R_6$

The first clock pulse transfers P_1 and Q_1 into R_1 and R_2. The second clock pulse transfers the product of R_1 and R_2 into R_3 and R_1 into R_4. The same clock pulse transfers P_2 and Q_2 into R_1 and R_2. It takes three clock pulses to fill up the pipe and retrieve the first output from R_5. From there on, each clock produces a new output and moves the data one step down the pipeline. When no more input data are available, the clock must continue till the last output emerges out of the pipeline.

4.4.1 Pipelining Performance

Any operation that can be decomposed into a sequence of suboperations of about the same complexity can be implemented by a pipeline processor. The technique is efficient for those applications that need to repeat the same task many times with different set of data. No matter how many segments there are in the system, once the pipeline is full, it takes only one clock period to obtain an output. Now consider that we are having k segment pipeline with a clock cycle time tp and we have to execute total n tasks. From the space time diagram depicted in Fig. 4.9 it is clear that first output is obtained when an instruction is passed through all the segments of the pipeline after that at each clock cycle we get the output. So the first task T_1 requires Ktp to complete its operation since there are k segments in the pipe. The remaining $(n–1)$ tasks will be completed in $(n–1)\ tp$ time. Since $(n–1)$ clock cycles are required because at every clock cycle output is coming from the pipe. So total clock cycles that are required to complete n tasks is [k + (n – 1)].

Next consider a non-pipeline unit that performs the same operation and takes a time equal to tn to complete each task.

The total time required is ntn. The speed up of a pipeline processing over an equivalent non-pipeline processing is defined by the ratio.

$$S = \frac{ntn}{\left[k + (n-1)\right]tp}$$

where tp – clock cycle time in pipeline

n – No. of tasks

k – Total no. of stages in pipeline

tn – Time taken to complete one task in non-pipeline system

when n becomes very large then

$$n >> k$$

So $K + (n - 1) \approx n$ under this condition

$$S = \frac{tn}{tp}$$

When we assume that the time to process a task is same as in pipeline and nonpipeline system then

$$tn = Ktp$$

and speed up ratio $$S = \frac{ktp}{tp} = k.$$

This shows that the theoretical maximum speed up that a pipeline can provide is k, where k is the number of segments in the pipeline.

In addition to speed up, two other factors are often used for determining the performance of a pipeline. They are efficiency and throughout. The efficiency E of a pipeline with k stages is defined as

$$E = \frac{S}{K}$$

The efficiency E represents the speed up per stage approaches its maximum value of 1 when $n \to \infty$. The throughout H also called as Bandwidth of a pipeline is defined as the number of input tasks it can process per unit of time. When the pipeline has k stages, H is defined as

$$H = \frac{n}{\left[K + (n-1)\right]tp} = \frac{S}{Ktp}$$

When $n \to \infty$ the throughput H approaches the maximum value of one task per clock cycle.

To get the theoretical speed advantage of a pipeline we use multiple functional units. It is necessary to construct k identical units that will operate in parallel. A K segment pipeline processor can be expected to equal the performance of k copies of an equivalent non pipeline circuit under equal operating conditions. Instead of operating with the input data in sequence as in a pipeline, the parallel circuits accept input data items simultaneously and perform all the tasks at the same time. This is single instruction multiple data organisation. Since the same instruction is used to operate on multiple data in parallel.

There are various reasons a pipeline system cannot operate at its maximum theoretical rate. Different segments may take different times to complete their suboperation. The clock cycle must be chosen to equal the time delay of the segment with the maximum propagation time. This causes the other segments to waste time while waiting for the next clock.

Moreover, it is not always correct to assume that a non pipe circuit has the same time delay as that of an equivalent pipeline circuit.

Pipelines are usually divided into two classes:

1. Arithmetic pipeline
2. Instruction pipeline.

An arithmetic pipeline divides an arithmetic operation into suboperation for execution in the pipeline segments. An instruction pipeline operates on a stream of instructions by overlapping the fetch, decode and execute phases of the instruction cycle.

4.4.2. Arithmetic Pipelining

The arithmetic logic units of a computer can be segmentized for pipeline operations in various data formats. This is shown in Fig. 4.11. Some functions of the arithmetic logic unit of a processor can be pipelined to maximize performance. An arithmetic pipeline is used to implement complex arithmetic functions like floating point addition, multiplication and division.

Pipeline arithmetic units are usually found in very high speed computers. Floating point operations are easily decomposed into suboperations. We will now show an example of a pipeline unit of floating point adder. This pipeline is linearly constructed with four functional stages. The inputs of this pipeline are two normalized floating point numbers.

$$A = a \times 2^p$$
$$B = b \times 2^q$$

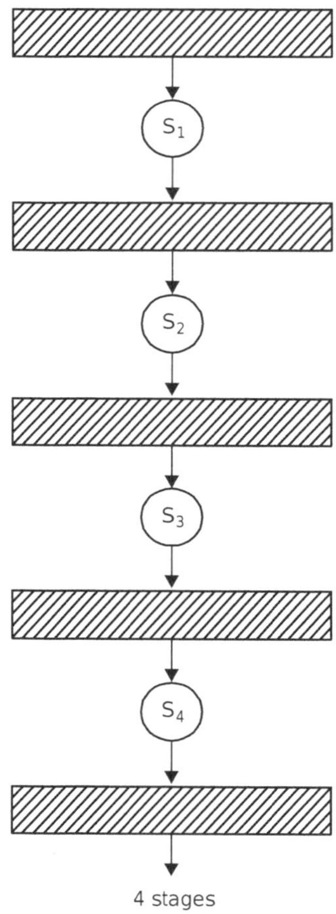

Fig. 4.11 Arithmetic pipelining

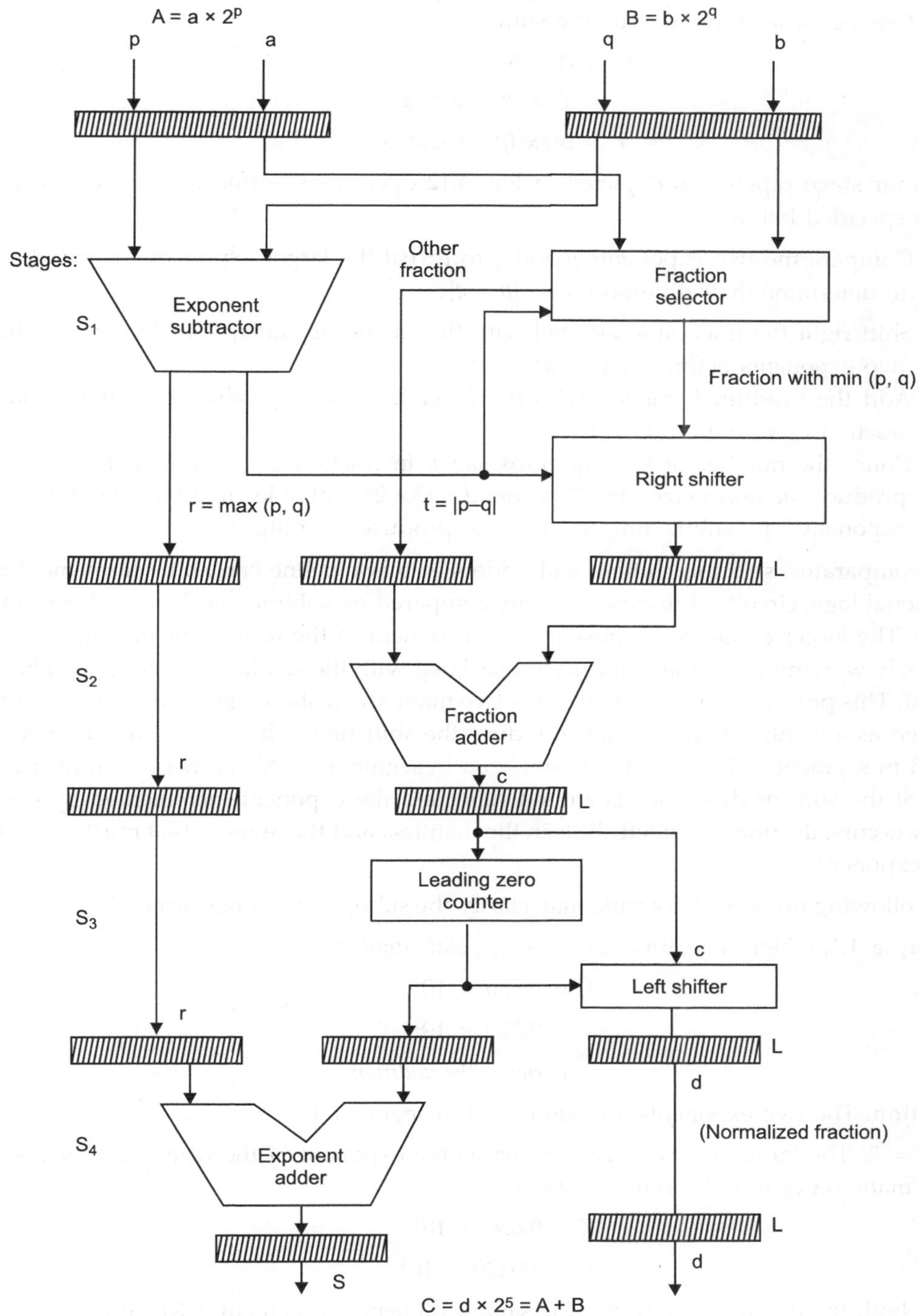

Fig. 4.12 Pipelined floating point adder

Where a and b are two fractions and p and q are their exponents. For simplicity base 2 is assumed. Our purpose is to compute the sum

$$C = A + B$$
$$= C \times 2^r = d \times 2^s$$

where $r = \max(p, q)$ and $5 \leq d < 1$

The four stage pipeline is depicted in Fig. 4.12 operations performed in the four pipeline stages are specified below:

1. Compare the two exponents p and q to reveal the larger exponent $r = \max(p, q)$ and to determine their difference $t = |p - q|$.
2. Shift right the fraction associated with the smaller exponent by t bits to equalize the two exponents before fraction addition.
3. Add the preshifted fraction with the other fraction to produce the intermediate sum fraction C, where $0 \leq C < 1$.
4. Count the number of leading zeros say u in fraction C and shift left C by u bits to produce the normalized fraction sum $d = C \times 2^u$ with a leading bit 1. Update the large exponent S by subtracting $S = r - u$ to produce the output exponent.

The comparator, selector, shifters and adders in this pipeline can all be implemented with combinational logic circuits. The exponents are compared by subtracting them to determine their difference. The larger exponent is chosen as the exponent of the result. The exponent difference determines how many times the mantissa a associated with the smaller exponent must be shifted to the right. This produces an alignment of the two mantissa. It should be noted that the shift must be designed as a combinational circuit to reduce the shift time. The two mantissa are added or subtracted in segment 3. The result is normalized in segment 4. When there is an overflow, the mantissa of the sum or difference is shifted right and the exponent incremented by one. If an underflow occurs, the number of left shifts in the mantissa and the number that must be subtracted from the exponent.

The following numerical example may clarify the suboperations performed in each segment.

Example 4.1: *Given two normalized floating point numbers.*

$$X = 0.850 \times 10^4$$
$$Y = 0.220 \times 10^2$$

Perform the addition.

Solution. The two exponents are subtracted in segment 1

4 – 2 = 2. The large exponent 4 is chosen as the exponent of the result. The next segment shifts the mantissa of y to the right to obtain.

$$X = 0.850 \times 10^4$$
$$Y = .00220 \times 10^4$$

Now both the mantissa are under the same exponent. In segment 3 we add the 2 mantissa and produces the sum

$$Z = .85220 \times 10^4$$

Now we have to normalize our result. Our result is already in normalized form it has a fraction with a non-zero first digit.

So $\boxed{Z = .85220 \times 10^4}$ **Ans.**

4.4.3. Instruction Pipeline

Pipelining processing can occur not only in the data stream but in the instruction stream as well. An instruction pipeline reads consecutive instructions from the memory while previous instructions are executing in the other segments. The execution of a stream of instructions can be pipelined by overlapping the execution of the current instruction with the fetch, decode and operand fetch of subsequent instructions. Almost all high performance computers are now equipped with instruction execution pipelines. It is depicted in Fig. 4.13

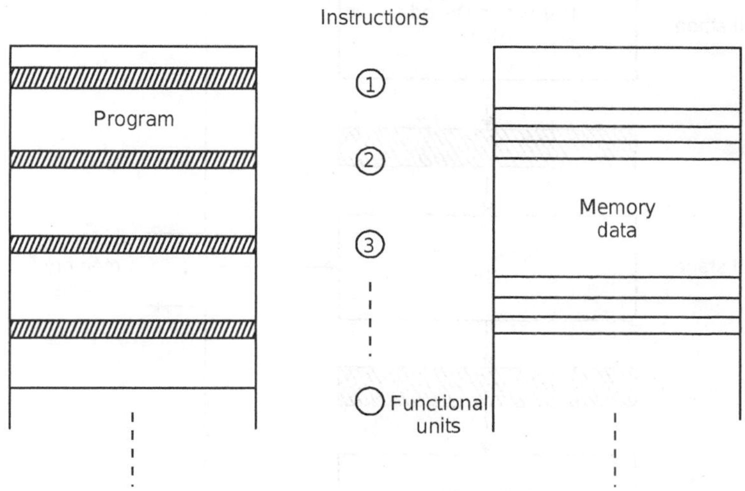

Fig. 4.13 Instruction pipelining

In a von-Neumann architecture, the processor of executing an instruction involves several steps. First the control unit fetches the instruction from the memory. Then the control unit decodes the instruction to determine the type of operation to be performed. When the operation requires operands, the control unit also determines the address of each operand and fetches them from memory. Next the operation is performed on the operands and finally the result is stored in the specified location.

An instruction pipeline increases the performance of a processor by overlapping the processing of several different instructions. Instruction pipeline often consists of five stages.

1. Fetch the instruction from memory (IF)
2. Decode the instruction (ID)
3. Operand fetch (OF)
4. Execute the instruction (EX)
5. Write back the result (WB).

Stages of instruction pipeline are shown in Fig. 4.14.

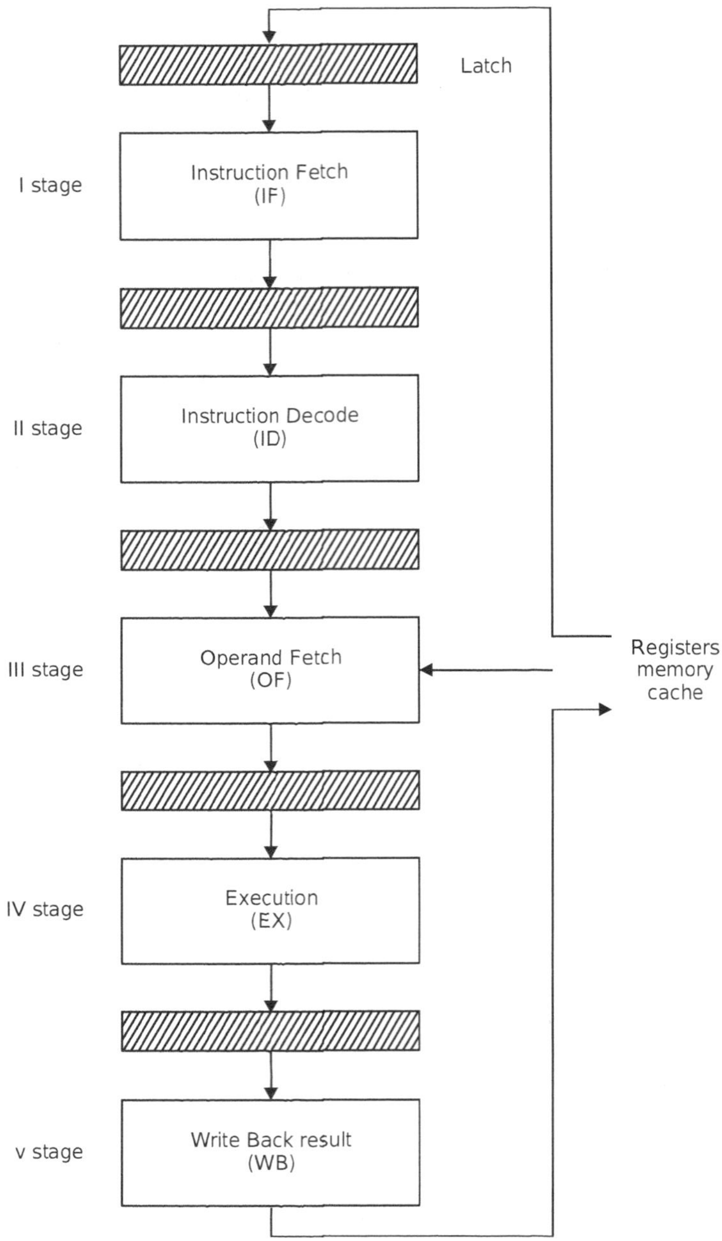

Fig. 4.14 Stages of instruction pipelining

4.4.3.1 Four Segment Instruction Pipeline

Now we taking an example of four segment instruction pipelining. We are considering that each instruction passes through the following four segments.

(*i*) Fetch the instruction (IF)

(*ii*) Decode the instruction and determine the effective address (DA) (*iii*) Fetch the operand (OF)

(*iv*) Execute the instruction and write back the result (W1 Ex).

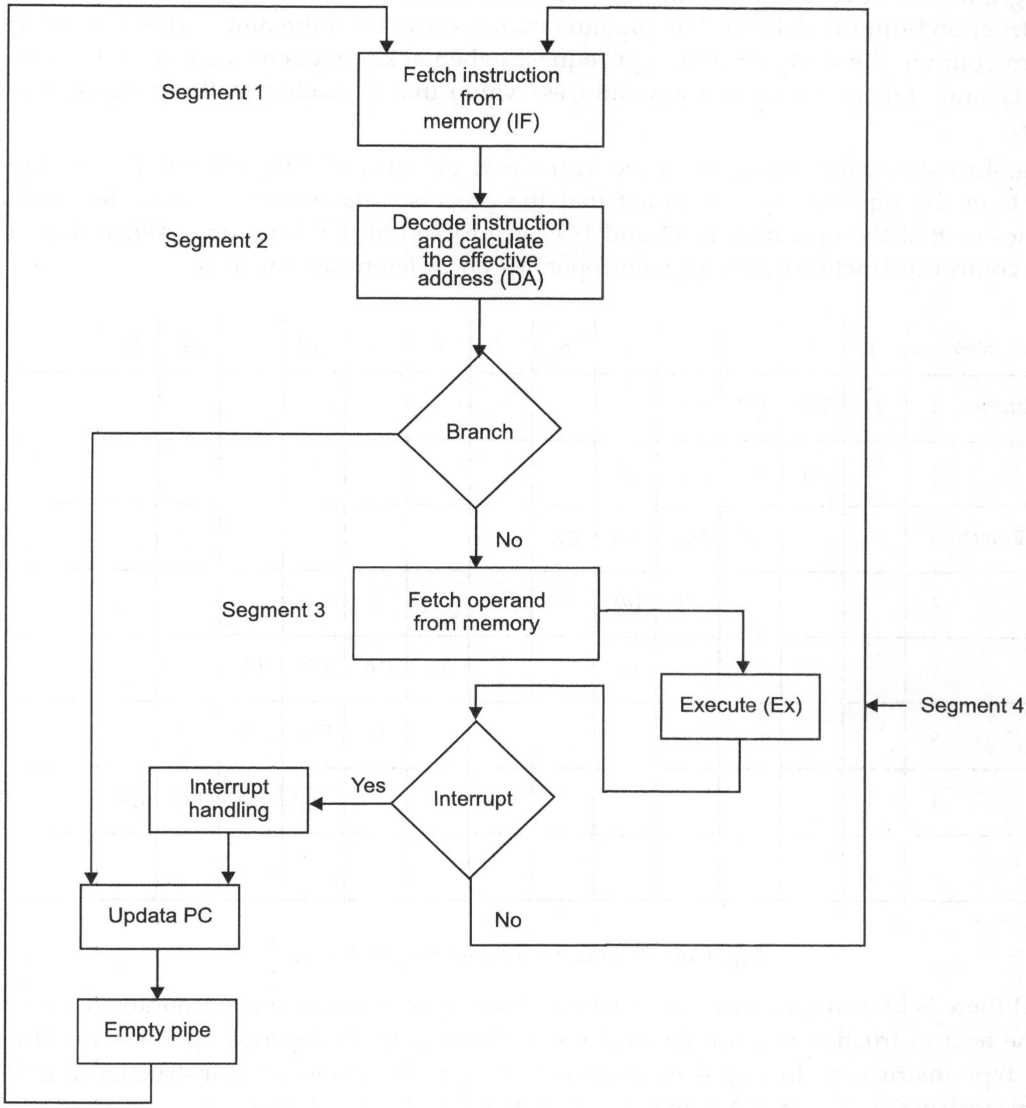

Fig. 4.15 Four segment instruction pipeline

Fig. 4.15 shows how the instruction cycle in the CPU can be processed with a four segment pipeline. Instructions are fetched from consecutive memory locations. In the Ist cycle Ist instruction is fetched from the memory. In the second cycle Ist instruction is executing in segment 2 while IInd instruction is fetched from memory. while an instruction is being executed in segment 4, the next instruction is in sequence is busy fetching an operand from memory in segment 3. The effective address may be calculated in a separate arithmetic circuit for the third instruction.

This sequence is followed when there is no decision making instructions in the program. When program control instructions are encountered then we cannot proceed normal execution of the program. In that case the pending operations are completed and all information stored in the instruction buffer is deleted. The pipeline than restarts from the new address stored in the program counter. Similarly an interrupt request, when acknowledged will cause the pipeline to empty and start again from a new address value that is loaded in the program counter register.

Fig. 4.16 shows the operation of the instruction pipeline. FI, DA, FO and EX are the four segments of the pipeline. It is assumed that the processor has separate instruction and data memories so that the operation in FI and FO can proceed at the same time. When there is no branch control instructions each segment operates on different instructions.

Step	1	2	3	4	5	6	7	8	9	10	11	12	13
Instruction 1	FI	DA	FO	EX									
2		FI	DA	FO	EX								
(Branch) 3			FI	DA	FO	EX							
4				FI	DA	FO	EX						
5					FI			FI	DA	FO	EX		
6									FI	DA	FO	EX	
7										FI	DA	FO	EX

Fig. 4.16 Timing of instruction pipelining

Let there is branch type instruction when branch type instruction is encountered we cannot fetch the next instruction because the next instruction execution depends upon the result of the branch type instruction. In step 4 instruction 1 is being in segment Ex, instruction 2 is in FO segment, instruction 3 is in FO segment and instruction 4 is in FI segment.

Assume now that instruction 3 is a branch instruction. As soon as this instruction is decoded in segment DA in Step 4, the transfer from FI to DA of the other instructions is halted until the branch instruction is executed in step 6. If the branch is taken, the instruction is fetched in step 4. If the branch is not taken, the instruction fetched previously in step 4 can be used. The pipeline then continues until a new branch instruction is encountered.

When Ex segment needs to store the result of the operation while FO segment needs to fetch an operand. In that case, segment FO must wait until segment Ex has finished its operation.

In general, there are three major difficulties that cause the instruction pipeline to deviate from its normal operations:

(1) Data dependency

(2) Branch difficulties

(3) Resource conflicts.

In the later section we will discuss these issues.

4.4.3.2 *Data Dependency*

Data dependency conflicts arise when an instruction requires data from the other instructions like an instruction will depends upon the result of the previous instruction. This degrades the performance of the pipeline computers due to collision of data or address. A data dependency occurs when an instruction needs data that are not yet available.

Let there are two instructions:

ADD R1, A

ADD R2, R1

These two instructions are not independent instructions. First instruction add the contents of register R1 with a memory word designated by the symbol A and store the result in register R1 while second instruction add this contents of register R1 with the contents of register R1 and store the result in the register R2. If we are not having the result of first instruction we cannot fetch the second instruction from memory. This degrades the performance of pipelining.

This is represented by Fig. 4.17.

Step 1	1	2	3	4	5	6	7	8	9
2	FI	DA	FO	EX					
3					FI	DA	FO	EX	

Fig. 4.17 Data dependency

So we are required total 8 clock cycles to execute these two instructions. An address dependency may occur when an operand address cannot be calculated because information needed by the addressing mode is not available. Pipelined computers deal with such conflicts between data dependencies in a variety of ways.

There are three techniques to handle this problem.

(1) Hardware interlocks

(2) Operand forwarding

(3) Delayed load.

The most straightward method is to insert hardware interlocks. Hardware interlock is a circuit that detects the instructions whose source operands depends upon the result of the various upcoming instruction in the pipeline. Detection of this type of instructions resolve the conflict because we delay the execution of these instructions by enough clock cycles. This program maintains the program sequence by using hardware to insert the required delays.

Another technique is operand forwarding. In this technique suppose we are transferring the result of an instruction into a destination register then if the result is needed by some another instruction then we transferred that result as a source in the next instruction, instead of passing it to the destination register. We use special hardware to detect a conflict and then avoid it by routing the data through special paths between pipeline segments. This method requires additional hardware paths through multiplexers as well as the circuit that detects the conflict.

Delayed load is a method that also resolves the data conflicts. This responsibility is driven by compiler. A compiler is a system program that translates the high level programming language into a machine language program. The compiler for such computers is designed to detect a data conflict and reorder the instructions as necessary to delay the loading of the conflicting data by inserting no operation instructions. This method is referred to as delayed load.

4.4.3.3 Handling of Branch Instructions

One of the major problem with the pipeline computers is the presence of branch instructions. A branch instruction is of two types.

(1) Conditional branch instruction

(2) Unconditional branch instruction.

An unconditional branch always load the program counter with the target address with specifying any condition. In a conditional branch the control selects the target instruction if the condition is satisfied or the next sequential instruction if the condition is not satisfied. Branch instruction breaks the normal sequence of the instruction stream causing difficulties in the operation of the instruction pipeline. Pipelined computers employ various hardware techniques to minimize the performance degradation caused by instruction branching.

To handle the conditional branch we prefetch the target instruction with the instruction that is following the branch. Both are saved until the branch is executed. If the branch condition is successful, the pipeline continues from the branch target instruction. An extension of this procedure is to continue fetching instructions from both places until the branch decision is made.

Another possibility is the use of a branch target buffer or BTB. The BTB is an associative memory included in the fetch segment of the pipeline. Each entry in the BTB consists of

(*a*) Address of the previously executed branch instruction.

(*b*) Target instruction.

It also stores the next few instructions after the branch target instruction. When the pipeline decodes a branch instruction, it searches the associative memory BTB for the address of the instruction.

If it is in BTB, the instruction is available directly and prefetch continues from the new path. If the instruction is not in BTB, the pipeline shifts to a new instruction stream and stores the target instruction in the BTB. In this case branch instructions that have occurred previously are readily available in the pipeline without interruption.

A variation of the BTB is a loop buffer. This is a small very high speed register file maintained by the fetch segment of the instruction pipeline. When a program loop is detected in the program, it is stored in the loop buffer in its entirely, including all branches. The program loop can be executed directly without having to access memory until the loop mode is removed by the final branching out.

A procedure employed in most RISC processors is the delayed branch. In this procedure the compiler detects the branch instructions and rearrange the machine language code by inserting useful instructions that keep the pipeline operating without interruptions. An example of delayed branch is the insertion of a no-operation instruction after a branch instruction. This causes the computer to fetch the target instruction during the execution of the no operation instruction.

4.4.3.4 Resource Conflicts

When two segments access the memory or any other computer hardware at the same time then resource conflict occurs. When two segments are sharing the same resource then there is problem of resource sharing. Main computer hardware resources are CPU, memory and I/O devices. When one segment stores the result of an intstruction in the memory and at the same time when one segment fetches the instruction from memory then one segment has to wait to access the memory and this degrades the performance of the pipelining system. When various segments access the same resource then deadlock occurs in the system and no instruction is able to complete its instruction. When resource conflict occurs in the computer, we have to maintain a policy for assigning the resources to the various segments. Like FCFS policy the segment that requests the resource first is assigned the resource first. Resource conflict degrades the performance of the pipeline computer by a large ratio. All the other segments enter in a wait state. When the resource is free then one of the segment that is waiting is assigned the resource that depends upon a particular policy.

4.5 RISC AND CISC ARCHITECTURE

Computer Architectures, in general have evolved toward progressively greater complexity such as large instruction sets, more addressing modes, more computational power of the individual instructions, more specialized registers and so on. An important aspect of computer architectures is the design of the instruction set for the processor. The instruction set chosen for a particular computer determines the way that machine language programs are constructed.

Early computer systems have very simple and small instruction sets, forced mainly by the need to minimize the hardware to implement them with the advent of integrated circuits, digital hardware circuits become cheaper, computer instructions increase in number and in complexity. These computers also employ a variety of data types and a large number of addressing modes. The trend into computer hardware complexity was influenced by various factors such as upgrading existing model to provide more customer applications, adding instructions that facilitate the translation from high level language into machine language programs. A computer with a large number of instruction is classified as complex instruction set computer abbreviated as CISC.

The basic concept of not adding useless instruction to the instruction set has invoked an increasing interest in an innovative approach to computer architecture, the reduced instruction set computer (RISC), computer designers have different view points, but the following two criteria are universally accepted goals for all systems.

(1) To maximize speed of operation or minimize execution time.

(2) To minimize development cost and sale price.

One way of accomplishing the first goal is to improve the technology of the components, thereby achieving operation at higher frequencies. Increased speed can be achieved by minimizing the average number of clock cycles per instruction. To accomplish both goals, the original designers of RISC focused on the aspect of the VISI realization. RISC architectures are load-store types of machines, they can obtain a high level of concurrence by separating execution of load and store operations from other instructions. CISC architectures may not be able to obtain the same level of concurrency because of their memory register type of instruction set. It supports all addressing modes having high degree of addressing flexibility. RISC approach take advantage of advancements in chip technology to reduce the clock cycle time. Because of the simple instructions, the performance of a RISC architecture is related to compiler efficiency.

There are a number of RISC and CISC processors on the market.

RISC processors: MIPS R4000
IBM RISC System 6000
Motorolo 88000 series

CISC processors: Intel pentium
IBM RISC System 16000.

4.5.1 CISC Characteristics

CISC means Complex Instruction set computer. A computer with large number of instructions is classified as complex instruction set computer, abbreviated as CISC. In early 1980, a number of computer designers recommended that computers use power instruction with simple constructs so they can be executed much faster within the CPU without having to use memory as often this type of computer is classified as reduced instruction set computer (RISC).

Complex instruction set is the desire to simplify the compilation and improve the overall computer performance, the task of the compiler is to generate a sequence of machine instructions for each high level language statement the task is simplified the statement directly. The essential goal of a CISC architecture is to attempt to provide a single machine instructions for each statement that is written in a high level language.

Examples of CISC

(1) Digital equipment corporation VAX computers

(2) IBM 370 computers.

Another characteristic of CISC architecture is the incorporation of variable length instruction format that requires register operands may be only two bytes in length, but instructions that require memory address may need five bytes to include the entire instruction code.

Packing variable instruction formats in a fixed length memory word requires special decoding circuits that according to their byte length.

Although CISC processors have instructions that use only processor registers, the availability of other words of operations stand to simplify the high-level language compilation. However, as more instructions and addressing modes are incorporated into a computer, the more hardware logic is needed to implement and support them, and this may cause the computations to slow them, and this may cause the computations to slow down. So major characteristics of CISC architecture are.

1. A large number of instructions-typically from 100 to 250 instructions.
2. Some instructions that perform specialized tasks and are used in frequently.
3. A large variety of addressing modes-typically 5 to 20 different modes.
4. Variable length instruction formats.
5. Instruction that manipulate operands in memory.

4.5.2 RISC Characteristics

The concept of RISC architecture involves an attempt to reduce execution time by simplifying the instruction set of computer. The major characteristics of RISC processor are:

1. Relatively few instructions
2. Relatively few addressing modes
3. Memory access limited to load and store instructions
4. All operations done within the register of the CPU
5. Fixed-length, easily decoded instruction format
6. Single-cycle instruction execution
7. Hardwired rather than microprogrammed control.

The small set of instructions of a typical RISC processor consists mostly of register-to-register operations, with only simple load and store operations for memory access. Thus each operand is brought into a processor register with a load instruction. All computations are done among the data stored in the processor registers. Results are transferred to memory by means of store instructions. The architectural feature simplifies the instruction set and encourages the optimization of register manipulation. The use of only a few addressing modes results from the fact that almost all instructions have simple register addressing other addressing modes may be included, such as immediate operands and relative mode.

By using a relatively simple instruction format, the instruction length can be fixed and aligned onward boundaries. An important aspect of RICS instruction format is that it is easy to decode. Thus the operation code and register fields of the instruction code can be accessed simultaneously by the control. By simplifying the instructions and their format, it is possible to simplify the control logic for faster operations, a hardwired control is preferable over a microprogrammed control. A characteristic of RICS processors is their ability to execute one instruction per clock cycle. This is done by overlapping the fetch, decode and execute phases of two or three instructions by using a procedure referred to as pipelining. A load or store instruction may require two clock cycles because access to memory takes more time than register operations. Efficient pipelining, as well as few other characteristics are sometimes attributed to RISC, although they may exist in non-RISC architectures as well. Other characteristics attributed to RISC architecture are:

(1) A relatively large number of register in the processor unit

(2) Use of overlapped register. Windows to speed-up procedure call and return

(3) Efficient instruction pipeline

(4) Compiler support for efficient translation of high-level language programs into machine language programs.

A large number of registers is useful for storing intermediate results and for optimize operand references. The advantage of register storage as opposed to memory storage is that registers can transfer information to other registers much faster than the transfer of information to and from memory. Thus register-to-memory operations can be minimized by keeping the most frequent accessed operands in registers studies that show improved performance for RICS architecture do not differentiate between the effects of the reduced instruction set and the effects of large register file. For this reason a large number of registers in the processing unit are sometimes associated with RICS processors.

SOLVED EXAMPLES

Example 1: *Suppose an unpipelined processor with a 25ns cycle time is divided into 5 pipeline stages with latencies of 5, 7, 3, 6 and 4 ns. If the pipeline latch latency is 1ns. What is the cycle time of the resulting processor. What is the latency of the resulting pipeline.*

Solution.

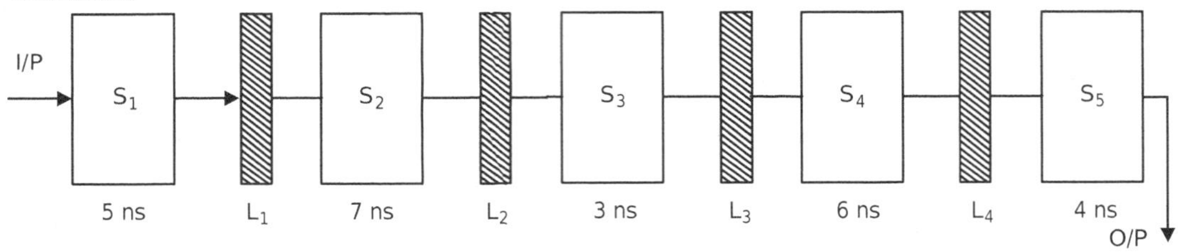

The longest pipeline stage is $7ns$. Latch latency is $1ns$.

Total latency $= 7 + 1 = 8ns$ **Ans.**

That is the cycle time. Since there are 5 stages in the pipeline, the total latency of the pipeline is $8 \times 5 = 40ns$ **Ans.**

Example 2: *Draw a space time diagram for five segment pipelining showing the time it takes to process & tasks.*

Solution.

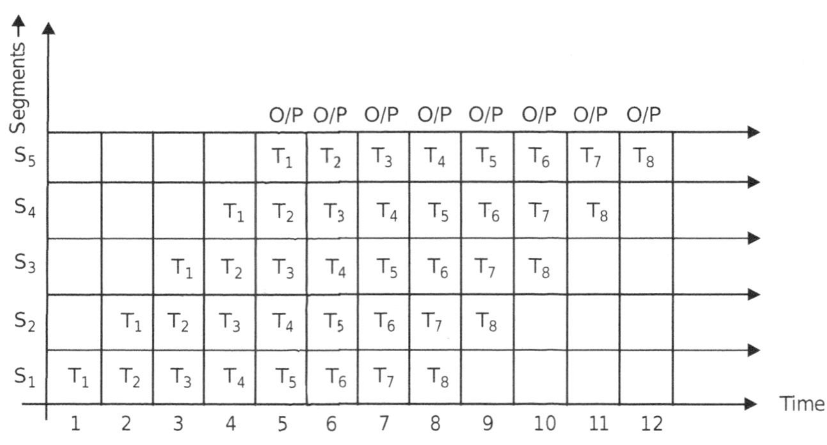

As there are five segments in the pipeline once the pipeline is full we get output at every clock cycle. The first output is produced in 5 clock cycle and then at every clock cycle completion we get output so next 7 tasks are completed in 7 clock cycles.

The total time taken by the pipeline to execute 8 tasks is

$$\text{T pipe} = [m + (n - 1)]\, tp$$
$$= [m + n - 1]tp$$
$$tp = 1$$
$$m = 5$$
$$n = 8$$
$$\text{T pipe} = (5 + 7)\,.\,1$$
$$= 12 \text{ cycle}$$

Example 3: *A nonpipeline system takes 50ns to process a task. The same task can be processed in a six segment pipeline with a clock cycle of 10ns. Determine the speed up ratio of the pipeline for 100 tasks. What is the maximum speed up that can be achieved.*

Solution. Part (*i*) Speed up ratio

tn = time taken by single task in a non-pipelined system

tn = 50*ns* (given)

tp = time period of a pipelined system

tp = 10*ns*

m = No. of segments in a pipeline = 6

n = No. of tasks to be completed = 100

T nonpipe = Time taken by the non-pipelined processor to process 100 tasks

$$\text{T nonpipe} = n \times tn$$
$$= 50 \times 100$$
$$= 5000\ ns.$$
$$\text{T pipe} = [m + (n - 1)]tp$$
$$= [6 + 99]10$$
$$= 105 \times 10$$
$$= 1050\ ns.$$

$$\text{Speed up ratio} = \frac{\text{T nonpipe}}{\text{T pipe}} = \frac{5000}{1050} = 4.7 \textbf{ Ans.}$$

Part (*ii*) The maximum speed up is when

$$n \to \infty$$

Then $$(m + (n - 1)) = n$$

$$\text{Speed up} = \frac{ntn}{[m + (n - 1)]tp} = \frac{ntn}{ntp} = \frac{tn}{tp}$$

$$= \frac{50}{10}$$

$$= 5 \textbf{ Ans.}$$

Example 4: *How many stages of pipelining are required to achieve a cycle time of 2ns and 1ns.*

Solution. We know that the pipeline cycle time

$$tp = \frac{t \text{ nonpipe}}{m} + t1$$

where $t1$ = Pipeline latch time

$$tp - t1 = \frac{t \text{ nonpipe}}{m}$$

To achieve a cycle time of $tp = 2ns$.

$$m = \frac{t \text{ nonpipe}}{tp - t1}$$

$$m = \frac{10}{2 - 0.5} = \frac{10}{1.5} = 6.67 \textbf{ Ans.}$$

To achieve a cycle time of $1ns$. The pipeline should have 20 stages as

$$m = \frac{10}{1 - 0.5} = 20 \textbf{ Ans.}$$

EXERCISES

1. Draw a space time diagram for a six segment pipeline showing the time it takes to process 8 tasks.
2. What is the Flynn's classification? *[Raj Univ. 2006]*
3. What is pipelining? How does it improve the performance of CPU explain?
4. What is parallel processing? How does it improve the performance of CPU?
5. Construct an arithmetic pipeline for floating point arithmetic operation.
6. What is pipelining? What is the maximum speed up that can be attained? Construct an instruction pipeline. It is possible to attain maximum speed up in an instruction pipeline.
7. A non-pipelined system takes $100ns$ to process a task. The same task can be processed in the six segment pipeline with a clock cycle of $20ns$. Determine the speed up of the pipeline for 50 tasks what is the maximum speed up that can be achieved.
8. What is the main differences between RISC and CISC architectures? Considering cost and technology, which design is better. Why?
9. What are the factors that degrades the performance of the pipeline system?
10. Explain the various possible hardware schemes that can be used in an instruction pipelining in order to minimize the performance degradation caused by a branch instruction.

Chapter 5

COMPUTER ARITHMETIC

5.1 INTRODUCTION

Arithmetic instruction in digital computers manipulate data to produce results necessary for the solution of computational problems. These instructions perform the basic arithmetic calculations. Basic arithmetic operations are addition, subtraction, multiplication and division. Other arithmetic functions are generated from these basic arithmetic operations.

An arithmetic processor is the part of a processor unit that executes arithmetic operations. In this chapter first we discuss about the representation of number. These are two representation:

1. Fixed point representation
2. Floating point represenation.

Fixed point numbers may represent integers or fractions. Negative numbers may be in signed magnitude or signed complement representation.

At an early edge we are taught how to perform the basic arithmetic operations in signed magnitude representation usually an algorithm will contain a number of procedueal steps which are dependent upon the results of the previous steps. A convenient method for presenting algorithms is a flow chart. The computational steps are specified in the flow chart inside rectangular boxes.

In this chapter we develop the various arithmetic algorithms and show the procedure for implementing them with digital hardware. We consider addition, subtraction, multiplication and division for the following types of data:

1. Fixed point binary data in signed magnitude representation.
2. Fixed point binary data in signed 2's complement representation.
3. floating point binary data.

5.2 REPRESENTATION OF NUMBERS

When an integer binary number is positive, the sign bit is represented by 0 and the magnitude by a positive binary number. When the number is negative, the sign is represented by 1 but the rest of the number may be represented in one of the three possible ways:

1. Signed magnitude representation
2. Signed 1's complement representation

3. Signed 2's complement representation.

The signed magnitude representation of a negative number consists of a magnitude and a negative sign. A positive number is represented by a sign bit 0 and the magnitude part for example, the signed positive number 14 is represented in 8 bit form then

Sign bit = 0

Magnitude = 0001110

Representation = 00001110

while a negative number can be represented by three different ways in eight bits. so -4 can be represented by the following three ways.

Signed magnitude representation	1 0000100
Signed 1's complement representation	1 1111011
Signed 2's complement representation	1 1111100

The signed magnitude representation system is used in ordinary arithmetic but is awkward when employed in computer arithmetic.

When two number of n digits each are added and the sum occupies $n + 1$ digits, we say that an overflow occured. When the addition is performed with paper and pencil, an overflow is not a problem since there is no limit to the width of the page to write down the sum. An overflow is a problem in digital computers because the width of registers is finite. A result that contains $n + 1$ bits cannot be accomodated in a register with a standard length of n bits. When an overflow occurs, a corresponding flip-flop is set.

If a positive number is added to a negative number, overflow does not occur because the sum is smaller than the largest of the two original numbers. An overflow occurs when numbers to be added are both positive or both negative and the result exceeds the storing capacity of the register.

Generally 2's complement representation is used when performing arithmetic operations with integers. For floating point operations, most computers use the signed magnitude representation for mantissa.

5.2.1 Fixed Point Representation

In fixed point representation all numbers are represented as integers or fraction. Signed integers or BCD numbers are referred to as fixed point numbers because they contain no information regarding the location of the binary point or decimal point. The binary or decimal point is assumed at the extreme right or left of the number. The fixed point method assumes that the binary point is always fixed in one position. The two positions most widely used are:

1. A binary point in the extreme left of the register to make the stored number a fraction.
2. A binary point in the exterme right of the register to make the stored number an integer.

The binary point is not actually present, but its presence is assumed from the fact that the number stored in the register is treated as a fraction or as an integer. It the binary or decimal point is at the extreme right of the computer word all numbers are positive or negative integers. If the radix point is assumed to be at the extreme left, all numbers are positive or negative fraction.

Suppose we have to multiply 2.58 × 50.38. The number will be represented as 258 × 5038. The result will be 1299804. The decimal point has to be placed by the programmer to get the correct result that is 1299.804. Thus in the fixed point of representation the user has to keep the track of radix point.

In scientific applications of computers fractions are frequently used. So a system that keeps track about the position of binary or decimal point is required. Such a system is called floating point representation of numbers. Many computers and all modern electronic calculators use floating point arithematic operations.

5.2.2 Floating Point Representation

A number which has both an integer part as well as fractional part is called real number or floating point numbers. A real number may be either positive or negative. The real number 54.378 can also be written as 5.4378×10^1, 146.58 as 0.14658×10^3 etc., such representations is known as scientific form of representation.

The floating point representation of a number has two parts.

1. Mantissa – represents a signed fixed point number.
2. Exponent – Designates the position of the decimal point.

In the general form a number N my be represents as

$$N = m \times r^e$$

Where

$$m = \text{mantissa}$$

$$e = \text{exponent}$$

$$r = \text{radix or base of the number}$$

Only the mantissa m and and the exponent e are physically represented in the register. The radix r and the radix point position of the mantissa always assumed.

For example, the decimal number 5348.96 is represented in floating point representation as shown below:

Sign	Mantissa	Sign	Exponent
0	.534896	0	04

A zero in the left most position of the mantissa denotes the plus sign. The mantissa may be either a fraction or integer. A floating point binary number is represented in a similar manner except it uses base 2 for the exponent. For the example, the binary number + 1011.11 is represented with an 8 bit fraction and 6 bit exponent as fallows:

Fraction	Exponent
01011110	000100

The fraction has a 0 in the left most position to denote positive. The binary point of the fraction follows the sign bit but is not shown in the register. The floating point number is equivalent to

$$m \times 2^e = + (.1011110)_2 \times 2^{+4}$$

A negative number – 563.5896 can be represented as shown below:

	Sign		Sign	
	1	.5635896	0	03
		↓		↓
		Mantissa		Exponent

The radix r and the decimal or binary point are not indicated in the register. These are assumed things which are taken into account by the electronic circuitary which makes computation and manipulation.

5.2.2.1 Normalized Floating Point Number

When the most significant digit of the mantissa is non-zero, the floating point number is said to be normalized. For example, the numbers $.005698 \times 10^5$ and and $.03698 \times 10^{-6}$ are not normalized floating point numbers. The corresponding normalized numbers are 0.5698×10^3 and 0.3698×10^{-7} are normalized numbers since most significant digit is non-zero. Normalized form is also called standard form. Floating point numbers are stored in the normalized form. While storing the floating point numbers the mantissa is shifted left until its most significant bit becomes non-zero and the exponent is adjusted accordingly. The process of shifting the mantissa left to make its most significant bit non-zero is called normalization.

5.2.2.2 Range of Stored Numbers

The range of the stored numbers depends on the word length of the computer and the number of bits assigned for the mantissa and the number of bits assigned for the exponent. Suppose a 16 bit word is employed to store numbers. Out of 16 bits, 9 bits are used for the storage of mantissa including the sign bit and 7 bits for exponent including sign bit. The maximum value of the number is represented in Fig 5.1.

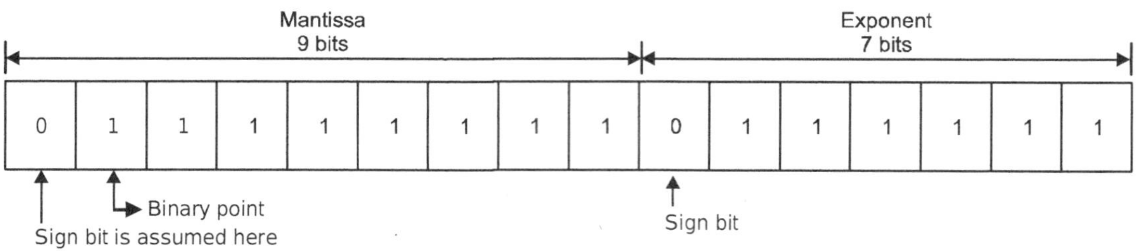

Fig. 5.1 Maximum value of number

The maximum value = 0.11111111E 0111111

E indicates exponent

$$\text{Maximum value} = (1-2^{-8})\times 2^{(2^6-1)}$$

Exponent sign bit is 0 indicates exponent is positive.

$$= (1 - 2^{-8}) \times 2^{63}$$
$$\cong 1 \times 2^{63}$$
$$\cong 10^{19}$$

The minimum value is represented in Fig. 5.2.

The minimum value = 0.10000000E 1111111

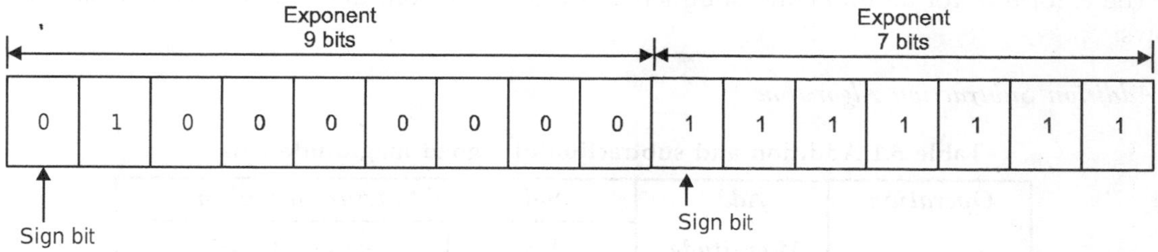

Fig 5.2 Minimum value of the number

$$\text{minimum value} = (2^{-1}) \times 2\ (2^{06} - 1)$$
$$= (2^{-1}) \times 2^{-63}$$
$$= 2^{-64}$$
$$= 2^{-19}$$

So the range will be 2^{-64} to 2^{63}

or 10^{-19} to 10^{+19}.

5.3 ADDITION AND SUBTRACTION

A negative fixed point binary number can be represented in signed magnitude, signed 1's complement or signed 2's complement form. Generally 2's complement representation is used when performing arithematic operations with integers. For floating point operations, most computers use the signed magnitude representation for mantissa. In this section we study the addition and subtraction algorithm when data is represented in signed magnitude form or when data is represented in signed 2's complement form.

It is important to realise that the adopted representation for negative numbers refers to the representation of numbers in the registers before and after the excution of the arithmetic operation. It does not mean that complement arithmetic may not be used in an intermediate step. For example, it is convenient to employ complement arithmetic when reforming a subtraction operation with numbers in signed magnitude representation. As long as the initial minuend and subtrahend have been used in an intermediate steps does not alter the fact that the representation is in signed magnitude.

5.3.1 Addition and Subtraction with Signed Magnitude Data

In signed magnitude form numbers are represented in everyday arithmetic calculations. Here we explain the addition and subtraction with the magnitude of two numbers A and B. There are eight different conditions to consider when we do addition and subtraction depending on the sign of the numbers and the operation performed. These different conditions are listed in Table 5.1 in column first. The other columns in the table show the actual operation to be performed with the magnitude of the numbers. The last column is needed to prevent a negative zero, when two numbers are equal the result should be zero.

The algorithm for addition and subtraction are derived from the table and can be stated as follows:

1. Addition Subtraction Algorithm

Table 5.1 Addition and subtraction of signed magnitude data

Operation	*Add Magnitude*	*Subtracted Magnitudes when*		
		A > B	*A < B*	*A = B*
(+A) + (+B)	+ (A + B)			
(+A) + (–B)		+ (A – B)	– (B – A)	+ (A – B)
(–A) + (+B)		– (A – B)	+ (B – A)	+ (A – B)
(–A) + (–B)	– (A + B)			
(+A) – (+B)		+ (A – B)	– (B – A)	+ (A – B)
(+A) – (–B)	+ (A + B)			
(–A) – (+B)	– (A + B)			
(–A) – (–B)		– (A – B)	+ (B – A)	+ (A – B)

We derive the algorithm for addition and subtraction from this above table. When the sign of A and B are identical in case of addition and when the sign of A and B are different in case of subtraction, then add the two magnitudes and attach the sign of A to the result. That are represented in add magnitude column. When the sign of A and B are different in case of addition operation and identical in case of subtraction operation then compare the magnitudes and subtract the smaller number from the larger.

If $A > B$

Sign of result = sign of A

If $A < B$

Sign of result = complement the sign of A.

If the two magnitudes are equal, subtract B from A and make the sign of the result positive.

The two algorithms are similar except for the sing comparision. The procedure to be followed for identical signs in the addition algorithm is the same for different signs in the subtraction algorithm and vice versa.

2. Hardware Implementation

To implement the addition and subtraction operation with hardware first of all we have to store these two numbers A and B in two registers. Let A and B are two registers that holds the numbers A and B. Sign of these two numbers are stored in two flip-flops As and Bs. The result of addition or subtraction can be transferred into the third register, however a saving is achieved if the result is transferred into A and As. Thus A and As together form an accumulator register. The following hardware components are used for implementation:

1. Complementer
2. Parallel adder
3. 4 1 bit flip-flops
4. Two registers

First a parallel adder is needed to perform the microoperation A + B. A comparator circuit is needed to establish if A > B, A = B or A < B. Figure 5.3 shows a block diagram of the hardware for implementing the addition and subtraction operation. A complementor is needed for performing complement of the numbers. As we know subtraction can be accomplished by means of complement and addition, secondly the comparision can be determined from the carry after subtraction. So there is no need for comparator circuit. The figure consists of registers A and B and sign flip-flops As and Bs. Subtraction is done by adding A to the 2's complement of B. The output carry is transferred to flip-flop E, where it can be checked to determine the relative magnitudes of the two numbers. The add overflow flip-flop AVF holds the overflow bit when A and B are added. The A register provides other micro-operations that may be needed when we specify the sequence of steps in the algorithm.

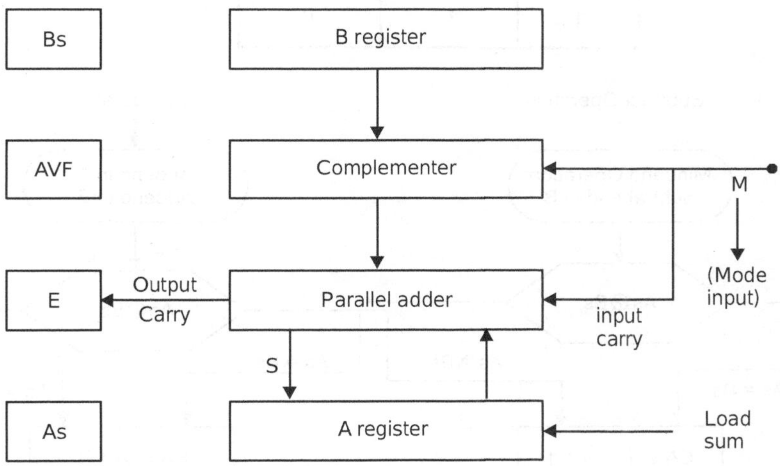

Fig 5.3 Hardware implementation

The addition of A plus B is done through the parallel adder. The sum output of the adder is applied to the input of the A register. The complementer provides an output of B or the complement of B depending upon the value of mode input M. The complementer consists of ex-OR gates and the parallel adder consists of full adder circuits that we have studied in Chapter-2. In case of addition initial carry is assumed 0 so the M signal is also applied to the input carry of the adder.

when M = 0

Input Carry = 0

Output = $\underline{A+B}$ (Addition operation)

When M = 1

Input Carry = 1

Output of B Register = $\overline{B}$

Output = $A+\overline{B}+1 = A-B$ (Subtraction operation).

3. *Hardware Algorithm*

The flow chart for the hardware algorithm is shown in fig 5.4. First of all we have to compare the sign of A and B that are stored in flip-flops As and Bs. The two signs are compared with exclusive OR gate.

Table 5.2 Truth table for Ex-OR gate

A	*B*	*o/p*
0	0	0
0	1	1
1	0	1
1	1	0

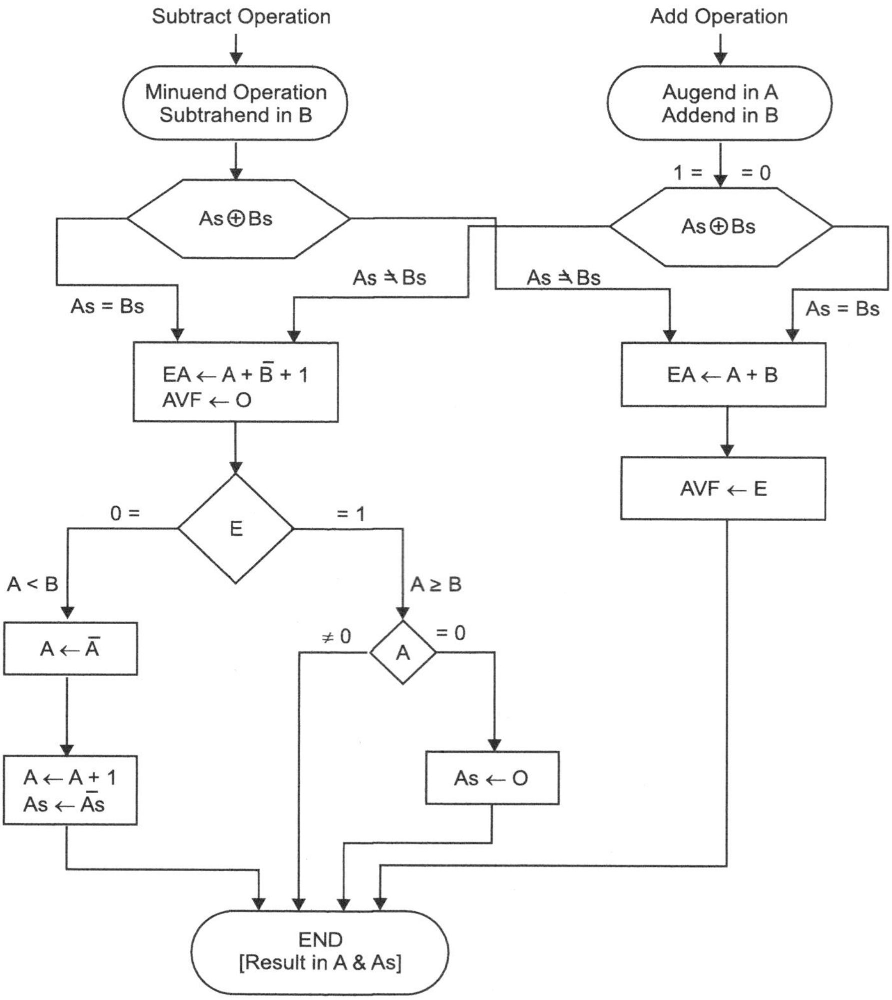

Fig. 5.4 Flow chart for add and subtract operation

From the truth table it is clear that when signs are identical output of Ex-OR gate will be 0 and when signs are different the output of Ex-OR gate will be 1. For addition operation same signs of numbers indicate that we have to add the magnitude and for subtraction operation different signs dictate that the magnitudes be added. The magnitudes are added with a microoperation EA $\leftarrow$ A + B, where EA is a register that combines E and A. The carry in E after the addition constitutes an overflow, if it is equal to 1. The value of E is transferred into the add overflow flip-flop AVF.

The magnitudes are subtracted by adding A to the 2's complement of B. No overflow can occur if the numbers are subtracted so AVF is cleared to O. A 1' in E indicates that A $\geq$ B and the number in A is the correct result. If the number is 0 then sign As must be made positive to avoid a negative zero. A '0' in E indicates that A < B. For this case it is necessary to take the 2's complement of the value in A. This operation can be done with one microoperation $A \leftarrow \overline{A}+1$. However, we assume that the A register has circuits for microoperations complement and increment, so the 2's complement is obtained from these two microoperations. In other paths of the flow chart, the sign of the result is same as the sign of A, so no change in As is required. However when A < B the sign of the result is the complement of the sign of A. It is necessary to complement as to obtain the correct sign. The final result is found in register A and its sign in As. The Value of AVF indicates overflow situation.

5.3.2 Addition and Subtraction with Signed 2's Complement Data

The left most bit of a number represents the sign of the number. If it is 0 number is positive sign bit 1 indicates that number is negative. The complete number that is negative can be represented in 2's complement form.

Let + 13 is represented as 8 bit binary equivalent 00001101 0 and – 13 as 11110011. Notes that 11110011 is 2's complement of 00001101 and vice versa. Sign bit is not treated separately it is treated the same as the other bit of the number.

The addition and subtraction in signed 2's complement form is very straight forward method. The addition of two numbers in signed 2's complement form consists of adding the numbers with sign bits treated the same as the other bits of the number. A carry out of the sign bit position is dicarded. The subtraction consists of first taking 2's complement of the subtrahend and then adding it to the minuend.

When two numbers of n digits are added and the sum occupies $(n + 1)$ digits then an overflow is detected. An overflow can be detected in 2's complement form by unspicting last two carries out of the addition operation. When the two carries are applied to an exclusive OR gate, the overflow is detected when output of Ex-OR gate is high.

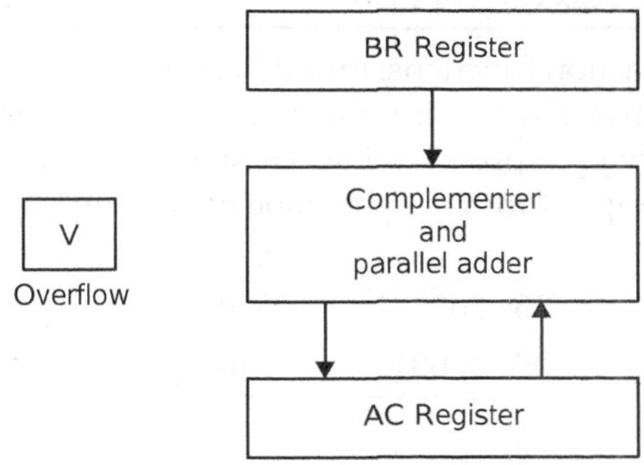

Fig. 5.5 Hardware implementation

(1) Hardware Implementation

Hardware Implementation is shown in Fig. 5.5. Now the sign bits are not separated from the number. The two numbers are stored in the register AC (accumulator) and register BR. Using hardware circuit parallel adder and complementer we perform addition and subtraction operation. It there is any overflow then flip-flop V is set to 1. The output carry is discarded.

(2) Hardware Algorithm

Flow chart for hardware algorithm is shown in Fig 5.6. The sum is obtained by adding the contents of AC and BR. The overflow bit V is set to 1 if the last two carry when applied to exclusive OR gate output is 1 and otherwise it is cleared to 0. The subtraction operation is accomplished by adding 2's complement of BR register to the AC register. Taking the 2's complement of BR has the effect of changing a positive number to negative and vice versa.

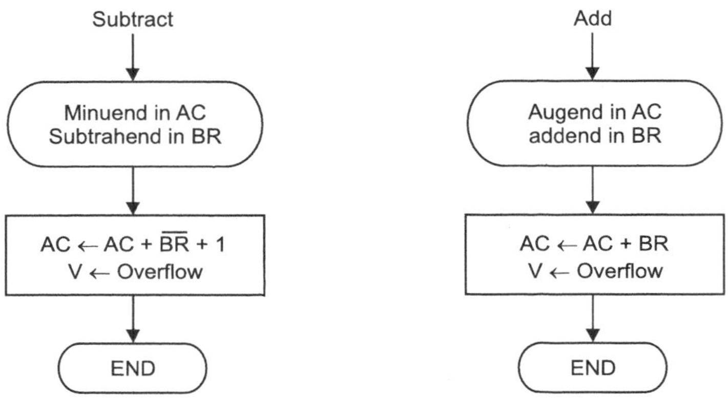

(a) Subtraction Operation 5.6 (b)

Fig. 5.6 Addition and subtraction is signed 2's complement form

An overflow must be checked during this operation because the two numbers added could have the same sign. The programmer must realize that if an overflow occurs there will be an erroneous result in the AC register.

This is very simple algorithm for this reason most computers adopt this representation over the more familiar signed magnitude.

5.4 MULTIPLICATION ALGORITHM

After addition and subtraction functions, multiplication is one of the most important arithmetic operation. Multiplication of two fixed point binary numbers in signed magnitude representation is done with paper and pencil by a process of successive shift and add operations. Multiplication of two *n* bit numbers in its simplest form can be done by adding of *n* partial products. Let we have to multiply 23 × 09.

23	10111	Multiplicand
09	01001	Multiplier

```
           10111
          00000×
         00000×
        10111×
       00000×
  ----------------
(207) 011001111    Product.
```

If the multiplier bit is 1, the multiplicand is copied down, otherwise zeros are copied down. The numbers copied down in successive lines are shifted one position to the left from the previous number. Finally the numbers are added and their sum forms the product. The sign of the result is determined from the signs of the multiplicand and multiplier.

5.4.1 Hardware Implementation for Signed Magnitude Data

Practically it is not possible that we store the intermediate results in registers because so many partial products are generated. Instead of providing registers to store and add simultaneously as many binary numbers as there are bits in the multiplier, it is convenient to provide an adder for the summation of only two binary numbers and successively accumulate the partial products in a register. Second, instead of shifting the multiplicand to the left, the partial product is shifted to the right, which results in leaving the partial product and the multiplicand in the required relative positions. Third, when the corresponding bit of the multiplier is 0, there is no need to add all zeros to the partial product since it will not alter its value.

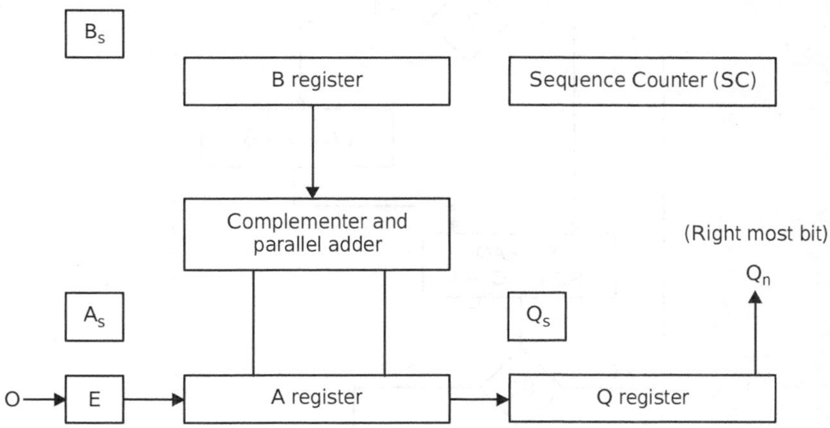

Fig. 5.7 Hardware for multiplication

Fig 5.7 represents the hardware for multiplication operation. The multiplier is stored in the Q register and its sign is stored in register Qs. The initial value of sequence counter (SC) is set to the no., of bits in the multiplier. After forming each partial product sequence counter is decremented by 1. When the contents of the counter reaches zero, the product is formed and the process stops.

Initially the multiplicand is in register B and the multiplier in register Q. Partial product is obtained by adding A and B. Partial product is transferred to the EA register. Both the partial product and multiplier are shifted to the right. This is represented by the statement SHREAQ. The least significant bit of A is shifted into the most significant position of Q, the bit from E is shifted into the most significant position of A and O is shifted into E. After the shift, one bit of the partial product is shifted into Q, pushing the multiplier bits one position to the right. In this manner, the rightmost flip-flop in register Q, designated by Qn will hold the bit of the multiplier.

Hardware Algorithm

Fig. 5.8 represents the flow chart for the multiply operation. Multiplicand is in B register and multiplier is in Q register. Corresponding signs are present in register Bs and Qs respectively. Both the signs are compared and the corresponding sign of result is calculated. Both A and Q

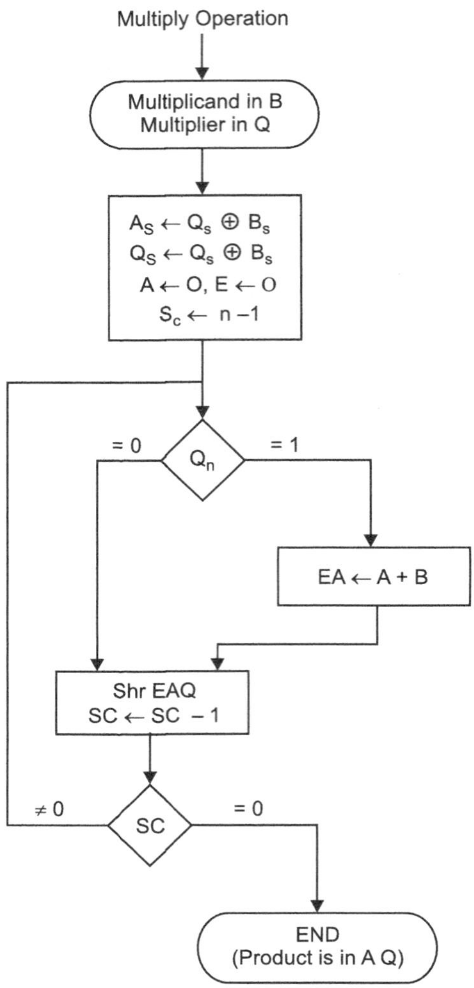

Fig. 5.8 Flow chart for multiplication operation

are set to correspond to the sign of a product since a double length product will be stored in registers A and Q, registers A and E are initialized to 0 and SC is set to the value equals to number of bits in the multiplier.

After the initialization, the low-order bit of the multiplier in Qn is checked. If it is 1 the multiplicand in B is added to the present partial product in A. If it is 0, nothing is done. Register

EAQ is shifted to the right that produces 1 bit result. The value of sequence counter (SC) is decremented by 1. The value of sequence counter is checked if it is not zero, the process is repeated with the new value of Qn. The process stops when SC = 0. The partial product formed in A is shifted into Q, one bit at a time and eventually replaces the multiplier. The final product is available in both A and Q, with A holding the most significant bits and Q holding the least significant bits.

The following numerical example represents the multiplication operation using table 5.2.

Let Multiplicand B = 11000 (– 8)
Multiplier Q = 01100 (+12)

Multiplicand B = 11000	E	A	Q	SC
Multiplier in Q	0	00000	01100	101
Qn = 0 Shr EAQ	0	00000	00110	100
Qn = 0 Shr EAQ	0	00000	00011	011
Qn = 1 add B shr EAQ	1 1	11000 11100	00011 00001	 010
Qn = 1 add B shr EAQ	1 1	10100 11010	00001 00000	 001
Qn = 0 Shr EAQ	1	11101	00000	000

The value of SC becomes zero so we have to stop.

The result is 1110100000. It is a negative number, its 2's complement is 0001100000. Which is the result.

5.4.2 Booth Multiplication Algorithm

In the shift and add form of multiplier, the multiplicand is added to the partial product at each bit position where a 1 occurs in the multiplier. Therefore, the number of times that the multiplicand is added to the partial product is equal to the number of 1's in the multiplier. Also when the multiplier is negative, the shift and add method requires an additional step to replace the multiplier and multiplicand with their 2's complement.

Booth multiplication algorithm gives a procedure for multiplying binary integers in signed 2's complement representation. The main point of Booth's multiplication is that the string of o's in the multiplier requires no addition, but just shifting and the string of 1's can be treated as a number from bit weight 2^k to weight 2^m can be treated as $2^{k+1} - 2^m$.

For example, the binary number (0011100) has a string of 1's from 2^4 to 2^2. Here (K = 4, m = 2). The number can be represented as $2^{k+1} - 2^m = 2^5 - 2^2$

$$= 32 - 4 = 28.$$

that is decimal equivalent of the binary number 0011100. Therefore the multiplication M × 28 where M is the multiplicand and 14 the multiplier can be done as $M \times 2^5 - M \times 2^2$. We know that arithmetic left shift multiply a number by two and arithmetic right shift divide a number by a factor of 2. So this multiplication can be obtained by shifting the binary multiplicand M five times and subtracting M shifted left twice.

As in all multiplication schemes, booth algorithm requires examination of the multiplier bits and shifting of the partial product. While shifting, the multiplicand may be added to the partial product, subtracted from the partial product or left unchanged according to the following three rules:

1. The multiplicand is subtracted from the partial product upon encountering the first least significant 1 in a string of 1's in the multiplier.
2. The multiplicand is added to the partial product upon encountering the first 0 in a string of 0's in the multiplier.
3. The partial product does not change when the multiplier bit is identical to the previous multiplier bit.

Booth multiplication algorithm is also known as 2's complement multiplication algorithm. This algorithm works for positive or negative multipliers in 2's complement representation.

Hardware Implementation

Hardware implementation of booth algorithm is shown in Fig. 5.9. Numbers are represented in 2's complement form so sign bits are not separated from the rest of the registers. We require the inspection of two bit so an extra flip-flop (Qn+1) is appended to Q register.

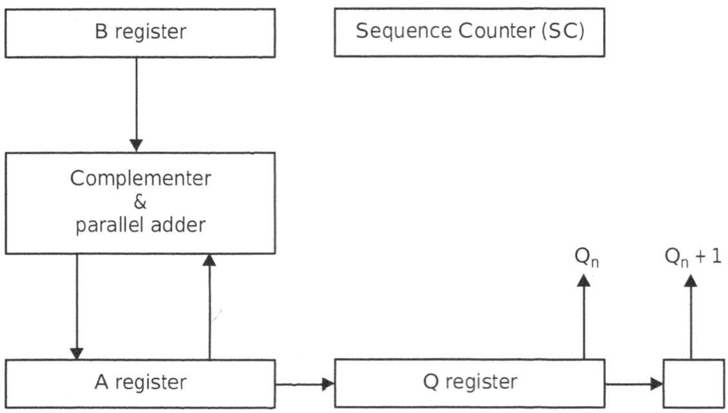

Fig 5.9 Hardware for booth algorithm

The function of SC is same as it was in the previous algorithm. Addition and subtraction is performed using the hardware circuit complementer and parallel adder. Multiplicand is in register B and partial product is obtained by adding A and B.

Hardware Algorithm

The flow chart for the booth algorithm is depicted in Fig. 5.10. Multiplicand is in register B and multiplier is in register Q. Initially register A is cleared. Bit Qn + 1 are initially cleared to 0 and the initial value of the sequence counter is equal to the number of bits in the multiplier. Now double bit inspection is performed. There are four deficient cases that we have to consider.

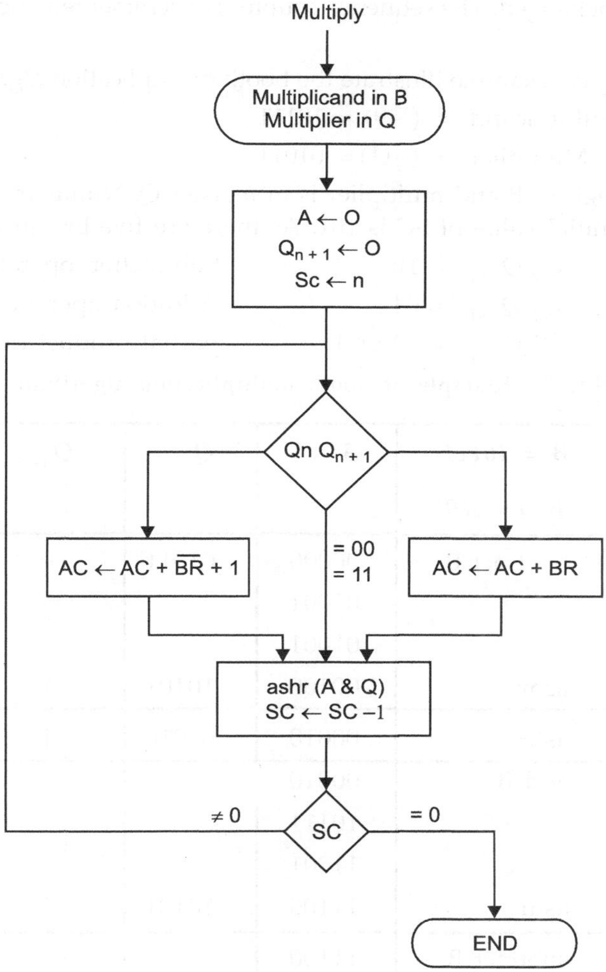

Fig. 5.10 Booth algorithm

Case I: When Qn Qn + 1 = 10

This implies that the first 1 in a string of 1's has been encountered. This requires a subtraction of the multiplicand from the partial product in A.

Case II: When Qn Qn + 1 = 01

This implies that the first 0 in a string of 0's has been encountered. This requires the addition of the multiplicand with the parital product in register A.

Case III: When Qn Qn + 1=00

partial product will not change.

Case IV: When Qn Qn + 1=11

partial product will not change.

As addition and subtraction operation are following each other, an overflow cannot occur. The next step is to shift right the partial product and the multiplier. It is arithmetic right shift and leaves the sign bit in A unchanged. The sequence counter is decremented and this is repeated until Sc = 0.

The following numerical example illustrate the booth multiplication algorithm using table 5.3.

Multiplicand = (– 9) = 10111

Multiplier = (+11) = 01011

Multiplicand is in register B and multiplier is in register Q. Numbers are represented in 2's complement form. The initial value of SC is 101. As there are five bits in the multiplier.

It $Q_n\ Q_{n+1}$ = 10 – Subtraction operation

$Q_n\ Q_{n+1}$ = 01 – Addition operation

$Q_n\ Q_{n+1}$ = 00 or 11 – partial product do not change.

Table 5.3 Example of booth multiplication algorithm

$Q_n\ Q_{n+1}$	$B = 10111$ $\overline{B}+1 = 01001$	A	Q	Q_{n+1}	SC
1 0	Subtract B	00000	01011	0	101
		01001			
		01001			
	ashr	00100	10101	1	100
1 1	ashr	00010	01010	1	011
0 1	add B	00010			
		10111			
		11001			
	ashr	11100	10101	0	010
10	subtract B	11100			
		01001			
		00101			

5.4.3 Array Multiplier

Multiplication algorithms discussed in the previous section requires a sequence of add and shift microoperations. Checking the bits of the multiplier one at a time and forming partial products is a sequential operation. The multiplication of two binary numbers can also be done with one microoperation by means of a combinational circuit that form the product bits all at once. This is a fast way of multiplying two binary numbers since all it takes is the time for the signals to propagate through the gates that form the multiplication array. Array multiplier requires large number of logic gates.

Let us take an example of multiplying two 2 bit numbers. The multiplicand bits are $y_1\ y_0$ and multiplier bits are $x_1 x_0$. The product bits are $z_3 z_2 z_1 z_0$.

$$\begin{array}{cccccc} & & y_1 & y_0 & \text{(Multiplicand)} \\ & & x_1 & x_0 & \text{(Multiplier)} \\ \hline & & x_0y_1 & x_0y_0 & \\ & x_1y_1 & x_1y_0 & & \\ \hline z_3 & z_2 & z_1 & z_0 & \\ \hline \end{array}$$

The first partial product is obtained by multiplying the bits x_0 with y_0 and y_1. The multiplication of two bits produces a 1 if both the bits are 1, otherwise if produces a 0. Multiplication of two binary bits can be done using AND logic gate. The second partial product is obtained by multiplying the bits x_1 with y_0 and y_1. Both the partial products can be implemented using 4 AND gates. Now we have to perform the addition microoperation. The two partial product are added using two half adder circuits. 2 bit 2 bit array multiplier is shown in Fig. 5.11.

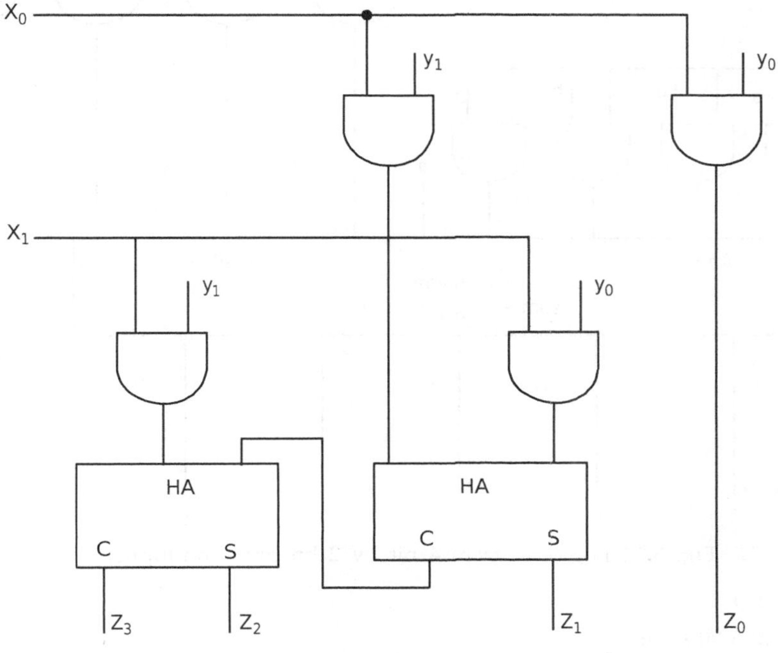

Fig 5.11 2 by 2 bit array multiplier

Note that the least significant bit of the product does not have to go through an adder since it is formed by the output of the first AND gate.

A combinational circuit binary multiplier with more bits can be constructed in a similar fashion. A bit of the multiplier is ANDed with each bit of the multiplicand in as many levels as there are bits in the multiplier. For J multiplier bits and K multiplicand bits we need j × k AND gates and (J–1) K bit adder to produce a product of $j + k$ bits.

For example, consider a multiplier circuit that multiplies a binary number of four bits with a number of two bits. Let the multiplicand is $x_3x_2x_1x_0$ and multiplier bits are y_1y_0.

		x_3	x_2	x_1	x_0
				y_1	y_0
		y_0x_3	y_0x_2	y_0x_1	y_0x_0
	y_1x_3	y_1x_2	y_1x_1	y_1x_0	
z_5	z_4	z_3	z_2	z_1	z_0

Product bits are $z_5\ z_4\ z_3\ z_2\ z_1\ z_0$.

The first partial product is obtained by multiplying yo with x_0, x_1, x_2 and x_3. The logic diagram is shown in Fig 5.12.

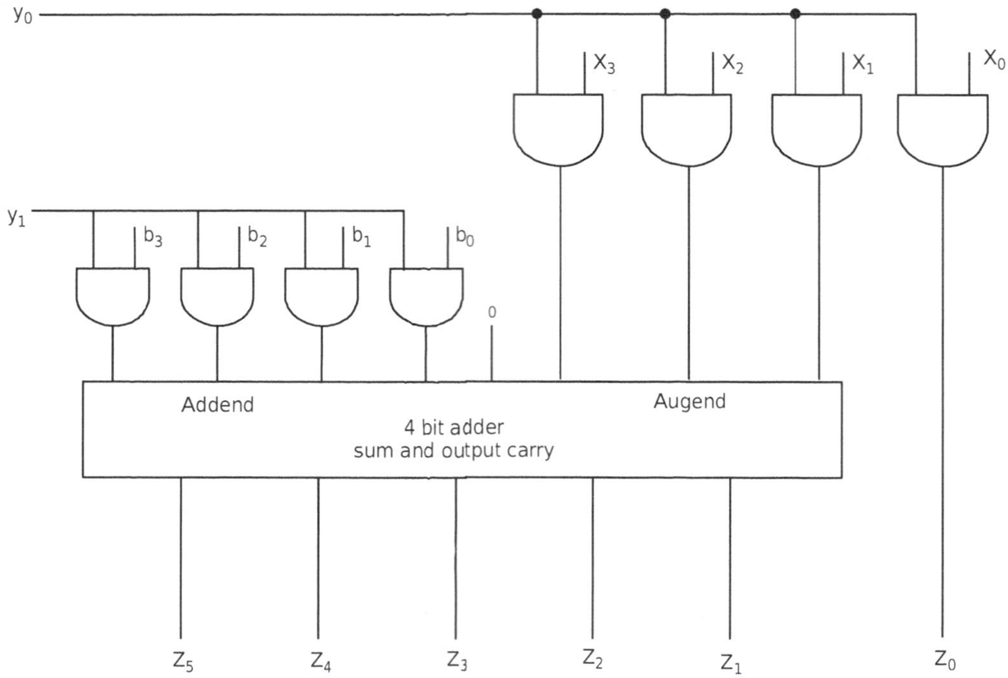

Fig. 5.12 Logic diagram 4 bit by 2 bit array multiplier

Since K = 4 and J = 2

We need j × k AND gates

⇒ 8 gates.

Since an Array multiplier requires a large number of gates and for this reason it was not economical until the development of integrated circuits.

5.5 UNSIGNED DIVISION

Division of two fixed point binary numbers in signed magnitude representation is done with paper and pencil by a process of successive compare, shift and subtract operations. In the previous sections we discussed multiplication by relating the way in which the multiplication operation can be done on paper to the way a logic circuit can do it. Binary division is simpler than decimal division because the quotient digits are either 0 or 1 and there is no need to estimate how many times the dividend or partial remainder fits in to the divisor.

5.5.1 Restoring Division Method

The conclusion from the long hand division algorithm is that the process of trial determination of the quotient digits is more difficult to automate in a logic circuit that the selection and addition of summands in the multiplication case.

The simplest circuit that implements binary division must methodically position the divisor with respect to the dividend and perform a subtraction. If the remainder is zero or positive, a quotient bit of 1 is determined, the remainder is extended by another bit of the divident, the divisor is repositioned and another subtraction is performed. If remainder is negative, a quotient bit of 0 is determined, the dividend is restored by adding back. The dividend and the divisor is repositioned for another subtraction.

The flow chart for restoring division is shown in Fig. 5.13. As n bit positive divisor is loaded into register M and n bit positive dividend is loaded into the register Q at the start of the operation.

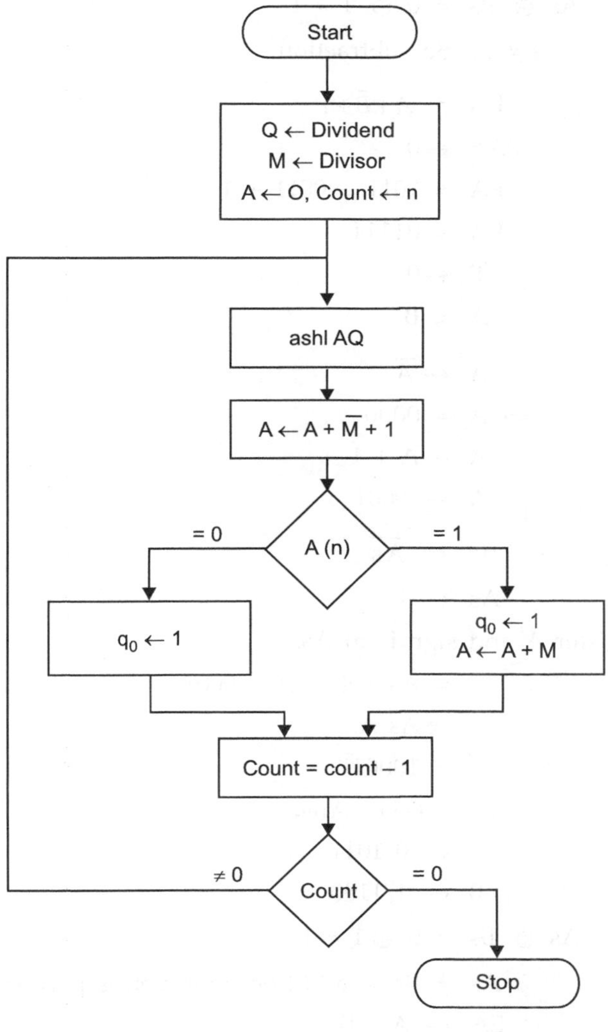

Fig. 5.13 Flow chart of restore division algorithm

Register A is cleared to 0. After the division is complete, the *n* bit quotient will be in register Q and the remainder will be in register A subtraction is performed using the complement method. The extra bit position at the left end of both A and M is for the sign bit for subtraction.

SOLVED EXAMPLES

Example 1: *Give step by step addition and subtraction process for* (+11) + (– 12) *and* (+11) – (– 12) *respectively.* [Raj. 2006]

Solution. (*i*) Addition Binary equivalent

A = +11 0 10 11

B = – 12 1 11 00 → sign bit

Step 1. As ⊕ Bs = 0 ⊕ 1 = 1

As ≠ Bs So subtraction

Step 2. $EA = A+\overline{B}+1$

AVF ←0

EA = 1011 + 0011 + 1

EA = 01111

Step 3. E ←0

So A < B

Step 4. $A \leftarrow \overline{A}$

⇒ A = 0000

A ←A + 1

A ← 0001

$As \leftarrow \overline{As}$

As ← 1

So answer is in register A and sign is in As.

= As = 1 A = 0001

⇒As A

= 10001

= (–1) **Ans.**

(*ii*) Subtraction A ← 0 1011

B ← 1 1100

As ⊕ Bs = 0 ⊕1 = 1

As ≠ Bs so addition operation is performed.

EA ← A + B

$$\begin{aligned} EA &\leftarrow 1011 + 1100 \\ &= 10111 \\ AVF &\leftarrow E \\ AVF &\leftarrow D \end{aligned}$$

Result. Sign bit in As = 0

$$\begin{aligned} \text{Subtraction in A} &= 10111 \\ &= (+23) \qquad \textbf{Ans.} \end{aligned}$$

Example 2: *Represent* – 1101011 *in the floating point representation for* 32 *bit word length.*

Solution. Given binary number = -1101011×2^7

Since the given number is negative, its 2's complement is used in the representation its 2's complement is 0010101.

So
$$\begin{aligned} \text{Mantissa} &= 0.0010101 \\ \text{Exponent} &= 7 \\ \text{The biased exponent} &= 7 + 128 = 135 \\ 135 &= 10000111 \end{aligned}$$

Since the number is negative, the sign bit for the mantissa will be 1. The 32 bit representation of the given number is

10010101	00000000	00000000	10000111
Mantissa			Exponent

Sign bit

Example 3: *What are the best case and worst cases in a Booth multiplier.*

Solution. The best case is when there is a continuous stream of 1's is in the multiplier. In this case we do two additions and subtraction operation.

Worst case when there are alternate '1' and '0' in the multiplier the number of additions and subtraction operations doubles than that of a simple multiplication.

EXERCISES

1. Explain the algorithm of addition and subtraction for signed magnitude data. Also give the hardware implementation of explained algorithm.
2. Design a data path for addition and subtraction of two numbers represented in single precision IEEE 754 format. Explain the operation of the data path.
3. Explain Booth's algorithm for performing multiplication of two binary numbers. What are the disadvantages over signed 2's complements using suitable block diagram?
4. Explain floating point number of any arithmetic operation, using block diagram.
5. Write short note on array multiplier.
6. Using add and shift method multiply x = 0110 and y = 1011.
7. Give a multiplication algorithm similar to the shift and add multiplication method but that proceeds with a left to right scan of the multiplier.
8. Design an array multiplier that multiplies two 4 bit numbers. Use AND gates and binary adders.

Chapter 6

Microprogrammed Control Unit

6.1 INTRODUCTION

A digital system is usually divided into two parts:

1. Execution unit
2. Control unit

The execution unit is a network of functional units that performs certain microoperations on data. The execution unit of the processor contains circuits to perform arithematic and logical operations on data and a storage unit where the data is stored.

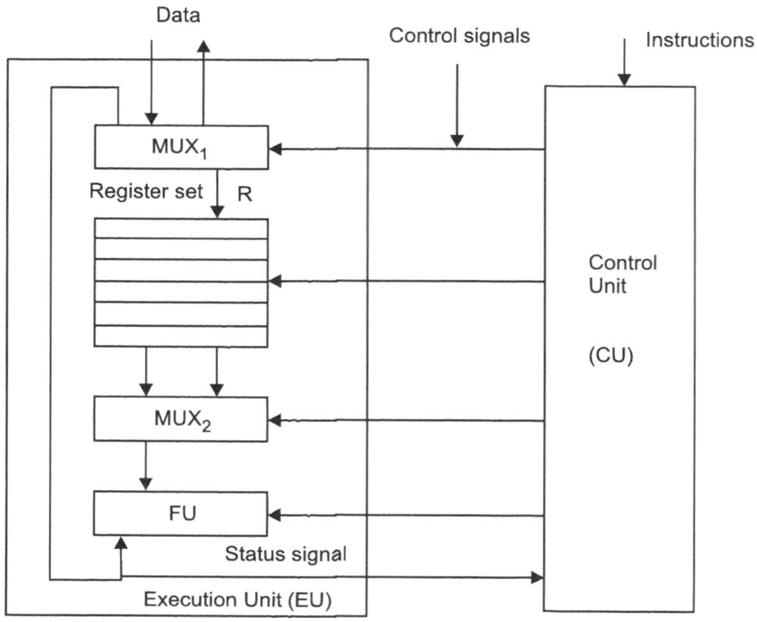

Fig. 6.1 Block diagram of a processor (EU + CU)

The function of the control unit in a digital computer is to initiate sequences of microoperations. The control unit issues control signals to the execution unit. These control signals enter the data path at control points, where they select the functions to be performed at particular times and to route the data through the appropriate parts of the execution unit. Hence logically the control unit reconfigures the execution unit to implement the specified instruction or program. Fig. 6.1 depicts a typical execution unit and control unit.

It contains a register set R for temporary storage of operands and to store the results. A function unit F which does the data processing and multiplers MUX_1 and MUX_2 to transfer data through the Execution Unit (EU). The control unit receives external instructions which it converts into a sequence of control signals that are applied to EU to implement a sequence of microoperations.

6.2 CONTROL UNIT

Central Processing Unit (CPU) consists mainly three parts:

(*i*) Register set

(*ii*) Control unit

(*iii*) ALU.

Register set is used to store the data temporarily during the execution of the various micro operations. Arithmetic logic unit performs the required microoperations. Control unit works as a supervisor. It itself does not do any thing just it provides an environment in which microoperations are executed. The function of the control unit is to initiate the sequence of microoperations. The total number of available microoperations in a system is finite. The complexity of the digital system is derived from the number of sequences of microoperations that are performed.

The control function that specifies a microoperation is a binary variable. When it is in one state, the corresponding microoperation is executed. In the opposite binary state it does not change the state of the registers in the system. The active state may be either 1 or it may be 0, depending upon the particular application.

Like in a bus organised system, 14 bit control word specifies the control signal that select the paths in multiplexers, decoders and arithematic logic units. The control variables at any given time can be represented by a string of 1's and 0's called a control word.

In general, there are two main approaches for realizing a control unit.

(*i*) Hardwired control unit

(*ii*) Microprogrammed control unit.

A more advanced development known as dynamic microprogramming permits a micropro-gram to be loaded initially from an auxiliary memory such as a magnetic disk. Control units that use dynamic microprogramming employ a writable control memory. A memory that is part of a control unit is known as control memory.

6.2.1 Hardwired Control Unit

When the control signals are generated by hardware using conventional logic design tech-niques, the control unit is called hardwired control unit. The hardwired approach to implementing a control unit views the controller as a sequential circuit based on different states in a machine. It can be viewed as a Finite State Machine (FSM) in which at each stage there are control signal that specifies the computer operation in response to externally supplied instruction.

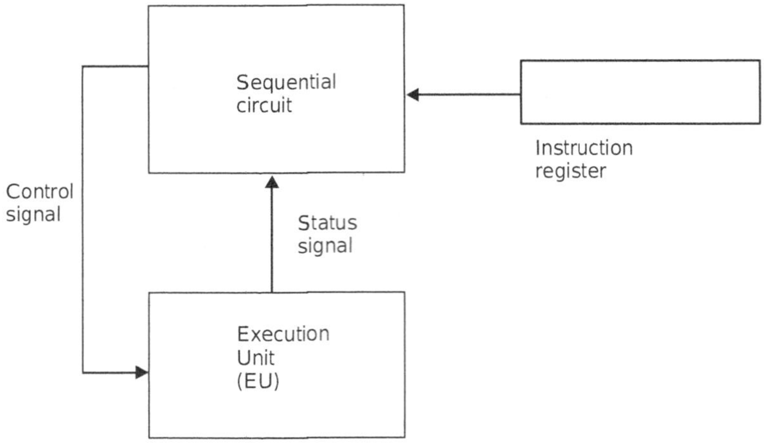

Fig. 6.2 Hardwired control unit

As shown in Fig. 6.2, externally supplied instruction are responded by control signals. It is designed with the aim of minimizing the number of gates used and maximizing the speed of operation. The main drawback of the hardwired control unit is that once the unit is constructed, it is difficult to implement the changes. The only way to implement changes in control unit is by redesigning the whole unit. A later change in the control unit requires the change of the whole circuit.

The reason for considering this a drawback is that a complete instruction set is usually not definable at the time, that a processor is being designed. However, the microprocessor design changes so rapidly, the life time of any particular processor is very short, making flexibility less of an issue. So today most of the control units are based on hardwired approach.

6.2.2 Microprogrammed Control Unit

The principle of microprogramming is an elegant and systematic method for controlling the sequences of micro operations in a digital computer. A control unit whose binary control variables are stored in memory is known as microprogrammed control unit. Each word in control memory contains within it a microinstruction. The microinstruction specifies the micro operations for the system. A sequence of microinstructions represent a microprogram. The control memory can be Read Only Memory (ROM). The contents of the words in ROM are fixed and cannot be altered by simple programming since no writing capability is there in ROM.

A microprogrammed control unit have two separate memories—a main memory and a control memory. The contents of the main memory can be altered when data are manipulated or when a program is changed. The main memory consists user program and the corresponding data. The control memory holds a fixed microprogram that cannot be altered easily. Each machine instructions initiates a series of microinstructions in control memory. These microinstructions generate the microoperations to fetch the instruction from main memory to evaluate the effective address, to execute the operation specified by the instructions, and to return control to the fetch phase in order to repeat the cycle for the next instruction.

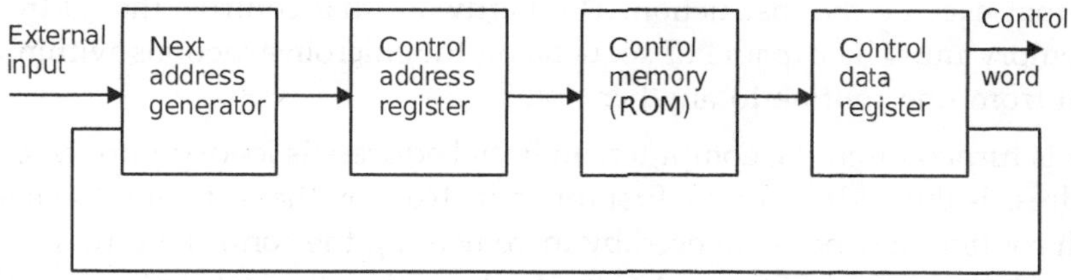

Fig. 6.3 Organisation of microprogrammed control unit

The organisation of microprogrammed control unit is shown in Fig. 6.3. The control memory is assumed to be a ROM, within which all control information is stored permanently. The control address register specifies the address of the microinstruction and the control data register holds the address of the microinstruction. The microinstruction specifies a control word that depicts the one or more microoperations to be performed. When these microinstructions are executed, the control must determine the next address. The location of the next microinstruction may be the next instruction, or it can be stored any where in the control memory. For this reason it is necessary to use some bits of the present microinstruction to control the generation of the address of the next microinstruction. The next address may be a function of external input conditions. The next address is calculated by the next address generator and it is transferred to control address register. The address of the next microinstruction is now in control address register and microinstruction is fetched from that address. Thus a microinstruction contains bits for initiating microoperations in the data processor part and bits that determine the address sequence for the control memory.

The next address generator is also known as sequencer as it determines the sequence of address that is read from the control memory. The address of the next microinstruction to be executed can be specified in several ways. By default control address register is incremented by one, loading into the control address register an address from the control memory, transferring an external address or loading an initial address to start the control operations.

The control data register holds the current micro instruction to be executed while the next address is computed and read from the memory. The data register is also known as pipeline register. It allows the execution of the microoperations specified by the control word simultaneously with the generation of the next microinstruction. The sequencer and the control memory are combinational circuits that do not need a clock.

Microprogramming makes control unit design more systematic as it organizes the control signals into formatted microinstructions. The control signals are embedded in a kind of low level software therefore it is also called as firmware.

Because the microinstructions are stored in memory, it is possible to add or change certain instructions without changing any hardware circuit. Once the hardware configuration is established, there should be no need for further hardware or wiring changes. Thus this technique is much more flexible than the hardwired approach. This approach is favoured by CISC architecture. It is slower than hardwired approach since extra time is required to fetch the micro instructions from the control memory. Most computers based on the Reduced Instruction Set Computer (RISC) architecture concept use hardwired control.

6.3 ADDRESS SEQUENCING

Microinstructions are stored in control memory in the form of groups with each group specifying a routine. Each computer instruction has its own routine in control memory to generate the microoperations that execute the instruction. The hardware that controls the address sequencing of the control memory must be capable of sequencing the microinstructions within a routine and be able to branch from one routine to another.

When power is turned on in the computer, an initial address is loaded into the control address register. This address is the address of the first micro instruction that activates the instruction fetch routine. The fetch routine may be sequenced by incrementing the control address register through the rest of its micro instructions. At the end of the fetch routine, the instruction is in the instruction register of the computer.

The control memory next must go through the routine that determines the effective address of the operand. A machine instruction may have bits that specify various addressing modes, such as indirect address and index registers. The effective address computation routine in control memory can be reached through a branch micro instruction which is conditioned on the status of the mode bits of the instructions. When the effective address computation routine is completed the address of the operand is available in the memory address register.

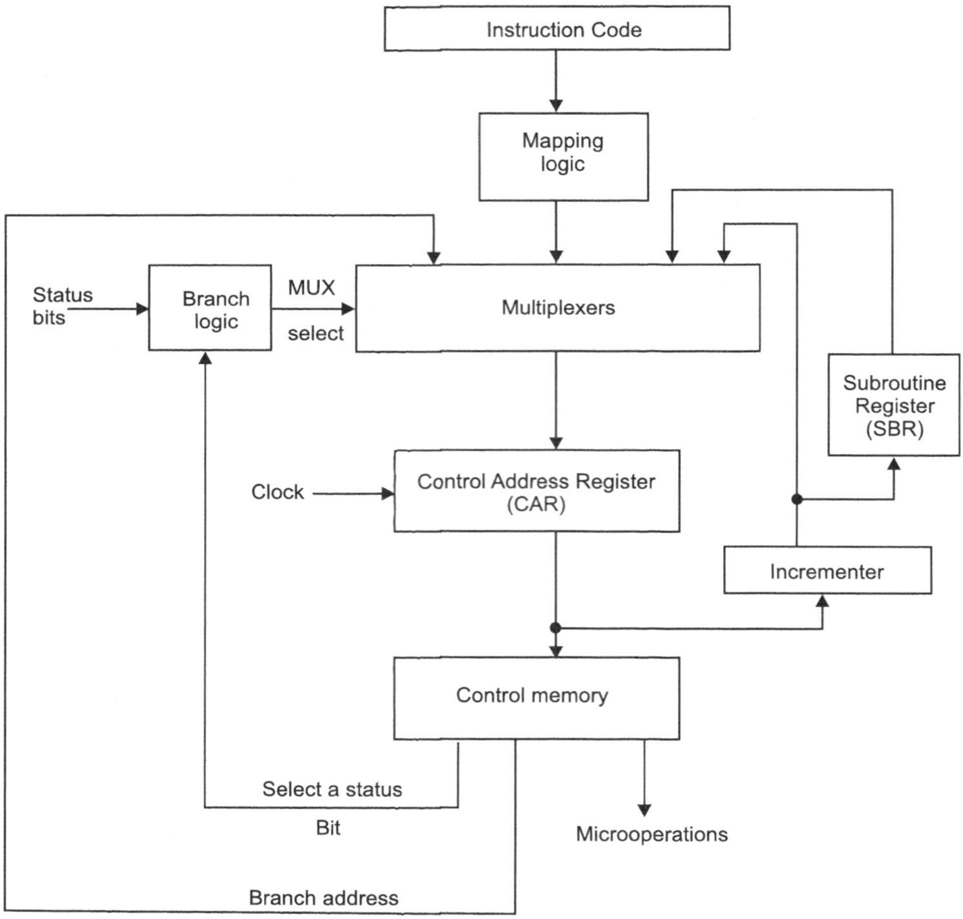

Fig 6.4 Address selection for control memory

The next step is to generate the microoperations that execute the instruction fetched from memory. The micro operation steps to be generated in processor registers depend on the opcode part of the instruction. Each instruction has its own microprogram routine stored in a given location of the control memory.

When the execution of the instruction is completed, control must return to the fetch routine. This is done by executing an unconditional branch micro instruction to the first address of the fetch routine.

The address sequencing capabilities are required in following four situations:

1. Incrementing of the control address register.
2. Unconditional branch or conditional branch depending on status bit conditions.
3. A mapping process from the bits of the instructions to an address for control memory.
4. A facility for subroutine call and return.

Fig. 6.4 shows a block diagram of a control memory and the associated hardware needed for selecting the next micro instruction address. This diagram represents four different paths from which the Control Address Register (CAR) receives the address. The incrementer increments the contents of the control address register by one, to select the next microinstruction in sequence. Branching is achieved by specifying the branch address in one of the fields of the micro instruction. Conditional branching is obtained by using part of the microinstruction to select a specific status bit in order to determine its condition. An external address is transferred via a mapping circuit. The return address for a subroutine is stored in a special register.

6.3.1 Conditional Branching

The branch logic of Fig. 6.4 provides decision making capabilities. The status bit conditions are special bits in the system that provides parameter information such as carry out, sign bit, mode bit of the instructions, and input and output status conditions. The value in these bits are checked and particular action is taken according to the value either it is 1 or 0. The status bits, together with the field in the microinstruction that specifies a branch address, control the conditional branch decisions generated in the branch logic.

The branch logic hardware may be implemented in a variety of ways. First the condition is tested and when the given condition is true, control is transferred to the specified address. If the condition is false, the address register is incremented. This is implemented using the digital component multiplexer. If there are eight status bit conditions in the system, three bits in the micro instruction are used to specify one of the eight status bit conditions. These three bits are used as selection variables for the multiplexer. A1 output in the multiplexer generates a control signal to transfer the branch address from the microinstruction into the control address register. A0 output in the multiplexer causes the address register to be incremented.

An unconditional branch micro instruction can be implemented by loading the branch address from control memory into the control address register. A reference to this bit by the status bit select lines from control memory causes the branch address to be loaded into the control address register unconditionally.

6.3.2 Mapping of Instructions

A special type of branch exists when a microinstruction specifies a branch to the first word in control memory where a micropogam routine for an instruction is located. The status bits for this type of branch are the bits in the opcode part of the instructions. To understand the mapping logic, let us consider an example, a computer with a simple instruction format as shown in

Fig. 6.5 has an operation code of four bits which can specify upto 16 distinct instructions. Let us assume that the control memory has 64 words. 64 words require an address of 6 bits. For each opcode there exists a microprogram routine in control memory that executes the instruction. One simple mapping process that converts the 4 bit operation code to 6 bit address for control memory is shown in Fig. 6.5.

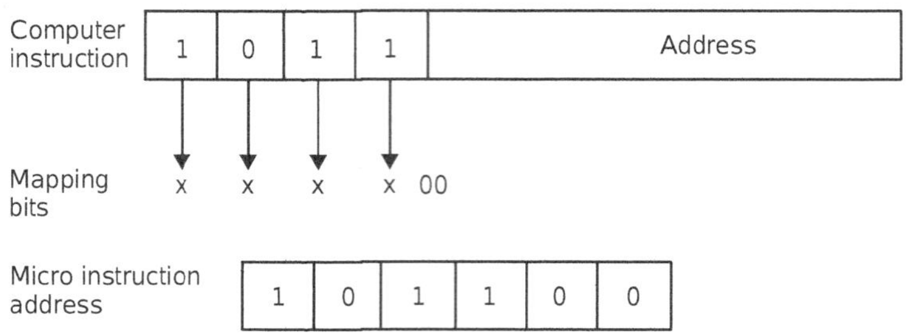

Fig. 6.5 Mapping from instruction code to microinstruction address

This mapping consists of transferring the four opcode bits and clearing the two least significant bits of the control memory address register. If the routine needs more than four micro instructions it can use addresses XXXX01 through XXXX11. If it used fewer, then four microinstructions, the unused memory locations would be available for other routines.

One can extend this concept to a more general mapping rule by using a ROM to specify the mapping function. In this configuration, the bits of the instruction specify the address of a mapping ROM. The contents of the mapping ROM give the bits for the control address register. In this way the microprogram routine that executes the instruction can be placed in any desired location in control memory. The mapping concept provides flexibility for adding instructions for control memory as the requirement arises.

6.3.3 Subroutines

Subroutines are a set of microinstructions to accomplish a particular task. It is in the form of subprograms when there is calling to the subroutine. The body of the subroutine is executed. A subroutine can be called from any point within the main body of the microprogram. Microinstructions can be saved by employing subroutines that use common sections of microcode. For example, the sequence of microoperations needed to generate the effective address of the operand for an instruction is common to all memory reference instructions. This sequence can be written in the form of a subroutine that is called from within many other routines to execute the effective address computation.

Microprograms that use subroutines must have a provision for storing the return address during a subroutine call and restoring the address during a subroutine return.

This may be accomplished by placing the incremented output from the control address register into a subroutine register and branching to the begining of the subroutine. Subroutine call and return is implemented using the last in first out data structure stack.

6.4 MICROINSTRUCTION FORMAT

The microinstruction format for the control memory is shown in Fig. 6.6.

3	3	3	2	2	7
F_1	F_2	F_3	CD	BR	AD

Fig 6.6 Microinstruction code format

The 20 bits of the micro instruction are divided into four functional parts. The three fields F1, F2 and F3 specify micro operations for the computer. CD stands for conditional branching that selects status bit conditions. The BR field specifies the type of branch to be used. The AD field Contains a branch address.

The 7 bits of address can specify a control memory that has 128 words.

The micro operations are divided into three fields of three bits each. The three bits in the fields F1, F2 and F3 specify 7 different microoperations. This gives a total of 21 microoperations. No more than three micro operations can be chosen for a micro instructions, one from each field. Binary code 000 specifies no operations. These distinct micro operations are represented in Tables 6.1, 6.2 and 6.3.

Table 6.1

F1	*Microoperations*	*Symbol*
000	None	NOP
001	AC ← AC + DR	ADD
010	AC ← 0	CLRAC
011	AC ← AC + 1	INCAC
100	AC ← DR	DRTAC
101	AR ← DR	DRTAR
110	AR ← PC	PCTAR
111	M [AR] ← DR	WRITE

Table 6.2

F2	*Microoperations*	*Symbol*
000	None	NOP
001	AC ← AC – DR	SUB
010	AC ← AC $\cup$ DR	OR
011	AC ← AC $\cap$ DR	AND
100	DR ← M [AR]	READ
101	DR ← AC	ACTDR
110	DR ← DR + 1	INCDR
111	DR [0–10] ← PC	PCTDR

Table 6.3

F3	*Microoperations*	*Symbol*
000	None	NOP
001	AC ← AC $\oplus$ DR	XOR
010	AC ← $\overline{AC}$	COM
011	AC ← Shl AC	SHL

100	AC ← Shr AC	SHR
101	PC ← PC + 1	INCPC
110	PC ← AR	ARTPC
111	Reversed	

Simultaneously two micro operations can be specified from F2 and F3. It is important to realize that two or more conflicting micro operations cannot be specified simultaneously for example, a micro operations field 011 001 000 has no meaning because it specifies two micro operations simultaneously incrementing AC and subtract DR from AC at the same time.

Each microoperations in table 6.1 is defined with a register transfer statement and is assigned a symbol for use in symbolic micro program. The CD field consists of two bits that are encoded to specify four status bit conditions as listed in Table 6.4.

Table 6.4

CD	*Condition*	*Symbol*	*Comments*
00	Always = 1	U	Unconditional branch
01	DR (15)	I	Indirect address bit
10	AC (15)	S	Sign bit of AC
11	AC = 0	Z	Zero Value in AC

The BR field contains two bits. It is used in conjunction with the address field AC, to choose the address of the next micro instructions. As shown in Table 6.5.

Table 6.5

BR	*Symbol*	*Function*
00	JMP	CAR ← AD if condition = 1
		CAR ← CAR + 1 if condition = 0
01	CALL	CAR ← AC, SBR ← CAR + 1 if condition = 1
		CAR ← CAR + 1 if condition = 0
10	RET	CAR ← SBR (Return from Subroutine)
11	MAP	CAR (2 – 5) ← DR (11 – 14)
		CAR (0, 1, 6) ← 0

There are two types of microinstruction formats.

(1) Horizontal format

(2) Vertical format.

6.4.1 Horizontal Format

Horizontal microinstructions has following attributes:

(*i*) Long formats

(*ii*) Ability to express a high degree of parallelism

(*iii*) Little encoding of control information

Ex. IBM system/360 uses horizontal format microinstruction.

(*a*) Here instructions of 30 bits which are portioned into separate fields

(*b*) There are 21 control fields shown in shaded.

(*c*) Remaining fields are used *n* generate next equivalent add and detect errors by means of parity facts for 3 bit control field consisting of 65 : 67 control input main add of CPU. This field indicates which one of several possible register should be connected to address input.

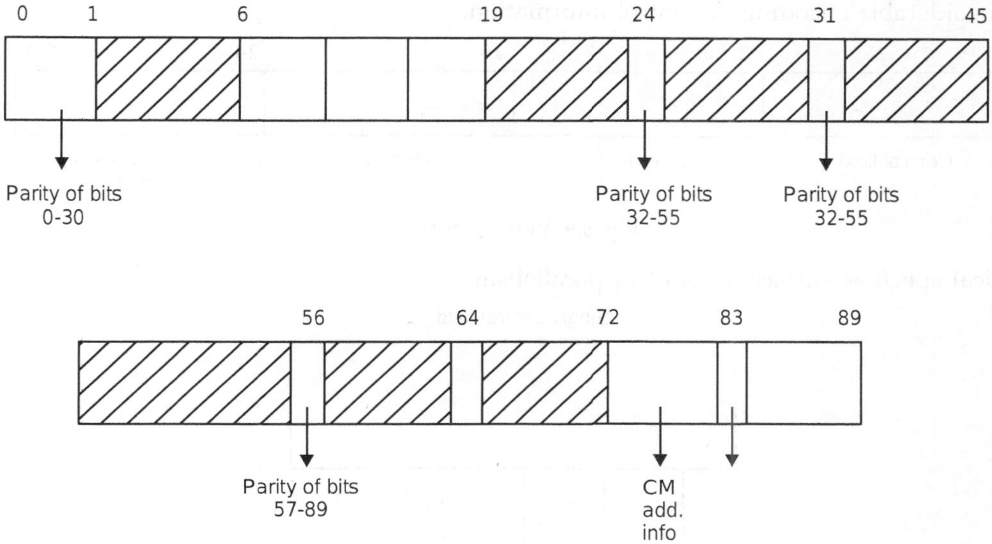

Fig. 6.7 Horizontal format

Bit 68 : 71 indentify function to be performed by adder with various ways of handling input carry bits.

The scheme of using control field for every control signal is wasteful of C.M. space because most of the combinations of control signals one nearer used.

For example register R can be loaded from any one of the four independent sources under control of 21 separate signals C_0, C_1, C_2, C_3.

The possible implementation is

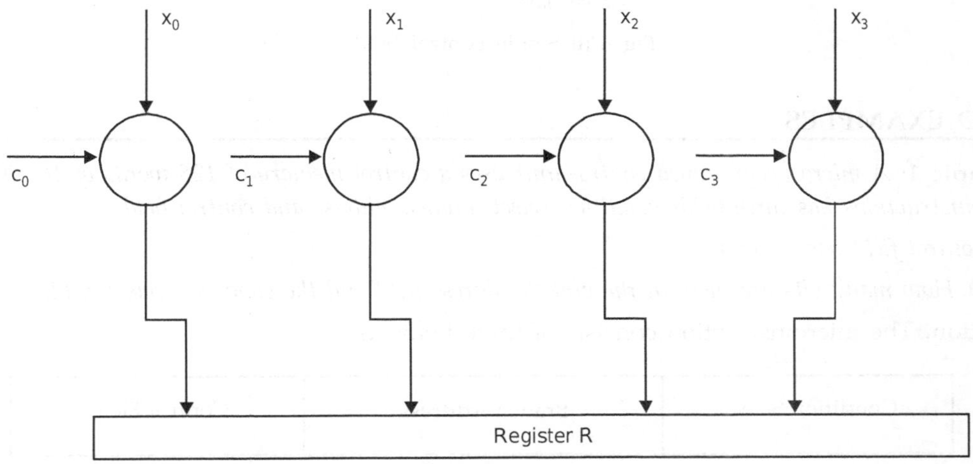

Fig 6.8 Implementation

6.4.2 Vertical Format

Vertical microinstructions has the following attributes:

(1) Short formats

(2) Limited ability to express parallelism

(3) Considerable encoding of control information.

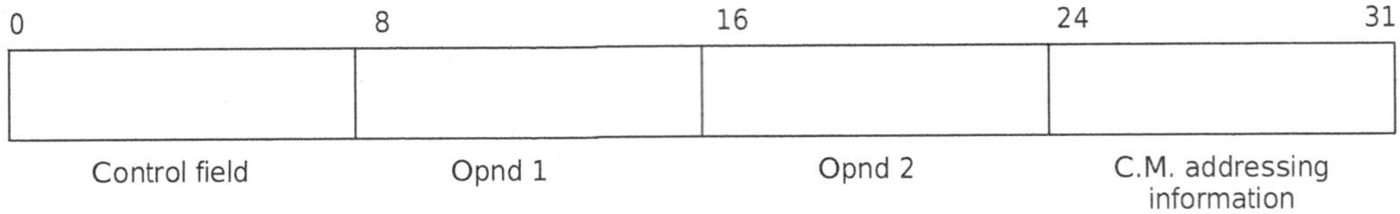

Fig 6.9 Vertical format

Vertical specifies surface amount of parallelism

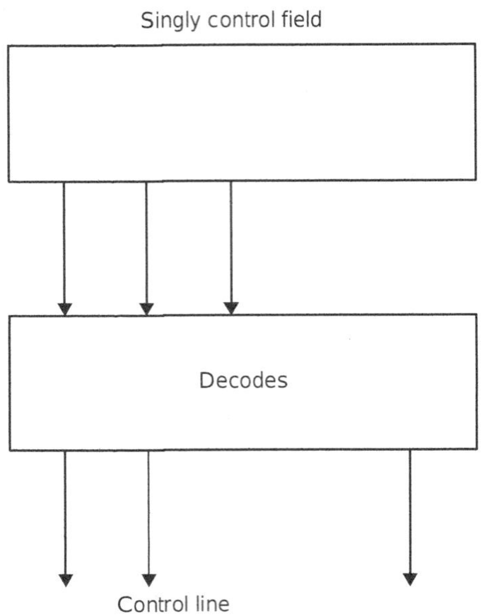

Fig 6.10 Single control field

SOLVED EXAMPLES

Example 1: *A micro programmed control unit uses a control memory of 128 words of 16 bits each. The microinstructions has three fields condition select, branch address and control field.*

The control field has 20 bits:

(i) How many bits are there in the branch address field and the condition select field.

Solution. The microinstruction consists of three fields as:

Condition Select	Branch Address	Control Field

As the microinstruction has 16 bits.

The control memory is having 128 words.

$$2^7 = 128$$

So we need 7 bits for the branch address field. The control field has 8 bits

Therefore,

$$\text{Bits in select field} = (16 - 2 + 7) = 7 \text{ bit.}$$

Example 2: *If there are 8 status bits in the systems how many bits of the branch logic are used to select a status bit.*

Solution. If there are 8 status bits in the system we need 3 bits for the branch logic to select a status bit as $2^3 = 8$.

Example 3: *How many bits are left to select an input for the multiplexer.*

Solution. Therefore out of 7 bits for condition select as 3 bits are used to select a status bit, 4 bits are used as multiplexer select.

EXERCISES

1. Define the following:
   (*a*) Microoperations (*b*) Microinstructions
   (*c*) Microprogram (*d*) Microcode
2. Explain how the mapping from an instruction code to a micro instruction address can be done by means of read only memory.
3. A microprogrammed control unit uses a control memory of 1024 words of 32 bits each. The micro instruction has three fields condition select, Branch address and control field. The control field has 16 bits.
4. How many bits are there in the branch address field and the condition select field?
5. If there are 16 status bits in the system. How many bits of the branch logic are used to select a status bit?
6. How many bits are left to select an input for the multiplexer?
7. Explain the organisation of a micro programmed control unit and describe its operations. *[Raj. Univ.]*
8. Explain the difference between hardwired control and microprogrammed control. Is it possible to have a hardwired control?

Chapter 7

MEMORY ORGANISATION

7.1 INTRODUCTION

The memory unit is an essential component of any digital computer system since it is needed for storing programs and data. Memory unit is capable of storing the programs and the data that are needed to perform a particular task. A CPU should have rapid , uninterrupted access to these memories so that it can operate at or near its maximum speed. The goal of every memory system is to provide adequate storage capacity with acceptable level of performance and cost. There is not enough space in one memory unit to accomodate all the programs used in a typical computer, not all the accumulated information is required by the processor at the same time. Therefore it is more economical to use low-cost storage devices to serve as a backup for storing the information that is not currently used by the CPU. Following all the some criterea on which we decide which memory unit is to be used.

1. Cost
2. Speed
3. Memory access time
4. Data transfer rate
5. Reliability
6. Memory cycle time.

In this chapter we will discuss about various memory device organisation. There are various types of memories some provides good speed but they are costly, some provide less speed but they are cheaper so we discuss the organisation of various memory units.

7.2 MEMORY HIERARCHY

The total memory capacity of a computer can be visualized by the hierarchy of components. This hierarchy system consists of all storage devices employed in a computer system from the slow but high capacity auxiliary memory to a relatively faster main memory, to an even smaller and faster cache memory accessible to the high speed processing logic. Fig. 7.1 depicts memory hierarchy system. The system can be visualized at three levels.

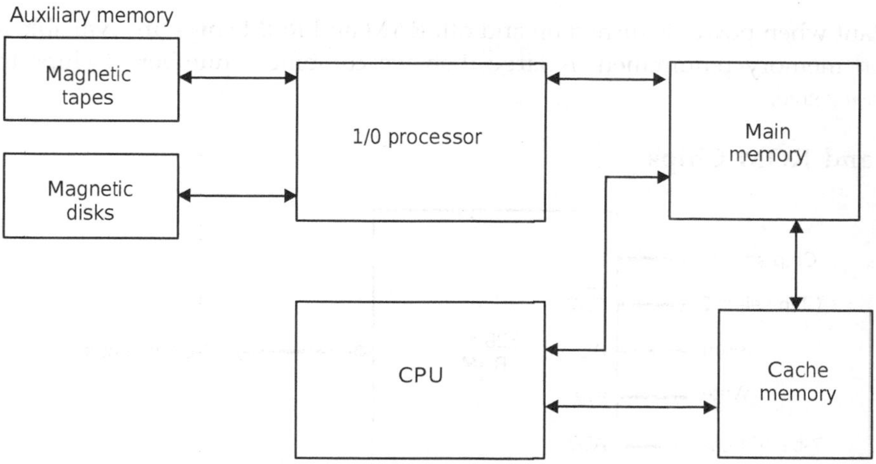

Fig. 7.1 Memory hierarchy

At the bottom level there is auxiliary memory. Auxiliary memory is slow but due to its low cost it is present in large volume. This memory is not directly connected with the CPU. Programs that are not currently needed in main memory are transferred into auxiliary memory that provides the space for the programs that is to be reside in main memory presently. At the second level there is main memory. It is the called central memory as it is directly connected to the CPU. The data and programs that are currently needed by the CPU, resides in the main memory only. At the top level there is a very special high speed memory called cache that provides speed that is comparable to the speed of CPU. It increases the speed of processing by making current programs and data available to the CPU at a rapid rate. This memory is used to compensate the speed difference between the main memory and CPU.

The access time of this memory is close to processor logic clock cycle time. By making programs and data available at a rapid rate, it is possible to increase the performance rate of the computer. I/O processor manages the data transfers between auxiliary memory and the main memory.

The memory hierarchy system consists of all storage devices employed in a computer system from the slow but high capacity auxiliary memory to a relatively faster main memory, to an even smaller and faster cache memory accessible to the high speed processing logic.

7.3 MAIN MEMORY

The main memory is the control storage device of a computer system. It is relatively large and fast memory that is used to store the data and programs that are currently needed by CPU. The principal technology behind the main memory is based on semiconductor integrated circuits. Integrated circuit RAM chips are available in two possible operating modes, static and dynamics. The main difference between SRAMs and DRAMs is how their bit cells all constructed. The dynamic RAM provides reduced power consumption and larger storage capacity in a single memory chip. The static RAM is easier to use and has shorter read and write cycles. Main memory is made up of RAM and ROM chips. RAM is used to store the programs and data that is to be changed while ROM is used for storing the programs that are permanently resident in the computer.

ROM portion of the main memory is needed for storing the initial program that is known as bootstrap program that runs on the computer when power is turned on. The contents of ROM remains constant when power is turned on and off. RAM and ROM chips are available in a variety of sizes. When memory requirement is large then we combine a number of chips to form the required memory size.

7.3.1 RAM and ROM Chips

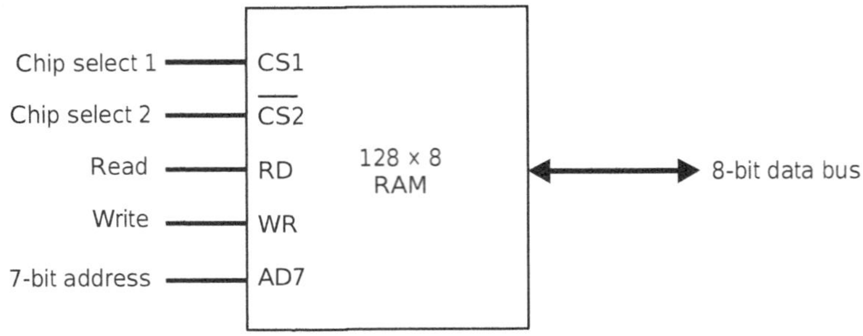

(a) Block diagram

Fig. 7.2 RAM chip

Fig. 7.2 depicts a typical RAM chip. RAM chips are better suited for communicating with the CPU. It has bi-directional data bus that allows the transfer of data in both the direction. A bi-directional bus can be constructed using three state buffers. A three state buffer output can be placed in one of the possible three states. The capacity of RAM chip is 128 × 8 means there are 128 words each word is of 8 bits.

For 128 words we require an address line of 7 bits since $2^7 = 128$. The read and write inputs specify the memory operation and the two Chips Select (CS) control inputs are for enabling the chip only when it is selected by the microprocessor. The function table is listed in Table 7.1.

Table 7.1 Function table

CS1	$\overline{CS2}$	*RD*	*WR*	*Memory function*	*State of data bus*
0	0	X	X	Inhibit	High Impedance
0	1	X	X	Inhibit	High Impedance
1	0	0	0	Inhibit	High Impedance
1	0	0	1	Write	Input data to RAM
1	0	1	X	Read	Output data from RAM
1	1	X	X	Inhibit	High Impedance

The unit is in operations only when CS1 = 1 and $\overline{CS2}$ = 0. In this combination the memory can be placed in a write or read mode. When WR input is enabled, a byte is stored from the data bus into a location that is specified by the address input lines. When RD input is enabled, the content of the selected byte is placed into the data bus.

A ROM chip is organised in a similar manner. Read Only Memories (ROMs) are memory divices that the CPU can read but cannot write. Computers use them for holding permanent information, for holding the constant values that specify the system configuration. Since a ROM can only read, the data bus can only be in an output mode. The block diagram is shown in Fig. 7.3.

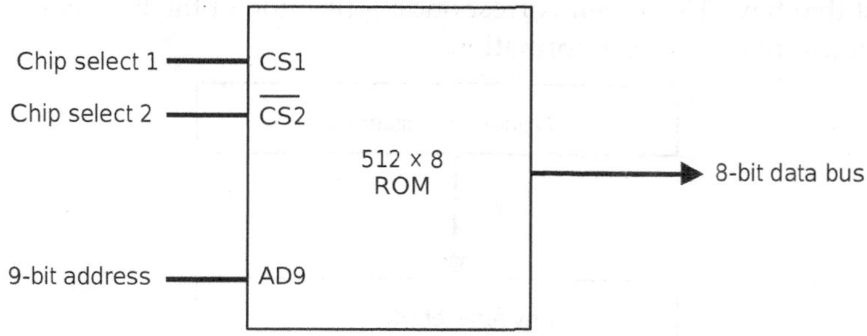

Fig. 7.3 Block diagram ROM chips

The nine address lines in the ROM chip specify anyone of the 512 bytes stored in it. The two chip select inputs must be CS1 = 1 and $\overline{CS2}$ = 0 for the unit to operate.

7.4 ASSOCIATIVE MEMORY

Many program and data processing applications require searching of data items that are stored in a table in memory. For searching the particular data item in a table first we choose a sequence of addresses, reading the content of memory of each address and comparing the information with the required data item being searched until a match occurs. The number of memory access depends upon the location of the data item and the efficiency of the search algorithm.

The time required to find an item that is stored in the memory can be reduced considerably if stored data can be identified by the contents itself rather then by the address. Associative memory is an approach towards this concept. A memory unit that is accessed by the contents is called associative memory or Content Addressable Memory (CAM). Every word in this memory is identified by the contents rather than any address. When a word is stored in associative memory, no address is given. The memory is capable of finding the empty or unused location to store the word. When a word is to be read from an associative memory, the content of the word or part of the word is specified. The memory locates all words which match the specified content and marks them for reading.

Associative memory provides parallel searching. Searching can be performed on the entire word or on a specific field within the world. This memory is expensive memory because there is a logic circuit that is corresponding to each word of the associative memory. So this memory is used where search time is very critical factor.

7.4.1 Hardware Organisation

The block diagram of associative memory is depicted in Fig. 7.4. It consists of a memory array and logic for m words where each word is containing n bit. There are two registers argument registers and the key registers, each is having n bits. Match register M is having m bits one for the each word. Each word of the associative memory is compared with the contents of the argument register when a match occurs corresponding bit in the match register is set. After the matching process, those bits in the match register that are set indicate that their corresponding words have been matched. Reading is accomplished by a sequential access to memory for those words whose corresponding bits in the match register have been set.

The key register provides a mask for choosing a particular field as key in the argument word. If the argument register is containing all 1's then whole word is compared otherwise, only those bits in the argument that have 1's in their corresponding position of the key register are compared. So it helps in providing the piece of information.

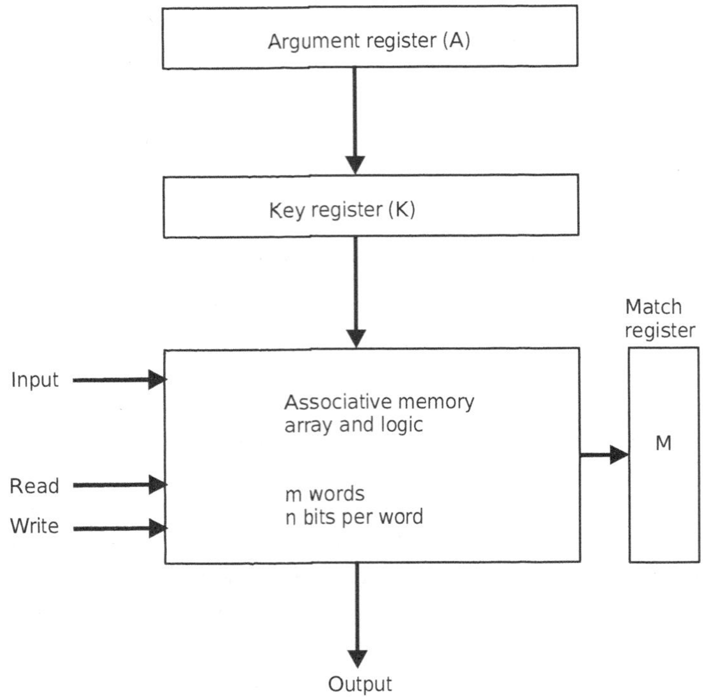

Fig. 7.4 Block diagram

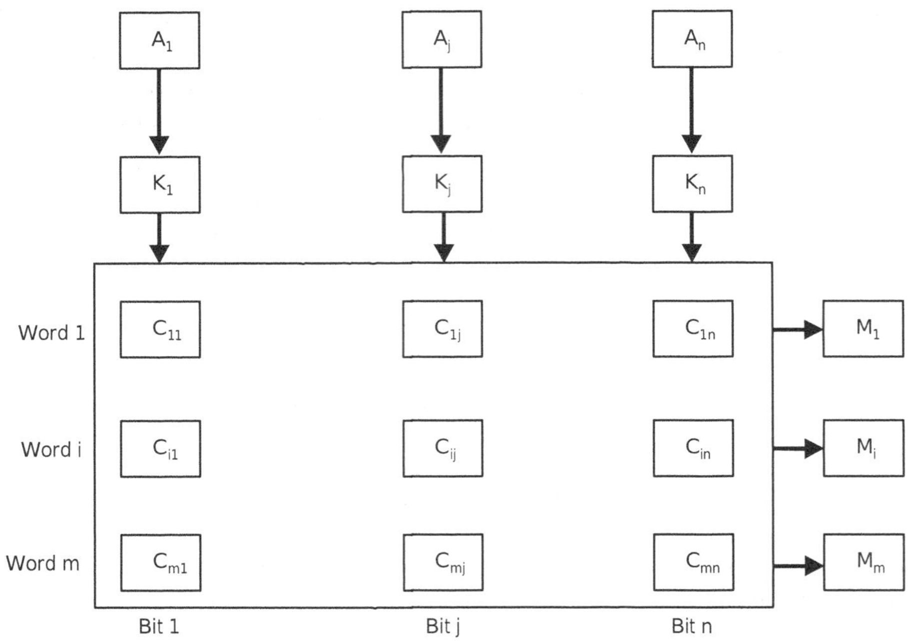

Fig. 7.5 Associative memory of *m* words, *n* cells per word.

Let us take an example:

A	111	10010	
K	101	10001	
Word 1	100	10010	No Match
Word 2	101	00010	No Match
Word 3	101	10000	Match

As there are four 1's in the key register, we have to match the corresponding four bits. Word 3 matches the unmasked argument field. The relation between memory array key register and argument register is shown in Fig. 7.5. The cells in the array are represented in the form of 2 dimensional array. Each cell is marked with the letter C having two subscripts. First subscript represents the word number and the second subscript represents the bit position in the number. Like cell *cij* represents the jth bit position is the ith word. A bit *Aj* in the argument register is compared with all the bits in column *j* of the array provided that *kj* = 1.

This is done for all columns *j* = 1, 2......, *n*. If a match occures between all the unmasked bits of the argument and the bits in word *i* the corresponding bit M*i* in the match register is set to 1.

7.4.2 Match Logic

The internal organisation is of a cell is shown in Fig. 7.6.

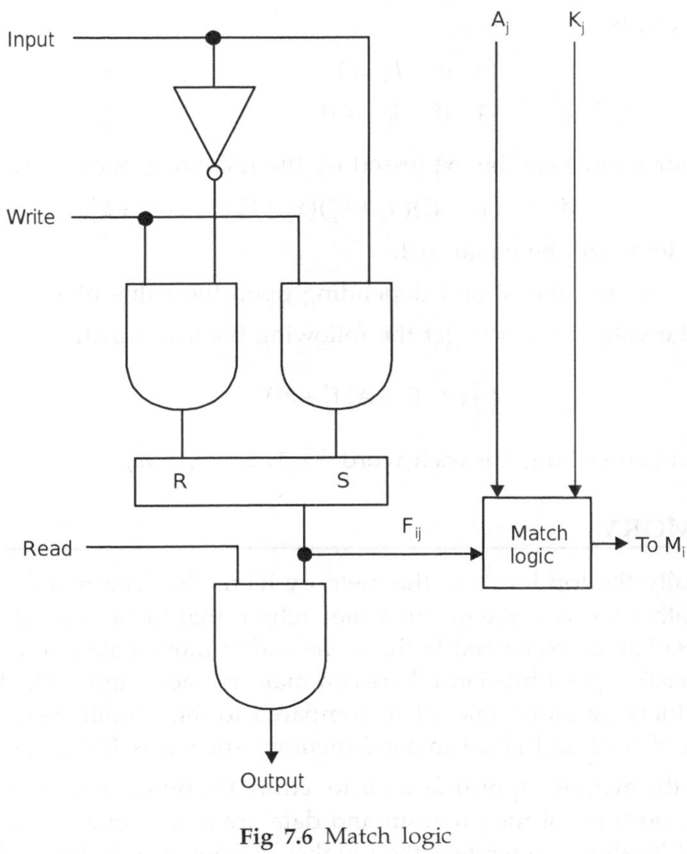

Fig 7.6 Match logic

This internal organisation consists of storage element flip flop F_{ij} and the circuit for reading, writing and matching the cell. The match logic can be derived from the comparision algorithm of two binary numbers. First we neglect the key bits and compare the argument in A with the bits stored in the cells of the words.

Word i is equal to the argument in A if $A_j = F_{ij}$ for $j = 1, 2......, n$. The equality of two bits can be expressed logically as

$$X_j = A_j F_{ij} + A'_j F'_{ij}$$

where

$$X_j = 1 \text{ if the bits are equal}$$

otherwise $X_j = 0.$

for any word i to be equal to the argument in register A, all X_j variables to 1. The boolean function for this condition can be defined as:

$$M_i = X_1 X_2 X_3......X_n.$$

This implies AND operation of all matched bits in the word.

Now we include the concept of key bit kj.

if $k_j = 0$, there is no comparision between A_j and F_{ij}.

if $k_j = 1$, A_j and F_{ij} must be compared.

This can be achieved by

$$x_j + k_j' = \begin{cases} x_j \text{ if } & k_j = 1 \\ 1 \text{ if } & k_j = 0 \end{cases}$$

The match logic for word i can be expressed by the following boolean function:

$$M_j = (x_1 + k_1')(x_2 + k_2')(x_2 + k_3')........(x_n + k_n')$$

when $k_j = 0$ each term will be equal to 1.

if $k_j = 1$ the term will be either 0 or 1 depending upon the value of x_j.

On substituting the value of x_j. We get the following boolean function.

$$M_i = \prod_{J=1}^{n} (A_j F_{ij} + A'_j f'_{ij} + k'_j)$$

we need m such functions, one for each word $i = 1, 2, 3......., m$.

7.5 CACHE MEMORY

Caches are generally the top levels of the memory hierarchy. The main structural difference between a cache and other levels in the memory hierarchy is that caches include hardware to track the memory addresses that are contained in the cache and to move data into and out of the cache as necessary. There exist a speed inbalance between main memory and CPU. Fetches from main memory require considerably more time when compared to the overall speeds in the processor, designers spend a lot of time and effort making memory speeds as fast as possible.

One way to make the memory appear faster is to reduce the number of times main memory has to be accessed. Active portions of the program and data are placed in a fast small memory, then due to the property of locality of reference, the number of references to the main memory will be drastically reduced. Such a fast small memory is called cache memory. It is placed between CPU and the main memory. The cache is the fastest component in the memory hierarchy and approaches the speed of CPU components.

Because cache memory is expensive, a computer system can have only a limited amount of it installed. Therefore, in a computer system there is a relatively large and slower main memory coupled together with a faster and smaller cache memory. The cache containes copies of some blocks of the main memory.

So when there is a request for a word by CPU, there will be no need to go to the larger and slower main memory.

The performance of a system can be greatly improved if the cache is placed on the same chip as the processor. The basic operations of the cache is that when the CPU needs to access the memory, first the cache is examined. If the word is present in the cache, it is read from the cache memory and it is known as a hit. If the word addressed by the CPU is not present in the cache memory then, the main memory is accessed to read the word. This is called a miss. A block of words containing the one just accessed is then transfered from main memory cache memory. The performance of the cache memory is measured in terms of the hit ratio. Hit ratio is defined as the number of hits divided by the total number of CPU references to memory. This high ratio verifies the validity of the locality of reference property.

Two types of operations can be requested by the CPU:

(1) Read operation

(2) Write operation.

7.5.1 Read Operation

When the CPU generates a read request for a word in memory. The generated request is first sent to the cache. We check that the word is present in the cache or not. If the word is residing the cache, it is sent to the CPU. If the word is not found in the cache, then request is transferred to the main memory. It is known a read miss. A copy of the word is stored in the cache memory for the future reference. If the cache is full a predetermined replacement policy is used to swap out a word from the cache in order to accomodate the new word. When a hit occurs, we do not require any fetch from the main memory. This speeds up the system.

7.5.2 Write Operation

An important aspect of cache organisation is memory write requests. In the read operation when the word is present in the cache memory the main memory is not involved in the transfer. When the CPU generates a write request for a word in memory, the generated request is first sent to the cache if the word currently resides in the cache. If the word is not present in the cache, a copy of the word is transferred into the cache. Next, a write operations is performed. There are two ways that the hardware may employ.

(1) Write through method

(2) Write back method.

7.5.2.1 Write Through Method

This is the simplest method. Main memory is updated every time whenever a memory write operations is performed. With cache memory updated in paralled if it contains the word at the specified address. The advantage of the write through method is that the main memory always has consistent data with the cache. Every time main memory is updated. The disadvantage of this method is that all write operations require access to the main memory, that is time consuming. It results in slowing down the speed of the system.

Write through caches are somewhat simpler to design and are sometimes used when another device is allowed to access the next level of the memory hierarchy.

7.5.2.2 Write Back Method

In write back method every word in the cache has a bit associated with it that is called dirty bit, which tells that the word is modified in the cache or not. When during the write operation, the word in the cache is modified then the dirty bit is set. All changes are performed in the cache only. When there is time to swapped out the word from cache then we check the value of the dirty bit. If dirty bit is set then the word is written back to the main memory in updated form.

The advantage of the write back method is that as long as a word stays in the cache it may be modified several times and, for the CPU, it does not matter if the word in the main memory has not been updated. The disadvantage of this method is that only extra bit has to be associated with each word, that makes the design of the system slightly more complex.

7.5.3 Basic Cache Organisation

The basic motivation behind using cache memories in computer systems is their speed. The transformation of data from main memory to cache memory is called a mapping process. The translations of the memory address, specified by the CPU is done into the possible location of the corresponding word in the cache.

Based on the mapping process, cache organisation is classified into three types:

(1) Associative mapping cache

(2) Direct mapping cache

(3) Set-associative mapping cache.

In the next section, we are going to discuss these three methods. To help in the discussion of these three mapping procedures we will use a specific example of a memory organisation. The main memory can store 32K words of 12 bits each. The cache memory is capable of storing 256 of these word at any given time. For every word stored in cache, there is a duplicate copy in main memory. The CPU communicates with both memories. We are considering that CPU generates a read request.

7.5.3.1 Associative Mapping Cache

In an associative mapping cache, both the address and the contents are stored as one word in the cache. This results in a memory word is allowed to be stored at any location in the cache making it the most flexible cache organisation. Fig. 7.7 illustrates this organisation. The address value of 15 bits is shown as a five digit octal number and its corresponding 12 bit word as a four digit octal number. CPU address (15 bits) is placed in the argument register and the associative memory is searched for a matching address. If the required address is found 12 bit data is read and it is sent to the CPU. If no match found, the request is transferred to the main memory. The data is transferred to the associative cache for the future reference. If the cache is full, a predetermined replacement policy is used. Since each associative memory cell is many times more expensive than a RAM cell, only the addresses of the words are stored in the associative part, while the data can be stored in RAM part of the cache because only the address is used for associative search.

The major disadvantage of this method is its need for a large associative memory, which is very expensive and increases the access time of the cache memory.

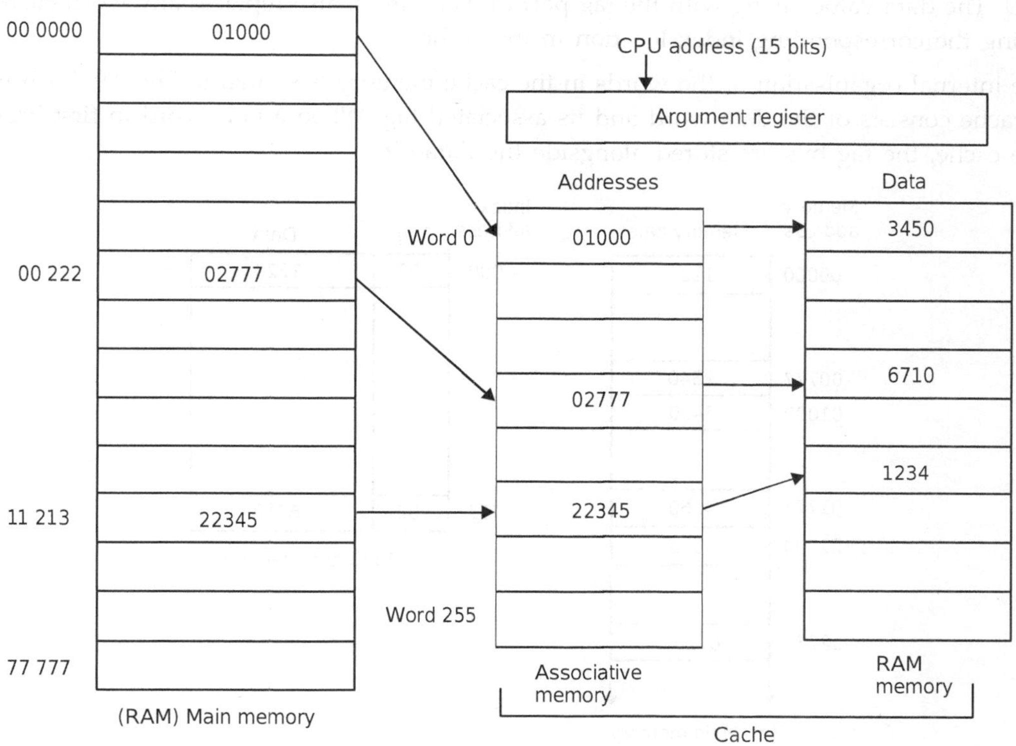

Fig. 7.7 Associative mapping cache

7.5.3.2 Direct Mapping Cache

Since associative memories are very expensive, an alternative cache organisation, known as a direct mapping cache may be used. In this organisation, RAM memories are used as the storage mechanism for the cache. In a direct mapping cache, CPU address is divided into two parts. An

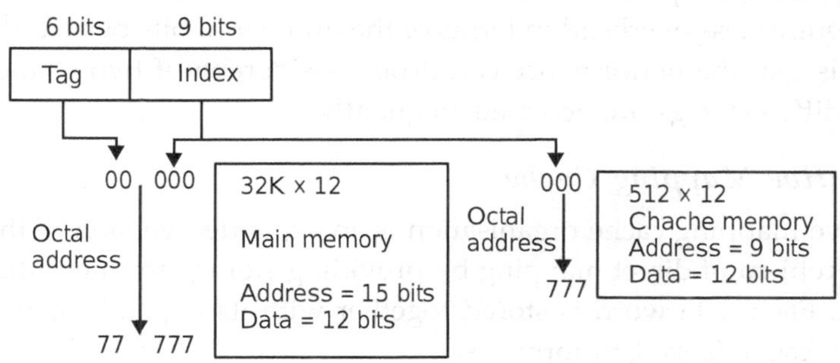

Fig 7.8 Direct mapping cache

index field and a tag field. The index field is used as an address to a location in the cache where the data are located. At this index a tag and a data value are stored in the cache. If the tag of the requested memory address matches the tag of the cache, the data value is sent to the CPU. Otherwise the main memory is accessed and the corresponding data value is fetched and sent to the CPU. The data value, along with the tag part of its address, also replaces any word currently occupying the corresponding index location in the cache.

The internal organisation of the words in the cache memory is shown in Fig. 7.9. Each word in the cache consists of the data word and its associated tag. When a new word in first brought into the cache, the tag bits are stored alongside the data bits.

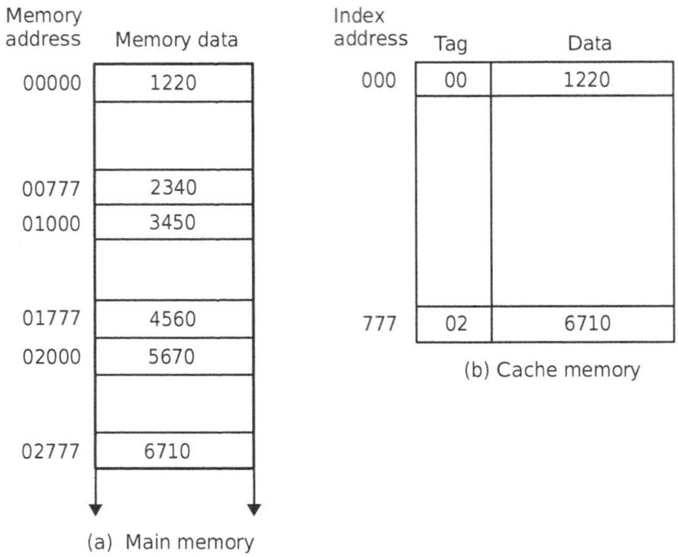

Fig. 7.9 Direct mapping example

When the CPU generates a memory request, the index field is used for the address to access the cache. The tag field of the CPU address is compared with the tag in the word read from the cache. If the two tags match, the desired word is present in cache. If there is no match, there is a miss and the required word is read from the main memory. It is then stored in the cache together with the new tag, replacing the previous value. The advantage of direct mapping over associative mapping is that it requires less overhead in terms of the number of bits per word in the cache. The major disadvantage is that the performance can drop considerably if two or more words having the same index but different tags are accessed frequently.

7.5.3.3 Set-associative Mapping Cache

The set-associative mapping cache organisation is an expanded version of the direct mapping cache. It solves the problem of direct mapping by providing storage for more than one data value with the same index. Each data word is stored together with its tag and the number of tag-data items in one word of cache is said to form a set.

A set-associative cache of set size k will accomodate k words of main memory in each word of cache. When the CPU generates a memory request, the index value of the address is used to access the cache. The tag field of the CPU address is then compared with both tags in the cache to determine if a match occures. The comparision logic is done by an associative search of the tags in the set similar to an associative memory search: thus the name set-associative.

When a miss occurs in set-associative cache and the set is full, it is necessary to replace one of the tag-data items with a new value.

Index	Tag	Data	Tag	Data
000	01	3450	02	5670
777	02	6710	00	2340

Fig. 7.10 Set-associative mapping cache

7.5.4 Cache Coherence

In a shared memory multiprocessor system, all the processors share a common memory the compelling reason for having separate caches for each processor is to reduce the average access time in each processor.

To ensure the ability of the system to execute memory operations correctly, the multiple copies must be kept identical. This requirement imposes a cache coherence problem. A memory scheme is coherent if the value returned on a load instruction is always the value given by the latest store instruction with the same address.

Conditions for Incoherence: Cache coherence problem exist in multiprocessors with private caches because of the need to share writable data.

To illustrate the problem, consider two processor configuration with private caches Fig. 7.11(*a*). During the operation an element X from main memory is loaded into the two processors P_1 and P_2. As a consequence it is also copied into the private caches of the two processors. Suppose X = 52. The load on x to the two processor result in consistent copies in the caches and main memory.

If one of the processors performs a store to x, the copies of x in the caches become inconsistent. Depending on the memory update policy used in the cache, the main memory may also be inconsistent with respect to the cache. This is shown in Fig. 7.11(*b*). A store to x (of the value of 120) into the cache of processor p_1 updates memory to the new value in a write-through policy. But in a write-back policy, main memory is not updated at the time of the store.

This problem may cause in DMA (Direct Memory Access) in the case of input, the DMA may modify location in main memory that also reside in cache without updating the cache. During a DMA output memory locations may be read before they are updated from the cache when using a write-back policy.

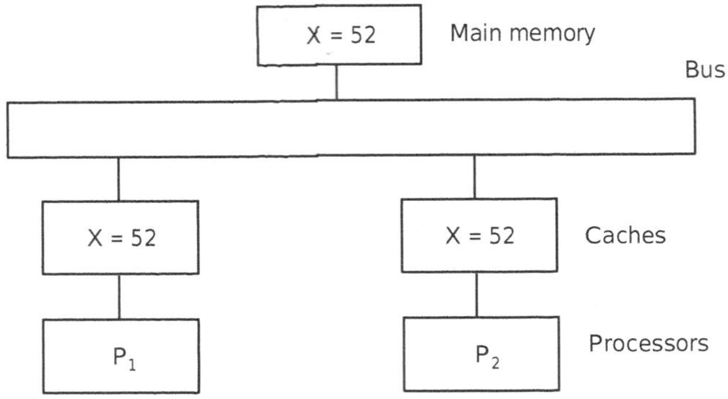

Fig. 7.11 ***(a)*** Cache configuration after a load on x

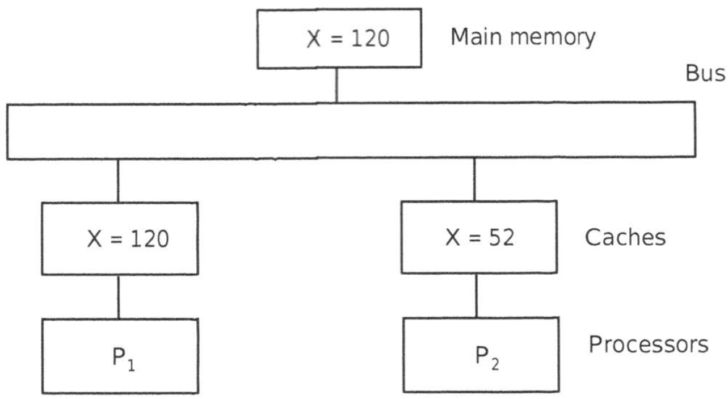

Fig. 7.11 ***(b)*** With write-through cache policy

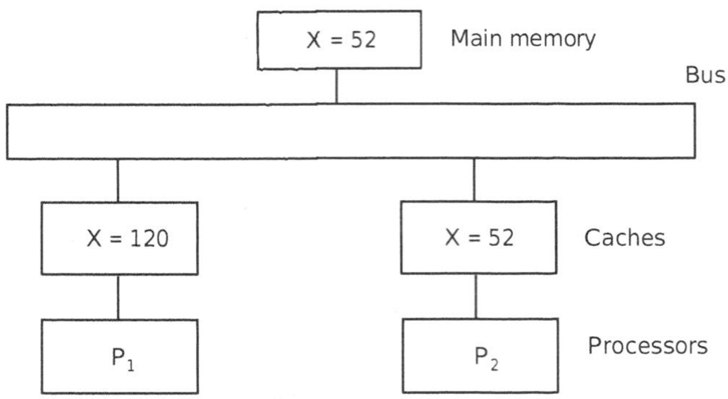

Fig. 7.11 ***(c)*** With write-back policy

Solutions to the cache Coherence problem: A simple scheme is to disallow private caches for each processor and have a shared cache memory associated with main memory. Every data access is made to the shared cache. But this scheme increase the average memory access time. In effect, this scheme solves the problem by avoiding it.

For performance considerations it is desirable to attach a private cache to each processor. One scheme that has been used allows only non-shared and read only data to be stored in cache. Such items are called cachable, shared writable data are non-cachable.

The compiler must tag data as either cachable or non cachable and the system hardware makes sure that only cachable data are stored in caches. The non-cachable data remain in main memory. This method restricts the type of data stored in caches.

Another scheme that allows writable data to exist in at least one cache is a method that employs a centralized global table in its computer. The status of memory blocks is stored in the central global table. Each block is identified as read only (RO) or read and write. All caches can have copies of blocks.

The cache coherence problem can be solved by means of a combination of software and hardware or by means of hardware-only scheme. This hardware-only solutions are handled by the hardware automatically and have the advantage of higher speed and program transparency in the hardware solutions, the cache controller is specially designed to allow it to monitor all bus request's from CPUs and IOPs.

Depending on the method used, they must then either update or invalidate their own cache copies when a match is detected. The bus controler that monitors this action is referred to as a shoopy caach controller. This is basically a hardware unit designed to maintain a bus watching mechanism overall the caches attached to the bus.

7.6 VIRTUAL MEMORY

Virtual memory is a technique that is used to both allow memory storage, such as harddisks, to serve as a level in the memory system and to provide protection between programs running on the same system. So that one program cannot modify another's data. In a memory system, programs and data are first stored auxiliary memory. When these programs and data are needed by the CPU then these are transferred into main memory. Virtual memory is a concept used in large computers permit the user to construct programs as though a large memory space were available, equal to the totality of auxiliary memory. Virtual memory allows a computer to act as if its main memory were much larger than it actually is.

In virtual memory we describe a hierarchical storage system of at least two levels, which is managed by the operating system to appear to a programmer as a single directly addressable main memory. A virtual memory system is a system wherein the logical address of an instruction of data word is likely to be different from its physical address. Each address that is referenced by the CPU goes through an address mapping from the virtual address to a physical address. The mapping is handled by the hardware automatically.

7.6.1 Address Space and Memory Space

An address that is used by the programmer is called virtual address and the set of these addresses is known as address space. An address in main memory is called physical address. It stored in memory address register. The set of such addresses is known as memory space. In most computers address space and memory space are identical. Virtual memory system allows address space to be larger than the memory space.

In a virtual memory system the operating system loads only part of a program, the currently active part in main memory one at a time. When the active part of the program requests a memory reference, the CPU resolves the effective address exactly as it would if the computer did not have virtual memory. However, it does not send the effective address directly to the main memory system. Instead, it send it to a memory map, which is part of the virtual-memory hardware. The memory map is the conceptual system translates virtual addresses into physical addresses.

7.6.2 Address Mapping Using Pages

Paging and segmentation are the two virtual memory management techniques which does this mapping of logical addresses into physical addresses. The memory map checks to see if the reference is active, that is present in main memory. If so, the memory map translates virtual addresses into physical addresses and the program executes just as if it were on a system without virtual memory. Virtual memory system generally use one or both of the two techniques paging and segmentation for mapping effective addresses into physical addresses.

Paging is a hardware-oriented technique for mapping physical memory. Using this technique large programs could run on computers with small physical memories. Paging is unrelated to the logical structure of the program, and the entire program must be created in a single unit, that is within a single logical address space for this technique to work.

In a paging system, the virtual memory hardware divides logical address into two parts:

(*a*) Virtual page number

(*b*) Page offset within the page.

The high order bits are the page number and the low order bits is the offset or displacement. the units of physical memory that hold pages are called blocks or frames.

Consider a computer with an address space of 8 *k* and a memory space of 4*k*. If we split each into group of 1*k* words then we get eight pages and four blocks as depicted in Fig. 7.12.

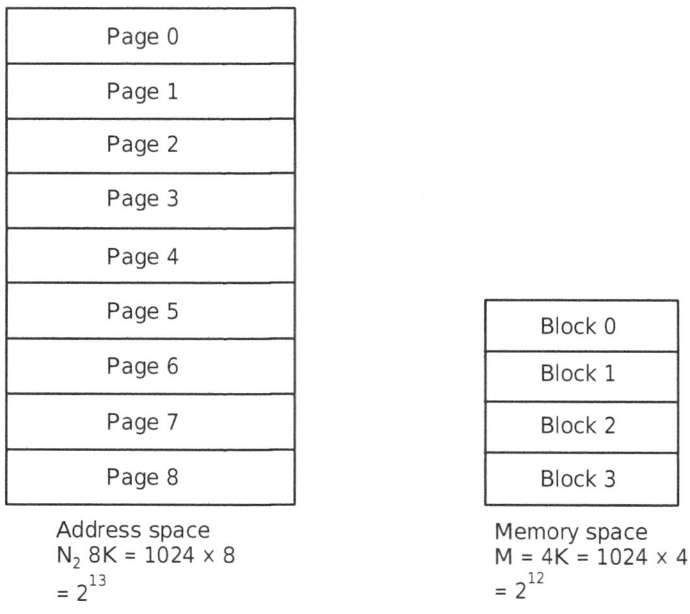

Fig. 7.12 Address space and memory space

In paged virtual memory system, the memory map is called a page map. The operating system maintains a page table, which holds various pieces of information about the program's pages Fig. 7.13 represents block diagram of a page table access.

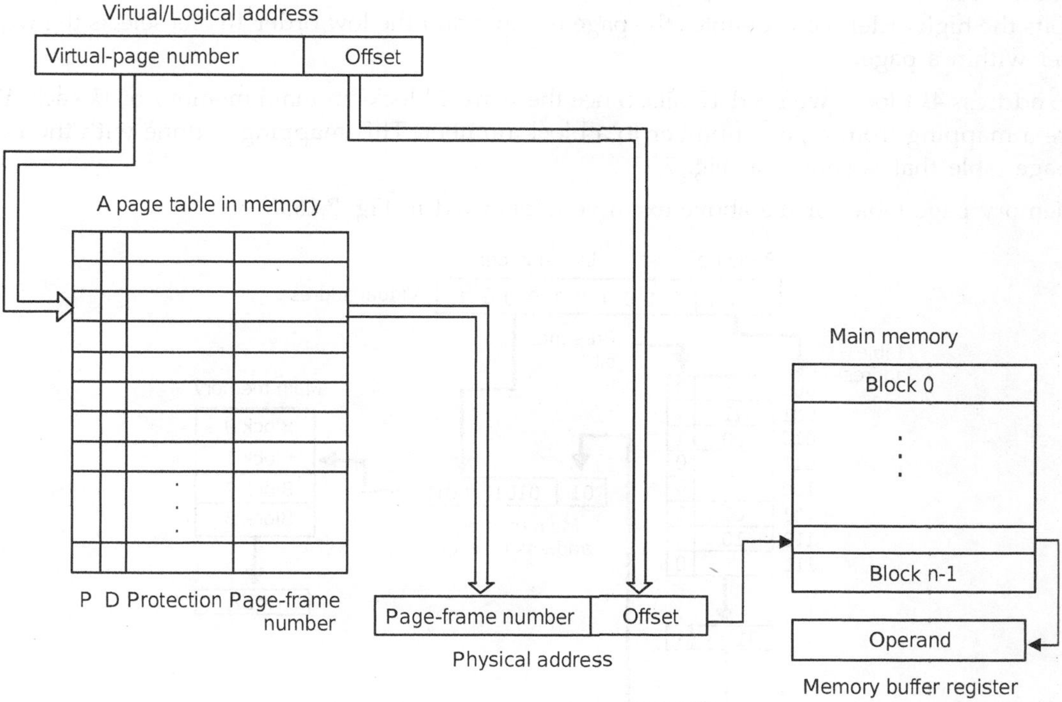

Fig. 7.13 Block diagram of a page table access the virtual address are represented as

Page number	Offset within page

Fig. 7.14 Virtual address

Page number tells the address of the page number and the offset field which tells the word within a page. In the above example virtual address is of 13 bits. To address 8 pages we need 3

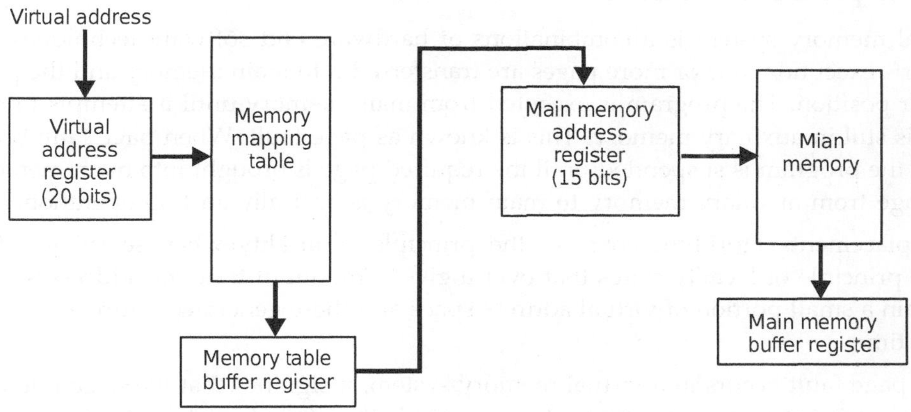

Fig. 7.15 Memory table for mapping virtual address

bits and to address a word within a page of size 1*k*, we need 10 bits. Therefore in the virtual address of 13 bits the high order 3 bits denotes the page number and the low order 10 bits selects the word number within a page.

To address 4*k* blocks we need 12 bits. Since these are 4 blocks in main memory of 1*k* each. We require a mapping from a page number to a block number. This mapping is done with the help of a page table that is shown in Fig. 7.15.

Memory page table for the above example is depicted in Fig. 7.16.

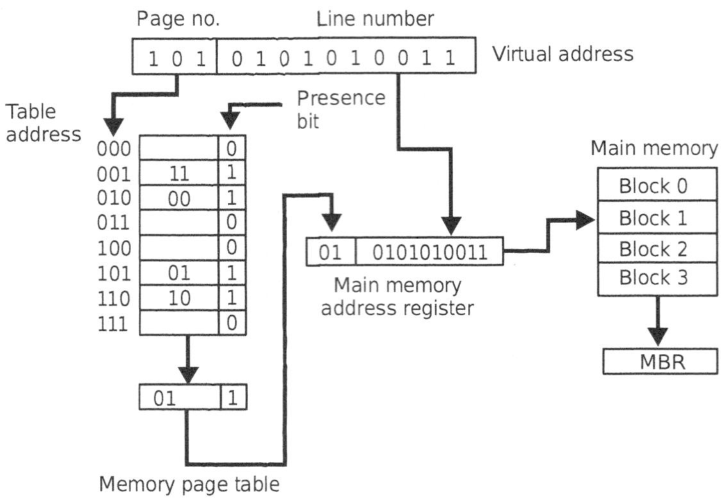

Fig. 7.16 Memory page table

The address in the page table denotes the page number and the content of the word gives the block number where the page is stored in main memory. The table shows that pages 1, 2, 5 and 6 are now available in main memory in blocks 3, 0, 1 and 2 respectively. A presence bit in each location indicates whether the page has been transferred from auxiliary memory into main memory.

7.6.3 Page Replacement Policies

A virtual memory system is a combinations of hardware and software techniques. When a program starts execution, one or more pages are transferred into main memory and the page table indicate their position. The program is executed from main memory until it attempts to reference a page that is still in auxiliary memory. This is known as page fault. When page fault occurs, the execution of the program is suspended until the required page is brought into main memory since loading a page from auxiliary memory to main memory is basically an I/O operation.

Most replacement algorithms consider the principle of locality when selecting a frame to replace. The principle of locality states that over a given amount of time the addresses generated will fall within a small portion of virtual address space and these generated addresses will change slowly with time.

When a page fault occurs in a virtual memory system, it signifies that the page referenced by the CPU is not present in main memory. A new page is then transferred from auxiliary memory to main memory. The goal of a replacement policy is to try to remove the page least likely to be referenced in the immediate future.

Most commonly used page replacement algorithms are:

(1) FIFO policy (2) LRU policy (3) OPR policy.

These replacement policies are used depending upon the application.

7.6.3.1 FIFO Policy

It is the simplest algorithm. As the name implies in this page replacement policy the page first loaded the main memory is replaced first. The FIFO algorithm selects for replacement the page that has been in memory the longest time. Each time is a page is loaded into memory, its identification number is pushed into a FIFO stack. FIFO will be full whenever memory has no more empty blocks. When a new page must be loaded, the page first loaded is removed. The disadvantage of FIFO is that it may significantly increase the time it takes for a process to execute because it does not take into consideration the principle of locality of reference and consequently may replace heavily used frames as well as rarely used frames with equal probability.

7.6.3.2 LRU Policy

The LRU method will replace the frame that has not been used for the longest time. The LRU algorithm can be implemented by associating a counter with every page that is present in main memory. When the page is referenced, its associated counter is set to zero. At fixed intervals of time, the counters associated with all pages presently in memory are incremented by n. The least recently used page is the page with the highest count. The counters are called aging registers as their count indicates their age, that is, how long ago their associated pages have been referenced.

SOLVED EXAMPLES

Example 1: *What is the bandwidth of a memory system that transfers 64 bits of data per request, has a latency of 25ns per operation and has a percentage time of 5 ns between operations.*

Solution. Given the latency of 25ns and percentage time of 5ns, one memory reference can initiate every 30ns and each memory reference fetches 64 bits (8 bytes) of data. Therefore, the bandwidth of the system is 8 bytes/30ns = 2.7×10^8 bytes/s.

Example 2: *Suppose a given cache has an access time of 10ns and miss rate of 5%. A given change to the cache will decrease the miss rate to 3%, but it will increase the cache access time to 15ns. Under what conditions does this result in greater performance.*

Solution. Average memory access time

$$t_A = (t_{hit} \times p_{hit}) + (t_{miss} \times p_{miss})$$

$$p_{mis} = 3\%$$

$$p_{hit} = 97\%$$

$$t_{hit} = (\text{access time of cache} = 15ns)$$

After change

Before change

$$t_{hit} = 10ns$$

$$p_{miss} = 5\%$$

$$p_{hit} = 95\%$$

For this change to reduce access time *ta* (after change) < *ta* (before change)

$\Rightarrow (15ns \times 0.97) + (t_{miss} \times 0.03) < (10ns \times 0.95) + (t_{miss} \times 0.05)$

Solving we get $T_{miss} > 252.5ns$

As long as the cache miss time is greater than this value, the reduction in cache miss frequently will be more significantly than the increase cache hit time.

As the cache miss time becomes larger, we become more willing to increase the cache hit time in order to reduce the cache miss rate, because cache miss becomes more and more expensive in terms of processing time.

Example 3: *An address space in virtual memory system is specified by 24–bits and the corresponding memory space by 16–bits.*

(*i*) *How many words are therein address space.*

(*ii*) *How many words are therein memory space.*

(*iii*) *If the page consist of 2k words, how many pages are therein the systems.*

Solution. (*i*) Virtual memory system is having 24–bits so total there will be 2^{24} words in the address space.

(*ii*) Words in the memory space = 2^{16}.

(*iii*) 2^{24} pages.

Example 4: *If a processor has 32 bet virtual addresses, 28–bit physical addresses and 2KB pages, how many bits are required for the virtual and physical frame numbers.*

Solution. 11 bits of each address are required specify the offset within the page therefore 32 – 11 = 21 bits are required to specifiy the virtual page number and 28 – 11 = 17 bits are required to specify the physical page frame number.

Example 5: *A system has 32 bit virtual addresses, 24 bit physical address and 2KB pages.*

(*a*) *How big is each page table entry if a single level page table is used.*

(*b*) *How many page table entries are required for this system.*

(*c*) *How much storage is required for the page table.*

Solution. (*a*) A page size of 2KB means that 11 bits are required for the offset field in the virtual and physical addresses. Therefore 13–bits are required for the PPN. Each page entry needs to hold the PPN for its page and the valid and change bits for a total of 15–bits which is rounded up to 16–bits.

(*b*) With a page size of 2KB, the virtual address space can hold 2^{21} pages, requiring 2^{21} page table entries.

(*c*) Each page table entry requires 2 bytes of storage, so the page table takes up 2^{22} bytes or 4MB.

Example 6: *A virtual memory system has an address of 8k words; a memory space of 4k words and page and block size of 1k words each. The following page reference change occur at a given time interval:*

4 2 0 1 2 6 1 4 0 1 0 2 3 5 7

determine the four pages that are resident in main memory after each page reference charge if the replacement algorithm used is:

(1) FIFO

(2) LRU. [Raj. Univ. 2000]

Solution. Here there are 8 pages and 4 blocks.

Page size = 4 block

(1) FIFO

4*	4*	4*	4*	6	6	6	6*	5	5
	2	2	2	2*	4	4	4	4*	7
		0	0	0	0*	2	2	2	2*
			1	1	1	1*	3	3	3

(2) LRU

4*	4*	4*	4*	6	6	6*	5	5
	2	2	2	2*	4	4	4*	7
		0	0	0	0*	2	2	2*
			1	1	1	3	3	3

Example 7: *A digital computer has a main memory of 64 k × 8 and a chache memory of 2K words. The cache uses direct mapping with a block size of 8 words.*

(*i*) *How many bits are therein the tag and index, fields of the address format?*

(*ii*) *How many bits are therein each words of cache and how are they divided into functions? Include a valid bit.*

(*iii*) *How many blocks can the cache accommodate?*

Solution. (*i*) Given memory of 64 K × 8 to address 64K words we need 16 address bit as $2^{16} = 64K$. The cache memory is of 2K word, to address 2K words we need 11 address bits ($2^{11} = 2K$). The index field addresses words in cache memory. Therefore the index field is 11 bits wide. The tag field is 5-bits wide (16 – 11 = 5). The 16-bit address is specified as

5	11
Tag	Index

(*ii*) Each word of cache contains the tag information and the data. The data is 8–bit wide and the tag field is 5-bits wide. If we include availed bit also then each word in cache has the

format

1	5	8
V	*Tag*	*Data*

= 14–bits wide.

(*iii*) The cache can accomodated 2K words. If a block size is of 8 words then the cache can

accommodated $= \frac{2K}{8} = \frac{2 \times 1024}{8} = 256$ block of 8 words each.

Example 8: *The logical address space in a computer system consists of 128 segments. Each segment can have upto 32 pages of 4K words each. Physical memory consists of 4K blocks of 4K words in each*

(i) Formulate the logical and physical address formats.

(ii) Give the logical address for segment 36, word number 2000 in page 15.

Solution. (*i*) The logical address is denoted as

Segment Number	Page Number	Word Number

Logical Address

Given (section 6.8.3) the system consists of 128 segments therefore segment number field must contain 7-bits as $2_7 = 128 \rightarrow$ Each segment can have up to 32 pages. Therefore to select one of the 32 pages we need 5-bits as $2^5 = \rightarrow 32$ Each page has 4K words to address these 4K words we need 12-bits as 2^{12} = 4K (4 × 1024 = 4096). Therefore the logical address is 24-bits wide 7 + 5 + 12 = 24-bits as shown

23 Segment number 16	Page number 11	Word 0
7-bits	5-bits	12-bits

The physical memory consists of 4K blocks of 4K words in each. We know the physical address is specification

Block	Word

Physical Address

As there are 4K blocks to be addressed. We need 12-bits for the block field 2^{12} = 4K. Also each block has 4K words, to address these 4K words we need 12-bits for the word field 2^{12} = 4K.

In total the physical address is also 12 + 12 = 24 bits wide as shown below

24 Block 11	Word 0
12-bits	12-bits

(*ii*) We have to address segment number 36. The segment field has 7-bits. therefore 7-bit address for segment $(36)_{10} = (0100100)_2$. The page to be addressed in segment 36 is page 15 is the page field has 5-bits. The page field contains $(15)_{10} = (01111)_2$. Finally word 2000 is to be addressed in page 15 of segment 36. The word field contains 12-bits. Therefore, the word field contains $(2000)_{10} = (011111010000)_2$.

Combining all the three field we have the logical address as

23	16	11 0
0100100	01111	011111010000
7-bits Segment number	5-bits Page number	12-bits word number

24-Bit Logical Address

EXERCISES

1. Draw the diagram for match logic for one word of associative memory. Derive the boolean expression of m_i, what additional logic is required to give a no match result for a word in associative memory when all key bits are 0? *[Raj. Univ. 2006]*
2. Explain the need of memory hierarchy. What is the main reason for not having large main memory for storing capacity of information in computer *[Raj. Univ. 2004]*
3. Explain the term locality of reference.
4. How do size of page and replacement policies affect the performance of a virtual memory system?
5. What is associative memory? How does is faciliate searching? Explain. *[Raj. Univ. 2001]*
6. Why does increasing the capacity of a cache tend to increase its hit rate?
7. What is the difference between a subroutine and an interrupt services routines?
8. A virtual memory has a page size of 1K words. There are eight pages and four blocks. The associative memory page table contains the following entries

Page	**Block**
0	3
1	1
4	2
6	0

Make a list of all virtual addresses that will cause a page fault if used by the CPU.

Chapter 8

INPUT–OUTPUT ORGANISATION

8.1 INTRODUCTION

The input-output subsystem of a computer provides an efficient communication mode between the central system and the outside environment. A computer serves no useful purpose if it is not able to receive the information from the outside world and transfer the result of the computation in a meaningful form.

Computer architects tend to focus their attention on the processor first, the memory system second and the I/O system third, if at all. This is because the benchmarks and metrics that have been used to compare computer systems have generally focused on the execution times of computationally intensive programs that do not use the I/O system much and partially it is because some of the techniques used to implement I/O systems.

Devices that are under the direct control of the computer are said to be connected online. Upon the command of the CPU, these devices are designed to read information into or out of the memory unit. Input-output devices attached to the computer are also called peripherals. Most commonly used peripherals are keyboards, display units and printers.

The input-output organisation of a computer is a function of the size of the computer and the devices connected to it. I/O system organisation can be divided into two major components.

1. The I/O devices themselves.
2. The technologies used to interface the I/O devices to the rest of the system.

Other input and output devices encountered in computer systems are digital incremental plotters, optical and magnetic character readers, analog-to-digital convertors and various data acquisition equipment.

8.2 PERIPHERAL DEVICES

Input-output devices attached to the computer are also called peripherals. Keyboard, display devices, printers, video display unit are the mostly used peripheral devices. The keyboard is a mechanical assembly on a panel mounted over a circuit beneath. It connects to computer via a serial interface. The entered character displayed on the screen provides an human computer interface. A keyboard is a device to enter text for alphanumeric characters. It also enters the commands with function, control and up-down keys. It sends an ASCII character on each entry as input to the computer. The mouse is a screen cursor pointing device. It is a device that provides a powerful human computer interface and graphical user interface in conjunction with the displayed text and icons on the computer screen.

Video monitors are the most commonly used peripherals. They consist of a keyboard as the input device and a display unit as the output device. Touch panel is a menu select and pointing device, in which a finger is used. Touch panel also displays a menu or icons for the menu. When a finger presses a menu or icon, the capacitance changes. This signals an input. The input is encoded and sent to an input-cum-display interface.

Printers provide a permanent record on paper of computer output data or text. Mainly there are three types of printers—Dot Matrix printer, Ink Jet printer and Laser Jet printer. A dot matrix printer depends on a concept that each character is mapped to a matrix. An Ink Jet printer uses a droplet, which is ejected through a thin nozzle. It is a non-impact technology. Video display unit has a large area and it displays text and picture in large area. A cathode ray tube (CRT) generates three electron beams from three electron guns. The beam focuses on the screen on a set of three adjacent pixels. Each set of pixels lights up in distinct colors—red, green and blue. LCD displays are light in weight and are much thinner compared to CRT-based VDU displays. A new form of LCD display is TFT (thin-film transistor) display. The display is sharp, as using a transistor use results in a fast control of the display.

8.3 INPUT-OUTPUT INTERFACE CIRCUITS

The input-output devices are sometimes also referred to as peripheral or external devices. External devices are not generally connected directly with the bus structure of the computer, so they need special circuits for interfacing with the CPU. These interface circuits allow I/O devices of different characteristics to be connected to a standard bus with a minimum special purpose hardware or software. The purpose of the communication link is to resolve the difference that exist between the central computer and each peripheral.

The major differences are:

1. Peripherals are electromechanical and electromagnetic devices and their manner of operation is different from the CPU and memory, which are electronic devices.
2. Data transfer rate is slower than CPU.
3. Data codes and formats in peripherals differ from the word format of CPU.
4. The operating modes of peripherals are different from each other.

To resolve these differences, computer systems include special hardware components between the CPU and peripherals to supervise and synchronize all input and output transfers. These components are known as interface units. Each device may have its own controller that supervises the operations of the particular mechanism in the peripheral.

8.3.1 I/O Bus and Interface Modules

Fig. 8.1 shows the communication link between processor and the various peripheral devices. The I/O bus consists of three lines:

1. Data Lines
2. Address Lines
3. Control Lines

Each peripheral device has an interface unit associated with it. An interface may control a single external device or two or more devices may be controlled by a single interface. Data, address and control lines together called system bus. The system bus from the CPU is attached to all external interfaces to communicate with a particular device. The CPU places a device address on the address lines. Each interface attached to the system bus contains an address decoder that monitors the address lines. When the interface detects its own address, it activates the path between the system bus and the device that it controls. The rest of the devices whose address does not match to the address in the bus are disabled by their interface. At the same time that the address is made available in the address lines the CPU provides an I/O command and executes it. The I/O command is an instruction that is executed in the interface and its attached I/O devices. The interpretation of the command depends on the peripheral that the processor is addressing.

There are four types of commands that an interface may receive. These are

(*i*) Control command

(*ii*) Status command

(*iii*) Data output command

(*iv*) Data input command.

(*i*) **Control command.** This command activate the peripheral device and inform it what to do. For example start printing. This command depends upon the particular I/O device each peripheral device has its own set of control commands, depending on its mode of operation.

(*ii*) **Status command.** This command tests the status conditions in the interface and the I/O device. For example, before sending command to peripheral checking the initial status of the peripheral. Before sending the print command, the CPU may wish to check the status of the printer. Errors may occur during the data transfer. Which are detected by the interface. These errors are notified by the CPU by setting the status bits in its status register.

(*iii*) **Data output command.** A data output command causes the interface to respond by transferring data from the bus into one of its registers. Consider an example, after the CPU has addressed the printer interface by means of control command and monitored the printer status by using status command, the CPU issues a data output command. The interface responds to the data output command and transfers the data from the data lines in the bus to its buffer register. The interface then communicates with the printer controller and sends the data to be printed.

(*iv*) **Data input command.** This command is just reverse of the data output command. In this command the interface receives an item of data from the peripheral and places it in its buffer register. The CPU checks if data is available by the status command and than issues a data output command. The interface responds by placing the data on the data lines where they are accepted by the processor.

8.4 ASYNCHRONOUS DATA TRANSFER

If the register in the interface share a common clock with CPU register, the transfer between two units is said to be synchronous. In other case the internal timing in each unit is independent from the other in that each uses own private clock for internal, register in this case the two units are said to be asynchronous to each other.

Asynchronous data transfer between two independent units requires that control signals be transmitted between the communicating units to indicate the time at which the data is transmitted.

There are various method to achieve this like strobe base, handshaking.

8.4.1 Strobe Control

The strobe control method of asynchronous data transfer employs a single control line to each time of transfer. The strobe may be activated either by source or by destination. The data will be valid on when the strobe is enable.

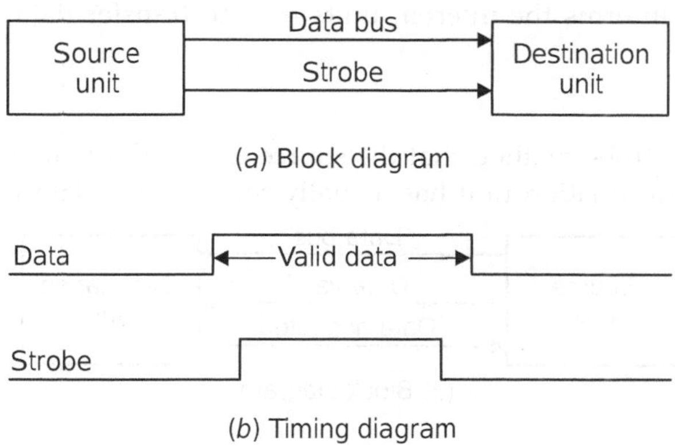

Fig. 8.1 Source initiated strobe for data transfer

Fig. 8.1 shows a source initiated transfer. In this fig. the data bus carries the binary information from source to source to destination typically the bus has multiple line to transfer an entire word. The strobe is a single line that informs the destination unit that valid data is available.

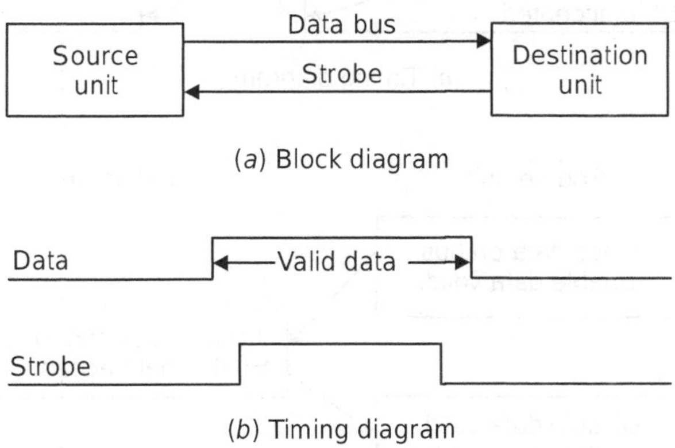

Fig. 8.2 Destination-initiated strobe for data transfer

As shown in above figure the source unit first places, the data on the data bus. After sometime or delay to ensure that the data is settle to steady value, the activates the strobe pulse. The information on data bus and the strobe signal remain in the active state for sufficient time period to allow the destination unit to receive the data the destination unit uses the falling edges of strobe pulse to transfer the contents of the data bus into one of its internal register. The source removes the data from the bus a brief period after it disables its strobe pulse. The source does not have to change the information in data bus the fact that the strobe signal is disabled indicates that the data bus does not contain valid data. New data will be available only after the strobe is enabled again.

In destination initiated transfer the destination unit activates the strobe pulse, informing the source to provide data. The source unit responds by replacing the requested binary information on data bus. The data must be valid and remain in the bus long enough for the destination unit to accept it. The falling edge of strobe pulse is used to trigger a destination register. The destination unit than disable the strobe. The source removes the data from the bus after some time. In many computers the strobe pulse is actually controlled by the clock pulse in the CPU. The CPU is in control of the buses and informs the internal units now to transfer data.

8.4.2 Handshaking

The disadvantage of strobe method that the source unit that initiate the transfer has no way of knowing whether the destination unit has actually received the data item that was placed in

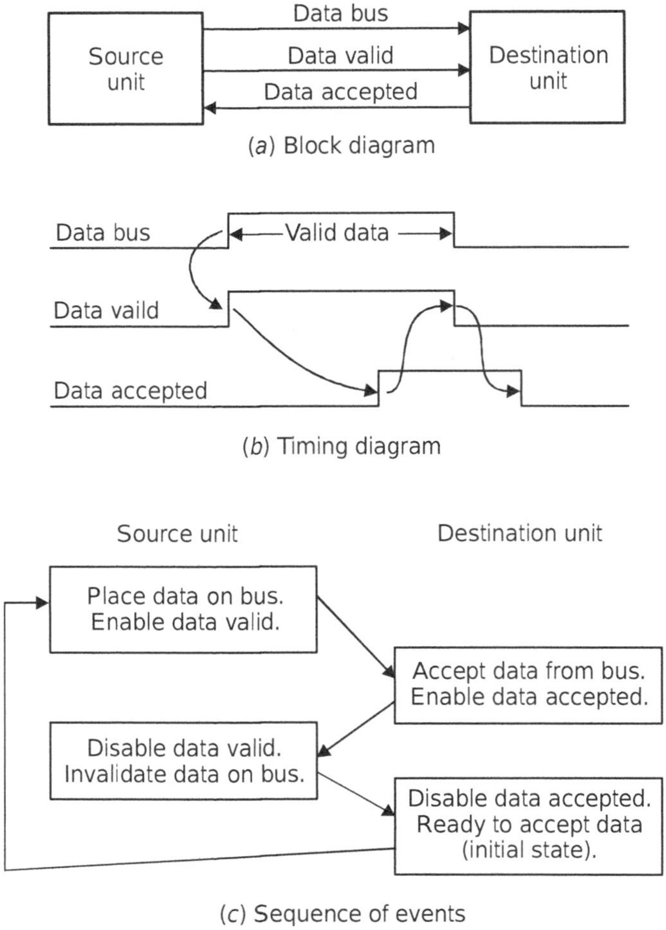

Fig. 8.3 Source-initiated transfer using handshaking

the bus. Similarly, a destination unit that initiates the transfer has no way of knowing whether the source unit actually placed the data on the bus. The solution of this problem is handshaking. It is a way to replay to unit that initiates the transfer. The basic principle of two wire handshaking method of data transfer is as follows. It uses two control line first from source to destination and used by source to inform destination unit whether there are valid data in the bus. Other control line is in the other direction from destination to source, used by destination unit to inform the source whether it can accept data. The sequence of control during transfer depends on unit that initiates the transfer.

In figure the two handshaking lines are data valid generated by source unit and data accepted, generated by destination unit timing diagram shows the enchange of signals between the two unit. The sequence of events shows the four possible states that the system can be at any given time the source unit initiates the transfer by placing the data on the bus and enabling its data valid signal. The data accepted signal is activated by the destination unit after it accepts the data from the bus. The source unit than disables its data valid signal, which invalidates the data on the bus. The destination unit then disables its data accepted signal and the system goes into its initial state. The source does not send the next data item until after the destination unit shows its readiness to accept new data by disabling its data accepted signal.

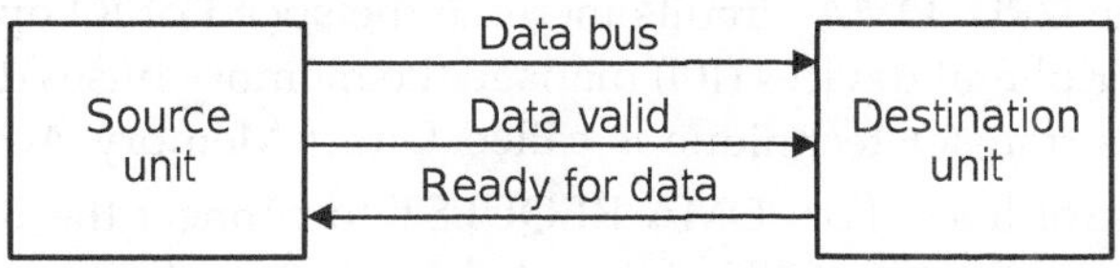

(*a*) Block diagram

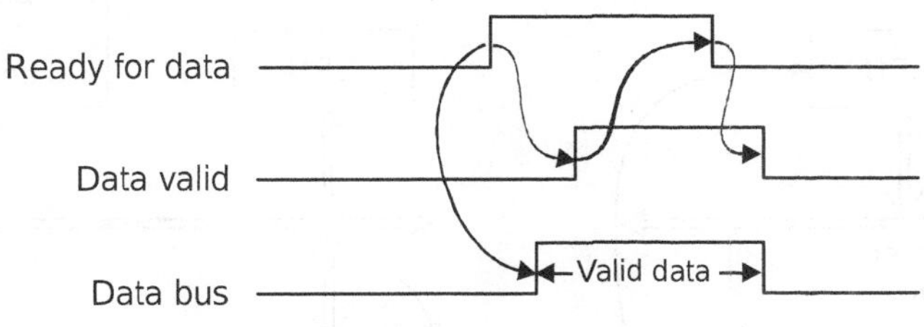

(*b*) Timing diagram

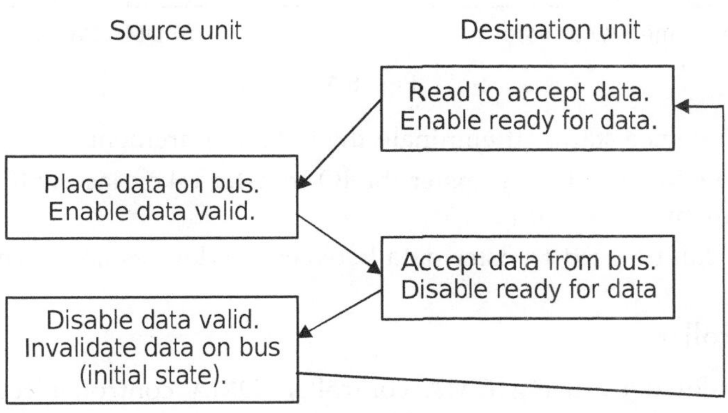

(*c*) Sequence of events

Fig. 8.4 Destination initiated transfer using handshaking

In this the name of the signal generated by destination unit has been changed to "ready for data" to reflect its view meaning. The source unit in this case does not place data on the bus until after its receives the "ready for data" signal from the destination unit. The handshaking procedure follows the same pattern as in the source initiated case.

If one unit is faulty, the data transfer will not be completed such an error can be detected by means of timeout mechanism, which produces an alarm if the data transfer is not completed within a predetermined time. It is completed by an internal clock that starts counting time when unit enables one of its handshaking control signals. If the return signal does not respond within a given time period the unit assumes that error has occured.

8.5 DIRECT MEMORY ACCESS (DMA)

The computer wastes a lot of time in testing IO device status and executing IO data transfer. This wastage of time has negative impact. Firstly a delay is suffered at the IO devices as it waits to be tested by the CPU. Secondly, because the data transmits through the CPU rather than directly to the main memory.

The transfer of data between a fast storage device such as magnetic disk and memory is often limited by the speed of the CPU. DMA circuits increase the speed of IO operations removing the CPU from the path and peripheral devices (IO) manage the memory buses directly would improve the speed of transfer. This transfer technique is called Direct Memory Access (DMA).

We need special control lines. For DMA-REQUEST to connect the IO devices to the CPU. When these control lines is active the CPU suspends its current activities at proper break points and attend to the DMA. So save CPU time or speeds up the IO transfer.

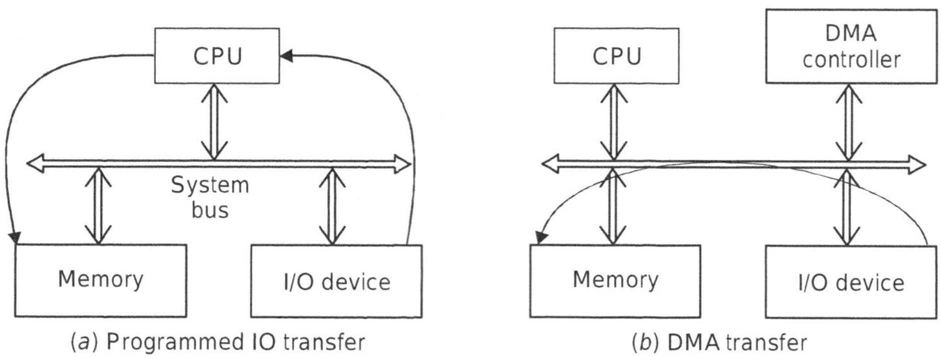

Fig. 8.5

1. Determine IO device status. It eliminate the CPU requirement.
2. Further in the DMA mode of transfer the IO transfer take place without the execution of IO instructions by the CPU.

Programmed IO can be used transfer data between IO devices and memory.

8.5.1 DMA Controller

DMA is implemented by using DMA controller. DMA controller receives data transfer instructions from the processor. Example, read data from an IO device. The CPU sends the IO device number as IO address, main memory buffer address number of bytes to transfer and direction of transfer (IO to memory or memory to IO).

After the DMA controller has received the transfer instruction. It generates all bus control signals to facilitate the data transfer.

DMA controller typically support more than one IO device.

DMA controller needs the circuits of an interface to communicate with the CPU and IO device. In addition, it needs an address register, word count register, set of address lines, address register and address lines are used for direct communication with the memory, word count register define the number of words that must be transferred. The data transfer may be done directly between the device and memory under control of the DMA.

DMA controller can support four independent devices; each device is attached to a specific DMA channel. These channels are also called IO channels. Each IO channel has registers to keep track of the address in memory, a byte count to indicate number of byte transfer and direction of transfer the following steps in DMA operation:

1. The processor initiates the DMA controller by identifying the IO device and supplying. The memory address, byte count and type of operation (I/P and O/P). This is referred to as channel initialization. The channel is ready for data transfer between the associated IO device and memory.
2. When IO device is ready to transfer data. It informs the DMA controller. The DMA controller starts the transfer operation.
   - Instruction obtain the bus.
   - Place the memory address and generate read and write control signals.
   - Complete the transfer and release the bus by the CPU or other DMA devices.
   - Update the memory address and count value.
3. After completing the operation, the processor is notified. This notification is done by an interrupt mechanism the processor can then check the status of transfer (successful or failure). DMA controller transfers one data word at a time.

The DMA is first initialized by the CPU after fact, the DMA starts and continues to transfer data between memory and peripheral unit until an entire block is transferred. That its buses are disabled. Then DMA puts the current value of its address register into the address bus. Initiates the RD or WR signal and sends a DMA acknowledge to the peripheral device RD and WR lines in the DMA controller are bidirectional. The direction of transfer depends on the status of the BG line when BG = 0 the RD and WR are I/P lines allowing the CPU to communicate with the DMA register.

When BG = 1 the RD and WR are O/P lines from DMA controller to memory.

When peripheral device receives a DMA ack. It facts a word in the data bus (for write) or receives a word from data bus (for read). Thus the DMA controller read or write operation done and address supplies for memory.

The peripheral unit can then communicate with memory through the data bus for direct transfer between the CPU is disabled.

8.5.2 DMA Transfer

The position of the DMA controller among the other components in a computer system.

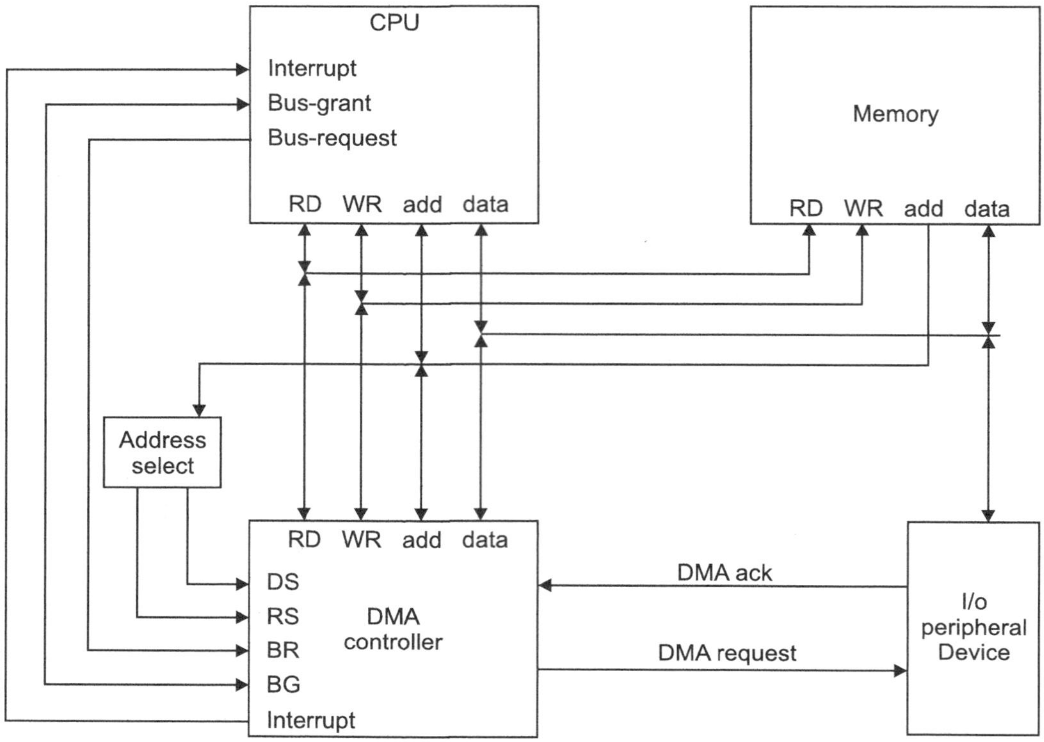

Fig. 8.6 DMA transfer

CPU communicates with the DMA by the address buses and data buses as with any interface unit the DMA has its own address which activates the DS and RS lines. CPU initializes the DMA through the data bus. The DMA receives the start control command. It can start the transfer between the IO peripheral device and the memory.

When peripheral device sends a DMA request the DMA controller activate the BR line informing the CPU. The CPU responds with its BG line informing the DMA.

For each word, that is transferred the DMA INCRM ents its address register and decrements its word count register. If the word count does not reach zero, the DMA checks the request line coming from the peripheral for a high–speed, device, the line will be active as soon as, and the process transfer is completed. A second transfer is then initiated and the process continue until the entire block is transferred. If the peripheral speed is slower, the DMA request line may come some what later. In this case the DMA disables the bus request line so that the CPU can continue to execute its program. When the peripheral request a transfer, the DMA request the buses again.

If the word count register reacher zero, the DMA stops any further transfer and removes its bus request. It also informs the CPU of the termination by means of an interrupt. When the CPU respond to the interrupt. It reads the content of the word count register. The zero value of this register indicates that all words were transferred successfully. The CPU can read this register at any time to check the number of words already transferred.

8.6 INPUT-OUTPUT PROCESSOR (IOP)

An I/O processor is classified as a processor with direct memory access capability that communicates with input-output devices. The IOP is similar to a CPU except that it is designed to handle the details of I/O processing. IOP is a specialized processor, which not only loads and stores into memory but also can execute instructions, which are among a set of I/O instructions. These instructions help in format conversions. The I/O device data in different format can be transferred to main memory using an IOP. IOPs are used to address the problem of direct transfer after executing the necessary format conversion or other instructions. In an IOP based system, I/O devices can directly access the memory without intervention by the processor.

In the communication between CPU and IOP the memory used as a message center where each processors leaves information for others. The sequence of operation may be carried out as depicted in Fig. 8.7. The CPU sends an instruction to test the input output path. The IOP responds by inserting a status word in memory for the CPU to check the bits of the status.

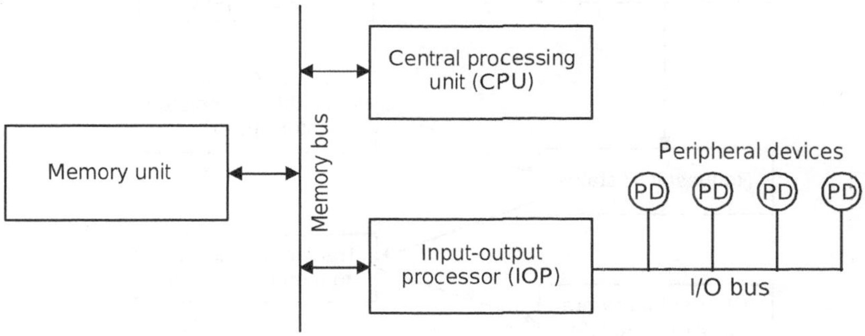

Fig. 8.7 Block diagram of computer with IOP.

Word indicates the condition of the IOP and I/O devices. Such as, IOP overload condition, device busy with another transfer, or device what to do next.

If all is in order, the CPU sends the instruction to start I/O transfer. The memory address received with this instruction tells the IOP where to find its program.

Instructions that are read from memory by an IOP are sometimes called commands, to distinguish them from instructions that are read by the CPU. The CPU informs the IOP where to find the commands in memory when it is time to execute the I/O program.

8.6.1 CPU IOP Communication

The communication between IOP and CPU take different forms, depending upon the particular computer considered. In most cases the memory unit acts as a message where each processor leaves information for the others.

The sequence of operation may be carried out as depicted in the flow chart. The CPU sends an instruction to test the IOP path. The IOP responds by inserting a status word in the memory for the CPU check. The bits of the status word indicates the condition of the IOP and I/O device, such as I/O transfer. The CPU refers to the status word in the memory to decide what to do next. If all is in order the CPU sends the instruction to start the I/O transfer. The memory address received with this instruction tells the IOP where to find its program, WR signal to write this at a fixed location in memory. And after that it will write the data in the defined memory location.

Similarly IOP can be used for the memory to memory communication.

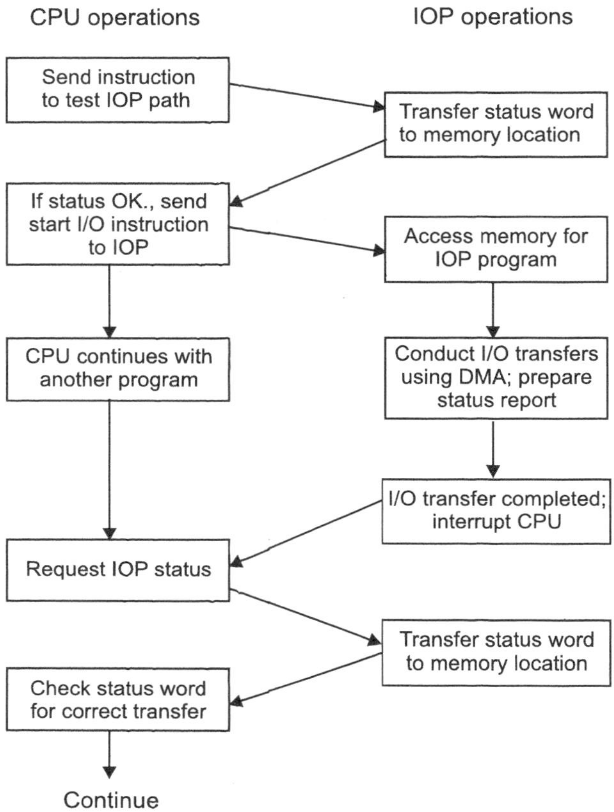

Fig. 8.8 CPU IOP communication

8.7 SERIAL COMMUNICATION

Serial communication is a device communication protocol that is standard on almost every PC. The concept of serial communication is very simple.

The serial port sends and receives bytes of information one bit at a time serial parts are used to physically connect asynchronous devices to a computer. They are located on the back of the system unit, using the multiport adapter.

Serial port require only a single wire or pin to send same data character to the device. To do this, first the data is converted from a parallel form to a sequential form, where bits are organised one after the other in a series. The data is then transmitted to the device with the least significant bit transmitted first. Once received by the remote device, the data is converted back in the parallel form. Fig. 8.9 depicts serial communication.

Serial transmission of a single character are simple and straight forward. The receiving system does not know where one character ends and the other begins. To solve this problem, both ends of the communication link must be synchronized or timed. Serial data transfers depend on accurate timing in order to differentiate bits in the data stream. The most striking difference between an I/O processor and a data communication processor is in the way the processor communications with the I/O devices.

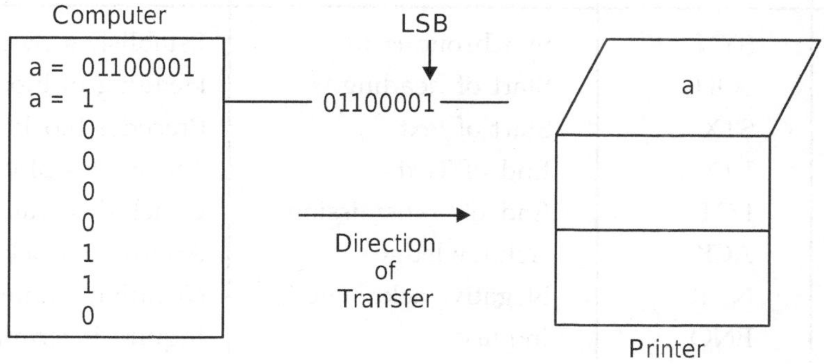

Fig. 8.9 Serial communication port

Data can be transmitted between two points in three different modes:

1. Simplex
2. Half-duplex
3. Full-duplex.

1. **Simplex.** Data can be transmitted only in one direction.
2. **Half-duplex.** Data can be transmitted in both the direction but not simultaneously.
3. **Full-duplex.** Data can be transmitted in both the direction simultaneously.

The communication lines, modems and other equipment used in the transmission of information between two or more stations in called a data link. The transfer of information in a data link is achieved by means of a protocol. The purpose of a data link protocol is to establish and terminate a connection between two stations, to identify the sender and receiver, to ensure that all message are passed correctly without errors and to handle all control functions.

There are:

(1) Character oriented protocol

(2) Bit oriented protocol.

These are discussed in the following sections.

8.7.1 Character Oriented Protocol

The character oriented protocol is based on the binary code of a character set. The code must commonly used in ASCII. It is a 7 bit code with an eight bit used for parity. The code has 128 characters of which 95 all graphic characters and 33 are control characters. The graphic characters include the upper and lowercase letters, the ten numerals and a variety of special symbols. The control characters are used for the purpose of routing data, arranging the test in a desired format and for the layout of the printed page. The characters that control the transmission are called communication control characters. These are listed in Table 8.1. Each character has a 7 bit code and is referred by a three letter symbol. The role of each character in the control of data transmission is stated briefly in the function column of the table.

Table 8.1 ASCII communication control characters

Code	*Symbol*	*Meaning*	*Function*
0010110	SYN	Synchronous file	Establishes Synchronism
0000001	SOH	Start of heading	Heading of block Message
0000010	STX	Start of text	Precedes block of text
0000011	ETX	End of Text	Terminates block of text
0000100	EOT	End of transmission	Concludes transmission
0000110	ACK	Acknowledge	Affermative acknowledgement
0010101	NAK	Negative acknowledge	Negative acknowledgement
0000101	ENO	Inquiry	Inquire it terminal is on
0010111	ETB	End of Transmission block	End of block of data
0010000	DLE	Data link escape	Special control characters.

The SYN character serves as synchoronizing agent between the transmitter and receiver. When the 7 bit ASCII code is used with an odd-parity bit in the most significant position. The assigned SYN character has the 8 bit code 00010110 which has the property that, upon circular shifting, it repeats itself only after a full 8 bit cycle. When the transmitter starts sending 8 bit character, it sends a few characters first and then sends the actual message.

Messages are transmitted through the data link with an established format consisting of a header field, a text field and an error-checking field, and an error-checking field. A typical message format is shown in Fig 8.10.

SYN	SYN	SOH	Header	STX	TEXT	ETX	BCC

Fig. 8.10 Typical message format

The two SYN characters assure proper synchoronization at the start of the message. Following the SYN characters is the header, which starts with an SOH. The header consists of address and control information. The STX character terminates the header and signifies the beginning of the text transmission. The text portion of the message is variable in length and may contain any ASCII characters except the communication control characters.

The text field is terminated with the ETX characters. The last field is a Block Check Character (BCC) used for error checking. It is usually either a Longitudinal Redundancy Check (LRC) or a Cyclic Redundancy Check (CRC).

The receiver accepts the message and calculates its own BCC. If the BCC transmitted does not agree with the BCC calculated by the receiver, the receiver responds with a Negative Acknowledge (NAK) character. The message is then retransmitted and checked again. The communication with the memory unit and CPU is similar to any I/O processor.

8.7.2 Bit Oriented Protocol

The bit oriented protocol does not use characters in its control field and is independent of any particular code. It allows the transmission of serial bit stream of any length without the implication of character boundaries. Messages are organised in a specific format called a frame. In addition to the information field, a frame contains address, control and error - checking fields. The frame boundaries are determined from a special 8 bit number called a flag. Examples are SDLC (Synchronous data link control) used by IBM, HDLC (High level data link control) adopted by the ISO and ADCCP (Advanced data communication control procedure) adopted by the American National Standards Institute.

Any data Communication link involves at least two participating stations. The station that has responsibility for the data link and issues the commands to control the link is called the primary station. The other station is a secondary station. Bit oriented protocols assume the presence of one primary station and one or more secondary stations. All communication on the data link is from the primary station to one or more secondary stations, or from a secondary station to the primary station.

The frame format is shown in Fig. 8.11. A frame starts with the 8 bit flag 01111110 followed by an address and control sequence.

The information field is not restricted in format or content and can be of any length. The frame check field is a CRC (Cyclic Redundancy Check) sequence used for detecting errors in transmission.

Flag 01111110	Address 8 bits	Control 8 bits	Information any no. of bits	Frame check 16 bits	Flag 01111110

Fig. 8.11 Frame format

The ending flag indicates to the receiving station that the 16 bits just received constitute the CRC bits. The ending frame can be followed by another frame, another flag or a sequence of consecutive 1's. When two frames follow each other, the intervening flag is simultaneously the ending flag of the first frame and the beginning flag of the next frame. If no information is exchanged, the transmitter sends a series of flag to keep the line in the active state. The line is said to be in the idle state with the occurrence of 15 or more consecutive 1's. frames with certain control messages are sent without an information field. A frame must have a minimum of 32 bits between two flags to accomodate the address, control and frame check fields. The maximum length depends on the condition of the communication channel and its ability to transmit long message error-free.

8.7.3 Data Transparency

The character oriented protocol was developed to communicate with keyboard, printer and display devices that use alphanumeric characters. There is a need to transmit binary information that is not in ASCII. An arbitrary bit pattern in the text message becomes a problem in the character oriented protocol. This is because any 8-bit pattern belonging to a communication control character will be interpreted errorneously by the receiver. When the text portion of the message is variable in length and contains bits that are to be treated without reference ot any particular code, it is said to contain transparent data. This feature requires that the character recognitation logic of the receiver be turned off so that data patterns in the text field are not interpreted as communication control information.

Data transparency is achieved by inserting a DLE character before each communication control character. The start of heading is detected from the double character DLE SOH and the text field is terminated with the double character DLE ETX.

The achievement of data transparency by means of the DLE character is inefficient and somewhat complicated to implement.

SOLVED EXAMPLES

Example 1: *What is the minimum number of bits that a frame must have in a bit oriented protocol?*

Solution. Format of the bit oriented protocol is defined as:

Flag 8 bits	Address 8 bits	Control 8 bits	Information Net fixed	Frame check 16 bits	Flag 8 bits

so the minimum number of bits in a frame is = Flag + Address + Control + Frame Check

(8 × 2 = 16 bits) (8 bits) (8 bits) (16 bits)

= 16 + 8 + 8 + 16

= 48 bits.

Example 2: *A typical CPU allows most interrupt requests to be enabled and disabled under software control but it does not provide facilities to disable DMA requests why?*

Solution. DMA is used for fast I/O devices. If such fast devices are forced to wait before being given access to the system bus, data can be lost. For example when a magnetic disk operation is initiated, I/O data must be sent to or from the disk unit at the fixed data transfer rate. Therefore DMA requests normally cannot be disabled. To delay a DMA request, we can insert a programmable mask flip-flop in the DMA request line to the CPU.

EXERCISES

1. Explain DMA based data transfer with the help of all diagrams. Give various applications in which it can be used. *[Raj. Univ. 06]*
2. Explain:
   (*i*) DMA (*ii*) IOP
   (*iii*) Priority Interrupt (*iv*) Character oriented Protocol. *[Raj. Univ. 06]*
3. What is an IO processor? How does it work? Discuss its organisation. *[Raj. Univ. 03]*
4. Can DMA and IO processor be used to achieve memory-to-memory data transfer? Discuss the concept. *[Raj. Univ. 03]*
5. Explain the system organisation in the presence of an I/O processor. How I/O processer and CPU interact with each other? *[Raj. Univ 03]*
6. Explain the difference between a bit oriented protocol and a character oriented protocol. *[Raj. Univ 01]*
7. What are the multiprocessors? Illustrate some of the multiprocessor structure with block diagram?
8. Why are the read and write control lines in a DMA one controller bidirectional? Under what conditions and for what purpose are they used as inputs? Under what condition and for what purpose are they used as outputs?
9. What is the basic advantage of using interrupt-initiated data transfer over transfer under program control without an interrupt?